Financial Management
2nd Edition

Financial Management

2nd Edition

M. G. Wright B.Com., FCCA, FCIS

Principal Lecturer, School of Management, Polytechnic of Central London. Consultant, Whitehead Consulting Group

McGRAW-HILL Book Company (UK) Limited

London · New York · St Louis · San Francisco · Auckland
Bogotá · Guatemala · Hamburg · Johannesburg · Lisbon · Madrid ·
Mexico · Montreal · New Delhi · Panama · Paris · San Juan · São
Paulo · Singapore · Sydney · Tokyo · Toronto

Published by
McGRAW-HILL Book Company (UK) Limited
Maidenhead · Berkshire · England

British Library Cataloguing in Publication Data

Wright, Maurice Gordon
  Financial management. − 2nd ed.
  1. Corporations − Finance
  2. Industrial management
  I. Title
  658.1'5   HG4026   80−40787

  ISBN 0−07−084550−6
  ISBN 0−07−084542−5 Pbk

12345 JWA 83210

PRINTED AND BOUND IN GREAT BRITAIN

To my wife Kathleen

Contents

PART 2   MANAGING SOURCES OF FUNDS

Preface

In the ten years since the first edition of this book was published events have reinforced the view that for a business to be successful its management must have a clear grasp of the essentials of financial management. Those managers who are able to express their plans and activities in financial terms, in a manner that enables them to understand the implications of those plans and events for the future financial health of the business, are likely to have a much greater propensity for success than those who do not.

Financial management must be considered as something much more than a description of the various institutions and individuals who contribute to the raising of funds for businesses. This is not to say that their role should not be considered—it is too vital to be ignored in any way—but rather that financial management has a leading part to play in the decision-making processes which determine aspects of profitability and growth.

For too long finance has been considered as a rather sterile function concerned with certain necessary recording activities and with banking matters, handling shareholders, often saying 'No' to projects put forward by other managers, and dealing with the Inland Revenue. If financial management is to make a significant contribution to the management revolution that is taking place this image must be drastically changed.

What then should be its role in the overall control of a business? Firstly, it should be concerned with identifying sources of profit and the factors which affect profit. That is to say with operating activities in the way in which the assets are used and, from a longer term point of view, the process of allocating funds to uses within the business. In these activities financial managers form part of a management team, applying their specialist advice and processing and marshalling the data upon which decisions will be based. The second major role is that of funds management. The need for funds is identified through a process of control of liquidity. How this need is to be satisfied, and from what sources, forms a crucial part of the overall planning of the business. As long-term planning proceeds, financial management must assess the implications of the policies proposed in terms of funds required and make arrangements to raise the long-term funds necessary to secure the financial basis of growth.

The method of raising long-term funds requires decisions as to the proportions of capital that are to be raised from shareholders and lenders, and upon

xiii

what terms. This decision will have important consequences for the overall cost of capital and will have significant effects upon the return on equity funds and the level of risk.

In the past the finance function has assumed the function of data processing for the business. This situation arose because money was the common measure in which the activities were recorded. This role is currently in a state of flux. The introduction of computers and the allied specialist techniques may well result in data processing being carried out as a service function independent of financial management. This book will, therefore, only be concerned with data processing in so far as it impinges on the decision-making processes.

If industry is to improve its efficiency, management must recognize that the financial area has as important a part to play in marketing, production, etc. It can only play that part, however, if financial management is shown to have a logical structure, particularly in the major decision areas. It is to the achievement of these objectives that this book is dedicated.

Welwyn
January 1980

M. G. Wright

Part 1
Managing assets for profitability

1

The role of financial management

Financial management is intimately interwoven into the fabric of management itself. Not only is this because the results of management's actions are expressed in financial terms, but principally because the central role of financial management is concerned with the same objectives as those of management itself: with the way in which the resources of the business are employed and how it is financed. Business is about making profits and profits will be determined by the way in which the resources of the business in terms of people, physical resources, capital, and any other specific talents are organized.

PROFITS AND OWNERSHIP IN THE PRIVATE SECTOR

The contentious topic of profit must be tackled at this stage or one's views of profits may obscure the purpose of the remainder of the book. In the author's view profits are the lifeblood of the private sector of industry and commerce. It is the measure of success and the raison d'être of the business. People save funds rather than consume them for various reasons, one being to earn a return on those funds to compensate for the delayed enjoyment and the risks that are incurred. In their investment policy, the providers of capital will try to maximize their *long-term gains*. This is particularly true today when a large part of new finance for the larger companies is provided by financial institutions, such as pension funds and insurance companies, which have a duty to the pension fund members and policy holders.

This is a fact that must be recognized if one is to understand the decisions made by managements. While we live in a world where businesses compete for the funds available for investment, then the preferences of those providers of funds must be considered. This is not to say, of course, that one should look only at the *short-term profit considerations*. The maximization of gains for the investor is a *long-term* objective which should dismiss short-term profits detrimental to the long-term interests of the business and its owners.

People who invest money in shares or in their own business are the *owners* of the business. It is on their behalf that the business is carried on, and in the

3

long run decisions made within the business should be made within the framework of the long-term gain implications for the owners. The growth of a class of professional managers with a minute interest in the shares of their companies tends to obscure the fact that they manage the business on behalf of the owners and not for some unspecified social purpose or for personal satisfaction.

Consideration of other resources used by the business

Stressing the owners' long-term requirements does not mean that employees, customers, or even society as a whole, are forgotten. Indeed, that maximization can only be achieved when full consideration is given to relationships with employees and customers. The effects of neglecting these aspects have been seen in several notable cases in the last decade. It is true that the really successful business can only be built up on the foundation of good employee and customer relations.

One of the tragedies of the strict division into 'functions' in the past is that decisions have frequently been made which only take into account the requirements of one function—all too often the financial one. It is rare for a business decision to affect only profit and nothing else. Usually, there are implications for marketing, employment, and for relations with the local community which, although they cannot be quantified, must be considered in the decision-making process.

Publicly owned businesses

The fact that a business is publicly owned does not mean it is unaffected by the requirements of profit. Indeed, Parliament may set specific targets for the nationalized industries in terms of the required return on capital employed and the need for commercial criteria in their decisions.

Where an objective of a nationalized industry is to satisfy some social need, this is now often segregated from the normal operations of the business. In the case of the railways, for example, it has been achieved by the Government, paying a subsidy to retain services not viable on normal commercial considerations.

THE ROLE OF FINANCIAL MANAGEMENT IN ORGANIZING RESOURCES

The part played by financial management can be divided into two main areas:

1. *Decisions on the capital structure.* This relates to decisions on the volume and sources of the funds to be used.
2. *Planning and control*
   (a) *The allocation of the available funds to specific uses.* Considerations of profitable employment of funds will be of prime importance

here. The financial manager's role will be to apply forecasting and appraisal expertise to the ideas of management.
(b)　*The provision of control information.*　This includes such aspects as budget reports.
(c)　*The analysis and appraisal of problems.*　Day-to-day problems will arise in managing activities within the framework set by the uses of funds decided upon.

THE VOLUME OF RESOURCES

An indication of the volume of resources used by listed companies operating mainly within the UK is given in Tables 1.1 and 1.2, and Fig. 1.1. These show that, on the basis of book values included in the companies' balance sheets, the funds employed have increased from nearly £33 000 millions in 1969 to £87 000 millions in 1977. These figures exclude non-listed companies and unincorporated businesses.

Figure 1.1

Sources of New Funds for Companies

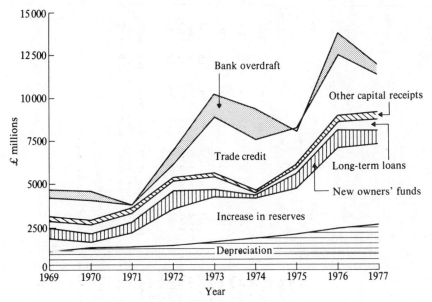

Source: *Annual Abstract of Statistics*, HMSO

Table 1.1

Sources of funds of over 1000 major UK companies

Year	1969		1970		1971		1972		1973		1974		1975		1976		1977	
Number of companies	1366		1308		1239		1168		1116		1058		1044		1006		975	
	£m	%	£m	%	£m	%	£m	%	£m	%	£m	%	£m	%	£m	%	£m	%
Trade and other creditors	6895	20.7	8131	22.6	8415	22.1	9736	22.4	13126	24.9	15858	26.2	17941	26.8	21357	27.2	23387	26.9
Bank overdrafts and loans	2505	7.5	3001	8.4	2911	7.7	3251	7.5	4611	8.7	6360	10.5	6227	9.3	7449	9.5	8151	9.4
Dividends and interest due[1]	611	1.8	621	1.7	693	1.8	1049	2.4	705	1.3	626	1.0	732	1.1	816	1.1	1010	1.1
Current tax	1868	5.6	1688	4.7	1595	4.2	1667	3.8	2215	4.2	1759	2.9	1497	2.2	1905	2.4	2050	2.4
Long-term loans	4443	13.4	4767	13.3	5250	13.8	5912	13.6	6672	12.7	6892	11.4	7339	10.9	8007	10.2	8551	9.9
Deferred tax	446	1.5	499	1.4	766	2.0	1162	2.7	1970	3.7	3360	5.6	4924	7.3	6288	8.0	5521	6.4
Shareholders' funds including minorities	16461	49.5	17188	47.9	18411	48.4	20694	47.6	23439	44.5	25667	42.4	28444	42.4	32622	41.6	38059	43.9
TOTAL SOURCES	33229	100.0	35895	100.0	38043	100.0	43472	100.0	52738	100.0	60522	100.0	67104	100.0	78444	100.0	86730	100.0

[1]Gross 1969–72. Net 1973 onwards.

Source: *Annual Abstract of Statistics*, HMSO

Table 1.2

Uses of funds in over 1000 major UK companies

Year	1969		1970		1971		1972		1973		1974		1975		1976		1977	
Number of companies	1366		1308		1239		1168		1116		1058		1044		1006		975	
	£m	%	£m	%	£m	%	£m	%	£m	%	£m	%	£m	%	£m	%	£m	%
Tangible fixed assets	12967	39.0	13707	38.2	14949	39.3	16672	38.3	19282	36.6	22116	36.5	24759	36.9	27538	35.1	30381	35.0
Goodwill	1255	3.8	1405	3.9	1572	4.1	1992	4.6	2278	4.3	2605	4.3	2441	3.6	2380	3.0	2286	2.6
Investment in unconsolidated subsidiaries	112	.4	153	.4	139	.4	146	.3	158	.3	142	.2	188	.3	297	.4	213	.2
Stocks and WIP	7913	23.8	8741	24.4	9053	23.8	9865	22.7	12627	23.9	16494	27.3	18189	27.1	21779	27.8	24353	28.1
Debtors	8148	24.5	8948	24.9	8757	23.0	9980	23.0	12479	23.7	13742	22.7	14853	22.1	17880	22.8	19662	22.7
Cash and near cash	2834	8.5	2942	8.2	3573	9.4	4817	11.1	5914	11.2	5422	9.0	6675	10.0	8568	10.9	9835	11.4
TOTAL ASSETS	33229	100.0	35895	100.0	38043	100.0	43472	100.0	52738	100.0	60522	100.0	67104	100.0	78444	100.0	86730	100.0

Source: *Annual Abstract of Statistics*, HMSO

Sources of funds

The total percentage of funds provided by short-term sources as shown in Table 1.1, i.e., trade and other creditors and bank overdrafts, increased from about 30 per cent to 37 per cent of total funds. Within the whole group the use of bank funds increased from around 7.5 per cent to 10 per cent. The other interesting trend is the changing balance between long-term loans and shareholders' funds. The former have declined from 13.4 to 9.9 per cent and the latter declined from 49.5 per cent to 43.9 per cent. These trends are further illustrated in Fig. 1.1.

A new trend is the increase in deferred tax from 1.5 per cent to 6.4 per cent. This results from the application of Statement of Standard Accounting Practice (SSAP) 11 on deferred tax. This was modified in 1978 so that provisions for future tax that the company is unlikely to have to pay are no longer required and have been released back to reserves. This proportion is therefore likely to decline in future years.

Despite a relative decline, shareholders' funds were important in the provision of new funds. The 1965 Finance Act which introduced corporation tax lead to large increases in the use of long-term debt (see Appendix A for tax implications). The crisis of 1973/74 underlined the risks of too extensive a use of loan capital and many companies have subsequently substantially improved their equity base.

Figure 1.1 underlines the role of profit and other retentions and depreciation in the provision of funds for investment within a business, depreciation alone providing over one fifth of all the funds available.

Employment of funds

The disposition of funds within the business is indicated in Table 1.2. The three principal forms in which funds are invested are: fixed assets, i.e., land and buildings, plant and machinery, stocks and work in progress, and debtors. Changes in the level of investment in each have not greatly altered over the period covered. Investment in tangible fixed assets has tended to decrease, although with the emphasis on the need for new capital investment, together with the financial incentives offered, one would have expected the change to be the other way. There has been a slight change in relative values of stocks and debtors, with the latter absorbing a smaller slice.

INTERRELATIONSHIPS AT DIFFERENT MANAGEMENT LEVELS

The linking of financial management with general management decisions at all levels is illustrated in Fig. 1.2. Included in this chart is data processing, which deals with the recording and analysis of events for the feedback of information to management. This is traditionally a function of financial management—

indeed, until a few years ago, one of the most important. The advent of the computer and its attendant specialists and, it must be faced, the lethargy of accountants, has left this area wide open for treatment as a specialist service operating outside the other functions.

Figure 1.2

Schematic outline of the finance function

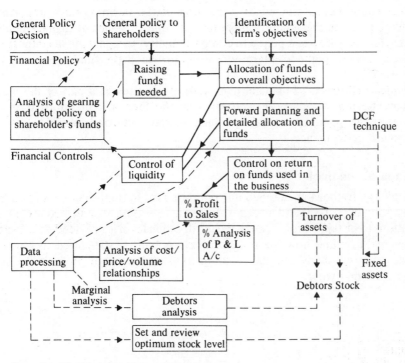

Reproduced by kind permission of *The Accountant*

Board of Directors level.   The two basic activities to which financial management makes an important contribution are the identification of the objectives of the business and, directly related to this, devising the corporate strategy for the business over the planning period. The strategy should include specific performance standards for all levels of management, including financial management. Additionally, but related to that strategy, board decisions should determine the relations of the business with its owners. These decisions include such matters as the proportion of funds to be raised as shareholder funds, as against borrowing, and dividend policy. The analysis of these relationships will provide significant parameters which will affect the company's internal investment policy, since management must relate the return requirements of investors with the earning capacity of investment in the business.

Financial policy.   Within the overall strategy set by management, the funds available to the business year by year will be put to use. This management decision will be reinforced by the financial analysis and appraisal of investment projects, and the feedback of operating information.

The funds needs created by expansion of the business have important implications for the liquidity position, and one of financial management's tasks here is to devise a policy to control liquidity, to signal the need for fund raising, and to point to alternative ways in which the funds need can be satisfied.

Financial controls.   Financial management operates as a part of the management team. Its purpose is to provide the feedback of information to facilitate the management tasks of planning, reporting, and control to ensure optimum performance.

Scope of the book

Within the framework outlined it is not proposed to treat the topics from the viewpoint of systems and methods. Instead, an outline of some major considerations to be taken into account at each decision level is provided. It will also attempt to outline how the decision process can be structured to reach a conclusion conducive to the maximization of long-term profitability and return to the owners.

2

Managing profitability

Accepting that the central purpose of a business is to earn a profit, the first problem is to determine those factors which make the level of profitability what it is. In this part of the book we examine aspects of managerial decisions which combine to produce the level of profitability as expressed in the Return on Capital Employed (ROCE). These decision areas will be related to:

1. The volume of sales.
2. The percentage of sales revenue absorbed by different cost areas, so determining the profit margin on sales.
3. The volume of funds required to support that level of activity through investment in fixed assets and working capital.

At present, the most important use of profitability measurement lies in deducing trends within a company. As soon as comparisons between two or more businesses are attempted, difficulties arise. Differing accounting practices and bases for valuation of assets become very important. While large differences between companies (or industries) are significant, finer comparisons should only be attempted under special conditions.

Two further general points should be borne in mind. Firstly, balance sheets are prepared on the 'going concern basis', i.e., at cost or revaluation less provisions for diminution in value, and do not purport to show the open market value. Secondly, in times of high inflation there are serious distortions in balance sheet values and the measurement of profit, unless some form of inflation accounting is adopted.

No doubt, in time, interfirm comparisons will assume greater significance. In the author's experience, when discussing ratios with managers, the question most asked is, 'What is the proper level for this ratio?' As managers become more aware of the possibility of comparing the level of performance of their firm with that of others in their industry, there will be much readier acceptance of interfirm comparison schemes, such as those of the Centre for Interfirm Comparisons.

Profitability

To say that X company made a profit of £1 million last year tells very little about the company and its profitability. This profit may have been earned by employing a capital of £5 million or £100 million. Any assessment of profitability must first measure the relationship between the profit and the funds committed to the business to earn that profit.

RETURN ON CAPITAL EMPLOYED

This is essentially a measure of the effectivenes of management in earning a return on the funds used in the business. At this stage no account is taken of how the funds are raised. It is measured by taking the operating profit of the business and expressing it as a percentage of the resources committed to the business. When used to show the trend over a number of years for a single company, such a percentage is a useful index of managerial efficiency in employing those resources.

What measurement of resources to use?

A number of different measures of capital employed have been used in the past. It is now becoming accepted that by capital employed we mean the *total long-term funds* employed in the business. In the balance sheet of a business, this can be defined either as the total of shareholders' funds and borrowed funds, or as the net assets of the business, i.e., total assets less current liabilities, the two values being the same.

The justification for this definition is that it measures those funds committed to the company on a long-term basis and on which it is expected to provide a return, whether in interest on borrowed funds or dividends to shareholders. Moreover, it is concerned with funds employed for a number of years, as distinct from funds provided by trade creditors or by bank overdrafts, which are used for only a short time and are soon replaced by different funds from the same or similar sources.

The question as to whether bank borrowing should be included in capital employed sometimes causes difficulties. Technically, a bank overdraft is repayable on demand and should be included in short-term funds. One must recognize, however, that some companies, as a matter of policy, rely consistently year by year on bank borrowing, effectively using it as a long-term source. Where such is the policy, the logical treatment is to include bank borrowing in the capital employed.

What level of profit to use?

The level of earnings measured against the capital employed must be considered from two points of view. Firstly, shall we take the measurement before or after tax? Secondly, should the earnings be taken before charging interest on long-term borrowing or after?

The treatment of tax will largely depend upon the purposes for which the ROCE is used. If one is looking at the return as the starting point for measuring the effect of internal operating activities, then a before-tax measurement may be desirable since it avoids the complications of tax with which most levels of management are not directly concerned.

On the other hand, when looking at the business as an entity for the purpose of appraisal, there may be considerable benefits in measuring earnings on an after-tax basis. After all, it is only out of after-tax profits that the business provides a return to its owners and accumulates retained profits to finance growth. Tax, in itself, will have an important impact on the availability of profit for these uses.

The other major consideration in determining 'What level of profit to use?' is the treatment of interest on long-term funds. Such an interest payment is effectively a part of the return on total long-term funds being appropriated to a particular part of those funds. As such, it forms part of the overall ROCE and should not be excluded from the measurement of profit.

Consider the following situation:

	£
Shareholders' funds	100 000
6% Debenture	40 000
Capital employed	£140 000

	£
(*EBIT*) Profit before interest	14 000
Interest	2 400
Profit before tax	£11 600

The ROCE is 14 000 × 100 / 140 000 = 10 per cent. This is the rate earned on the overall commitment of £140 000 long-term funds to the business. Taking away from the £14 000 profit the interest cost of £2400, the remaining profit of £11 600 is the return on the ordinary shareholders' funds only.

(*8%*)

Figure 2.1

X Ltd

Balance sheet as at 31 December 1980

EMPLOYMENT OF FUNDS: FIXED ASSETS	Cost £	Deprn £	£	£
Land and buildings	150 000	—	150 000	
Plant and machinery	275 000	150 000	125 000	
Vehicles	16 000	9 000	7 000	
	441 000	159 000	282 000	282 000

Figure 2.1—*contd.*

	£	£
CURRENT ASSETS		
Stock and work in progress	364 000	
Debtors and prepayments	195 000	
Cash in hand	35 000	
		594 000
Less:		876 000
CURRENT LIABILITIES		
Trade creditors	189 000	
Accrued liabilities	6 000	
Tax payable 1 January 1981	21 000	
Dividend	20 000	
		236 000
NET ASSETS		£640 000
SOURCES OF FUNDS:		
SHAREHOLDERS' FUNDS:		
7% preference shares	100 000	
200 000 £1 ordinary shares	200 000	
Capital reserves	63 000	
Retained profits	96 000	
	459 000	459 000
6% debentures 1990/95		150 000
Tax payable 1 January 1982		31 000
		£640 000

Profit and loss account for the year to 31 December 1980

	£	£
Sales (net)		1 280 000
Cost of goods sold		938 000
Gross profit		342 000
Operating expenses		251 000
Operating profit		91 000
Interest on debentures		9 000
Net profit		82 000
Tax at 50%*		41 000
Profit after tax		41 000
7% preference dividend	7 000	
Dividend on ordinary shares: 10p per share	20 000	
		27 000
Retained profit		£14 000

* The actual tax charge may differ from the amount calculated by multiplying the tax rate by the net profit since the Revenue will disallow the depreciation included in the expenses and substitute instead the capital allowances due for that year. There may also be other differences between what are considered as revenue and capital items, as between Income Tax law and the management's practice.

Using the figures for X Ltd in Fig. 2.1, the ROCE can be calculated as follows:

ROCE (before tax): 91 000 × 100/640 000 = <u>14.22%</u>

To calculate the after-tax ROCE, the operating profit must first be converted to an after-tax value. The basis for this (which readers will find a useful starting point when handling mixtures of before- and after-tax values later) can be taken from the profit and loss account as follows:

	Before tax	Tax @ 50%	After tax
	£	£	£
Operating profit	91 000*	45 500	45 500
Interest	9 000*	4 500	4 500
Net profit	82 000*	41 000*	41 000*

The figures with asterisks are taken directly from the profit and loss account. The rest are inserted by calculating the tax of £4500 saved by the interest payment. This is deducted from the gross cost of interest to give an after-tax cost of £4500. The tax and after-tax values of the operating profit are calculated by adding the second and third lines together:

ROCE (after tax): 45 500 × 100/640 000 = <u>7.1%</u>

Changes in the value of capital employed during the year

Where there are major changes in the total value of capital employed during the year, e.g., if an additional loan is raised or owners subscribe new funds, then it may be necessary to calculate the average capital employed during the year. A ROCE based upon the year-end figure only would give an untrue picture of the profitability for that year.

Return on capital employed in UK companies

Looking at a cross-section of over 1000 British companies from 1969 to 1977 (Table 2.1), it can be seen that the ROCE has fluctuated between 14.0 and 18.1 per cent before tax and 8.0 and 11.4 per cent after tax, the fluctuations following the pattern of alternate squeeze and boom in the economy.

DETERMINANTS OF RETURN ON CAPITAL EMPLOYED

A little reflection on the way in which the return on capital employed was calculated shows that the return depends upon the interrelation between three factors: the *volume of sales*, the *margin of profit* earned on those sales, and the *capital investment required* to sustain the sales volume.

Table 2.1

Return on capital employed in major UK industrial companies
1969—77

Year	Capital employed	Earnings before interest and tax	% on capital employed	Earnings before interest but after tax	% on capital employed
	£ millions	£ millions	%	£ millions	%
1969	21 349	3167	14.8	1988	9.3
1970	22 454	3135	14.0	2093	9.3
1971	22 428	3522	15.7	2373	10.6
1972	27 769	4512	16.2	3162	11.4
1973	32 081	5691	17.7	3359	10.4
1974	35 918	5753	16.0	3250	9.0
1975	40 707	5921	14.5	3263	8.0
1976	46 917	8474	18.1	4878	10.4
1977	52 131	9121	17.5	5612	10.8

Source: *Annual Abstract of Statistics*, HMSO

For a given sales volume, profitability is maximized if the margin of profit on sales is at its highest and capital employed at its lowest. The desirability or otherwise of increasing sales volume will depend upon both its effect on margins and on the level of capital employed. The increased profit potential of a higher level of sales may be more than compensated for by reduced margins and/or increased capital requirements—a condition of profitless expansion.

In analysing profitability, therefore, our next step after calculating ROCE is to examine the effect that margins have on profitability and the efficiency with which management employs the capital of the business in relation to the sales volume.

MARGIN ON SALES

The level of profit used in the calculation of the ROCE can now be expressed as a percentage of the sales value for the period. This ratio, therefore, expresses the operating profit before interest (and either before or after tax) as a percentage of sales value. For X Ltd the ratio is:

Margin on sales (after tax):

$$45\,500 \times 100/1\,280\,000 = \underline{3.55\%}$$

TURNOVER OF CAPITAL EMPLOYED

The efficiency with which management uses capital available may well be critical for the profitability of the business. Indeed, the data given in Table 2.3 on page 22 indicate that the cause of differences in profitability between UK and US companies in the electronics industries is that in the US, management has learned the art of managing funds successfully, particularly the way in which they are locked up in stocks and debtors.

Turnover of capital employed X Ltd:

$$1\,280\,000/640\,000 = 2 \text{ times per year}$$

Note that the determinants of profitability are now expressed in a mathematical relationship between the three ratios dealt with so far, i.e:

ROCE 7.1% = Margin on sales 3.55%

$$\times \text{ Turnover of capital employed 2 times}$$

RETURN ON EQUITY FUNDS

What has been examined so far is the return on *all* the long-term funds committed to the business. Investors in equity shares will be conscious of the return earned on the funds they have provided. This return is decided by two factors:

1. The return earned on capital employed.
2. The 'gearing' factor that is built into the capital structure.

The gearing factor (called 'leverage' in the USA) is built into the capital structure by the inclusion of fixed interest borrowing and fixed dividend shareholders' funds. The return on equity is, therefore, the end result of the policies pursued by management in its two fundamental financial roles: how the funds of the business are raised, and the control of the profitability of those funds in the uses selected.

As far as the equity holders of X Ltd are concerned, the return on their funds will be made up of the profits available to the *ordinary* shareholders as a percentage of ordinary shareholders' funds. The profits available are profit after tax of £41 000 less £7000 preference dividend.

Return on equity X Ltd: $34\,000 \times 100/359\,000 = 9.47\%$

In this case, the fact that £100 000 of the capital employed is in the form of fixed dividend shares and a further £150 000 in the form of 6 per cent debentures, has contributed to lifting the after-tax return from 7.1 per cent on capital employed to 9.47 per cent on equity. The possibilities and limitations of gearing will be explored further in Chapters 13 and 14. Meanwhile, the top of the pyramid of financial ratios can be expressed as follows:

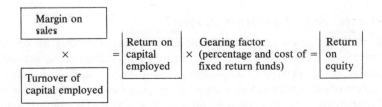

Return on equity in UK companies

The return on equity earned by over 1000 UK companies during the period 1969–77 is shown in Table 2.2. The rate changes from 9.8 to 14.1 per cent (and is of course on an after-tax basis). It is interesting that the average ROCE over the nine years was 9.9 per cent compared with the average return on equity over the same period of 11.96 per cent. The advantages that can be derived from gearing are clearly evident.

Table 2.2
Return on equity for major industrial companies in the UK 1969–77

Year	Equity funds	Profit available for ordinary shareholders	Return on equity
	£ millions	£ millions	%
1969	15 005	1650	11.0
1970	15 790	1730	11.0
1971	16 923	1965	11.6
1972	19 111	2694	14.1
1973	21 617	2783	12.9
1974	23 787	2560	10.8
1975	26 411	2529	9.8
1976	30 298	4030	13.3
1977	35 667	4690	13.1

Source: *Annual Abstract of Statistics*, HMSO

Industry variations

The way in which the margin on sales and the turnover of capital employed combine to form the return on capital employed will vary greatly between different industries. Some will be high turnover, low margin industries, some highly capital intensive.

DETERMINANTS OF MAJOR RATIOS

Having examined the make-up of the return on capital employed in terms of its two major components, it is now the turn of these components themselves to be examined. If management is to be able to control within certain limits the profitability of the business it manages, then it must be able to isolate and measure the major operating factors which lead to a particular level of profitability.

What determines the margin on sales?

Profit is the residual amount left out of gross income after all operating expenses have been met. The margin of profit will, therefore, be determined by movement in groups of expenditure relative to sales. The higher the proportion of sales revenue absorbed by any group of expenditure, the smaller the proportion of gross income remaining as profit. The identification of the significant operating costs, and their relationship to gross income through the medium of ratios, will form an essential part of the control of profit determinants.

Work along the lines of defining these significant relationships and arranging methods of measuring them are being explored by organizations such as the Centre for Interfirm Comparisons. The objective of such studies is to build up a 'pyramid' of ratios, showing the relationship of costs and uses of funds to sales volume in the build-up to the return on assets employed.

Turnover of capital employed

As mentioned previously, this ratio measures the efficiency with which the business utilizes its capital in relation to the volume of sales. The higher the turnover of capital, *all other things being equal*, the higher will be the return on capital employed. Profitability is determined as much by this factor as by any other.

A cornerstone of financial management is control of this ratio. It is achieved by devising control tools for the major uses of funds:

1. Fixed assets, i.e., land, buildings, plant and machinery, vehicles, ships, etc.
2. Stocks and work in progress.
3. Debtors and prepayments.

Knowing that these are the major uses of funds raises the question, 'Can methods be devised to control investment in these three fields so as to control the turnover of capital employed?' To some extent this is possible provided that one takes into account the time cycle of decision making within the business.

Turnover of fixed assets

Investment in fixed assets is essentially of a long-term nature. Therefore, the turnover of fixed assets ratio may indicate whether investment decisions have been good or bad, but will not provide a *control* tool. Such control can only be exercised *before the investment in fixed assets is made*. Once funds have been committed to this use the quality of the decision will affect the business for some years. If the decision was wrong, it can be recognized by writing off the investment as a loss, or one can try to minimize the adverse effects until the next decision point is reached, i.e., whether or not to replace the asset.

Because of the long-term nature of such investment, control will depend upon a system of *capital investment appraisal*. This will subject investment proposals to evaluation in terms of return and other factors before funds are committed (see Chapter 6).

Turnover of stocks and work in progress

Both this ratio and the following one, which is concerned with the level of investment in debtors, must be treated at two levels. Firstly, when looking at a company's published balance sheet where the data is necessarily restricted, the sophistication of analysis is severely limited. Secondly, management should have available within the business a range of additional information facilitating a more realistic measurement of the ratio, which can be incorporated into the information reporting system.

1. Assessing published accounts.   Taking the published balance sheet position first, what one requires is an assessment of the effectiveness of management in controlling the volume of funds absorbed by this use. Usually, the only figures available are the sales for the year and the year-end value of stocks, etc. The method of measurement is designed to show whether the percentage change in stocks over the period exceeds or falls short of the percentage change in sales. Taking the figures for X Ltd, the ratio is calculated as follows:

Turnover of stock and work in progress:

1 280 000/364 000 = 3.5 times per year

2. Internal control measurement.   The above method of calculation suffers from two chief defects. It is measuring sales valued at selling price against stocks, etc., which are valued at cost. Movements in the mark-up between cost and selling price will themselves influence the ratio. Secondly, it is a moot point just how relevant are sales in January or February of any year to stocks held at the end of the year. The general trend in sales and seasonal factors may have significant effects.

Management has available all the data needed to correct these defects. Instead of using the sales volume in the calculation, the proper figure is the *cost of goods sold*. Thus, both parts of the ratio are valued on the same basis. The recalculated figure for X Ltd will then be:

Turnover of stock and work in progress:

938 000/364 000 = 2.6 times per year

The cycle of events in most businesses would suggest that stock levels are related to the immediate past level of sales, or to future sales. When the turnover of stock is included in the management information system, it can be calculated using the cost of goods sold based on, say, the last three months' sales. This gives a much more proximate measurement.

It would also be desirable to calculate separate ratios for material stocks, work in progress, and finished stock (these figures are now published in annual reports), and for separate operating areas.

Debtors' ratio

The level of debtors or accounts receivable in the balance sheet is determined by two factors:

1. The volume of sales
2. The length of time it takes to collect amounts owing by customers.

A convenient way of expressing this ratio is in the number of days' sales that the debtors represent. This provides a ratio which compares debtors to sales and at the same time enables one to compare the actual collection time with the firm's allowed credit period.

The first step in ascertaining the ratio is to calculate the average daily sales for the period under review. Taking the sales value for X Ltd for the year to be £1 280 000, this would be £3500 per day, i.e:

Average Daily Sales = £1 280 000/365 = £3500

The number of calendar days in the period has been taken rather than the number of working days. This is a logical approach since the credit period allowed by the firm is expressed in calendar days.

To calculate the number of days' sales represented by debtors, the average daily sales are now divided into the total debtors:

Debtors ratio: £195 000/3500 = 56 days

X Ltd is, therefore, taking on average 56 days to collect the cash due in respect of sales. Every additional day adds £3500 to debtors with no extra return.

As with the stock ratio, when used for internal control purposes this ratio would be calculated on a much more proximate basis. Average daily sales would be based upon the last two or three months' sales rather than the annual sales.

COMPARATIVE RATIOS

Comparisons of profitability as between US and UK companies tend to suggest that in the US much more effective control of the employment of funds is exercised, and that this is the prime reason for their higher level of profitability. On comparisons made by the author, profit margins tended on the whole to be comparable between the two countries, the higher return on capital employed being achieved by a much more effective use of the capital available. These studies which have been carried out in the aerospace industries are supported by an investigation carried out in the electronics industry and reported in New Technology[1]: it is reproduced in Table 2.3. The key point of these ratios is that the higher US profitability is due entirely to more effective use of investment in assets.

[1] New Technology, Ministry of Technology, March 1968

Table 2.3

Comparison of ratios between UK and US electronics industries

	US companies		UK companies	
	(Base sales = 100 units)			
SALES		100.0		100.0
PROFITS before tax and loan interest		10.0		9.0
	Equiv. months' sales		Equiv. months' sales	
CAPITAL EMPLOYED				
Fixed capital				
Operating assets at WDV	2.0	17.0	2.8	23.0
Investment and other fixed assets	0.4	3.0	0.8	7.0
	2.4	20.0	3.6	30.0
Working capital				
Inventories	2.2	18.0	4.3	36.0
Debtors and prepayments	2.0	17.0	4.1	34.0
Creditors and accruals (deduct)	(1.8)	(15.0)	(2.4)	(20.0)
	2.4	20.0	6.0	50.0
Total capital employed	4.8	40.0	9.6	80.0
Profit to sales (%)		10.0%		9.0%
Ratio sales to capital employed		2.5		1.2
Profit to capital employed (%)		25.0%		11.3%
Sales per £ of fixed operating assets		£5.9		£4.4
Sales per employee (using £1 = $2.80)		£6000		£2700

Source: *New Technology,* Ministry of Technology, March 1968

There are obvious dangers in making comparisons between different firms in different countries, but the gap between the ratios produced by each, or the lessons which must be drawn from them, are too startling to ignore.

The ratios dealing with the investments in stock and debtors give management only an overall view of trends within their firms. A much more detailed analysis of optimum stock levels, credit terms for customers, and procedures for implementing management's policies in these respects are needed if the general level of profitability of UK companies is to be raised.

THE FINANCIAL STRUCTURE

The full structure of relationships between the ratios is now set out in Fig. 2.2. This also shows the management planning and control tools that are associated with operating ratios. Ratios of concern to investors (dealt with later) are added to complete the framework.

Figure 2.2

The financial structure of the firm

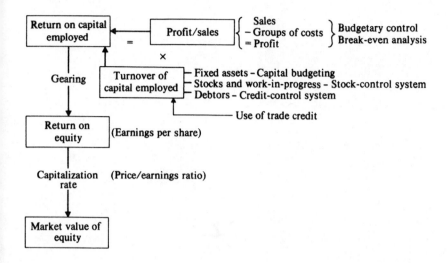

ASSET VALUATIONS

One of the difficulties in looking at the comparative profitability of a number of companies lies in the differences in practice in valuing the assets used in the business. This is particularly true of fixed assets. In modern times, there has been a continuing erosion of the value of money, contrasting with the accounting practice of recording asset values in terms of cost. In time, cost becomes less representative of the real value of the assets employed.

The effect that the process of inflation can have is shown in Fig. 2.3. It is assumed that the fixed assets in A were purchased five years ago and that inflation has averaged 6 per cent per annum over that period. If we calculate the return on capital employed using cost as the basis of valuation, less depreciation based on that value, then a return on capital employed of 10 per cent after tax is shown which management may consider adequate.

Consider, however, the real value of the assets employed. At present-day prices their book value is £382 000 and not the £305 000 shown, and the ROCE is 8 not 10 per cent, taking the same level of after-tax profits of £29 000. This return might not be one acceptable to management.

$$\frac{10\%}{\frac{30 \cdot 5}{305}} \qquad \frac{8\%}{\frac{30 \cdot 5}{382}}$$

Figure 2.3

Effect of inflation on the balance sheet values and return on capital employed

	A		B
			Adjusted for
			inflation at
	At cost		6% per year
	(£000's)		(£000's)
ASSETS EMPLOYED:			
Fixed assets:			
Freehold buildings			
at cost	100	As revalued	134
Plant and machinery			
at cost	250	As revalued	335
		Less depreciation:	
Less: depreciation 125		Original	
—	125	provision 125	
		Additional	
		provision 42	
		— 167	
		—	168
	225		302
Net current assets	80		80
NET ASSETS	£305		£382
SOURCES OF FUNDS:			
Share capital	200		200
Capital reserve	—	From revaluation of:	
		Buildings 34	
		Plant and machinery 85	
		Additional provision for	
		depreciation (42)	
		—	77
Retained profits	55		55
Total shareholders' funds	255		332
6% debenture 19x8/z2 →	50		50
	£305		£382
Recorded profit in the fifth year		*Recorded profits in future years*	
Profit before depreciation	86.0		86.0
Depreciation	25.0		33.5
	61.0		52.5
Less Interest on debenture	3.0		3.0
	58.0		49.5
Taxation at 50%	29.0		29.0
Profit after tax	£29.0		£20.5
Return on capital employed			
(after tax)	10%		5.8%

$$\frac{61}{\text{on tax } 30\cdot 5} \quad \frac{30\cdot 5}{305} = 10\% . \qquad \frac{52\cdot 5 - 30\cdot 5}{382} = 5\cdot 8$$
$$30\cdot 5$$

The reduction to 8 per cent is not, however, the whole picture. The plant and machinery will now take £335 000 to replace instead of £250 000. The profit and loss account shows £'s of different values. Sales and most of the items of expenditure are current year £'s, but depreciation is charged in terms of £'s of five years ago. If the real value of profits is to be stated correctly, the depreciation charge must be increased. Assuming a further five years' life for the plant, the total value to be depreciated is £335 000, less the depreciation already provided of £125 000 and the additional provision to cover the first five years' undercharge of £42 000. Depreciation of £33 500 per year will now be required rather than the previous figure of £25 000. As the Inland Revenue do not recognize that such a thing as inflation exists, they will continue to tax the profits on the old basis, so that the after-tax profits in real terms are only £20 500 instead of £29 000, bringing down the return on capital employed to 5.8 per cent which is very different from the 10 per cent shown by the pre-valuation figures.

In addition to the balance sheet effects there is the problem of measuring the profit itself. This is because the stocks, etc., being used up to meet sales are based on historic cost (or if LIFO is being used, on the most recent purchase price). If some form of inflation accounting is adopted the cost of goods and services used up should be based on replacement cost, thus further reducing ROCE.

EFFECT OF ASSET VALUATION ON SETTING PROFIT TARGETS

If the balance sheet values of the business do not adequately reflect the real value of the capital employed, the business may be setting the wrong target levels of profit. If there is an early recognition of the position, such as that in Fig. 2.3, management should want to review the current profit targets. If a return of 10 per cent after tax is considered appropriate for the type of business, then the level of after-tax profits in real terms should be £36 700 after allowing for the additional depreciation to be charged. If management finds that the type of business will not permit that rate of return, then it must consider the future of the business very carefully indeed. Either a means must be found of introducing new products/services, internally or by acquisition, or liquidation should be considered.

INVESTMENT RATIOS

The investor will be examining investments held and potential investment opportunities from a different point of view, namely the return that he expects to accrue to him, in terms of income and capital gain, in relation to the current share price in the stock market.

Earnings per share

This is a measure of the after-tax earnings of a business available to the class of shares being appraised divided by the number of shares at issue. Taking the figures previously used for X Ltd in Fig. 2.1, there are after-tax profits of £34 000 available to the ordinary shareholders, i.e., earnings after tax of £41 000, less the cost of the preference dividend of £7000. There are 200 000 ordinary shares issued, so the EPS are 34 000 × 100/200 000 = 17p.

Price/earnings ratio (P/E ratio)

The P/E ratio is a measurement of the number of years' purchase of the current EPS represented by the market price of the shares. If, in the previous example, the current price of the ordinary shares had been £1.70, the P/E would be 10 (£1.70/17p).

It is true, in assessing the implications of the P/E ratio, that the price of the share reflects investors' anticipations of the *future* earnings, whereas the P/E ratio relates this to the *past* earnings of the business.

Gross dividend yield

In making his investment decision, the investor, in addition to the P/E ratio, must also consider the gross dividend yield on the shares, i.e., the anticipated net dividend plus tax credit[1] as a percentage of the current market price for the shares. For X Ltd, the present dividend yield would be:

10p net dividend + 4.29p tax credit = 14.29p

equivalent gross dividend as a percentage
of the share price of £1.70 = $\dfrac{14.29 \times 100}{1.70}$ = 8.4%

That is to say that for every £100 invested at today's price in the ordinary shares of X Ltd, the investor receives a gross dividend of £8.40 per year.

Note that if investors' expectations for the future earnings improve they will be prepared to increase the amount that they are prepared to pay for the shares. Thus the P/E will rise and the gross dividend yield will fall.

Dividend cover (Times covered in the *Financial Times*)

This ratio measures the number of times that the cost of the dividend is covered by earnings available to that security on an annual basis. For X Ltd, the dividend cover for the preference and ordinary dividends is calculated as follows:

	Profit available £	Cost of dividend £	Times covered
Preference dividend	41 000	7 000	5.9 times
Ordinary dividend	34 000	20 000	1.7 times

[1] For consideration of the tax system see Appendix A.

3

Managing stocks and work in progress

As indicated in the previous chapter, the amount of capital employed that is 'locked up' in inventories of one sort or another will help determine the level of profitability achieved. This will arise from two causes:

1. There will be costs associated with storing and handling materials which will increase overall operating costs.
2. The higher the value of capital employed used in this way as against sales volume, the lower will be its turnover and consequently a lower return on capital employed will be earned.

Table 3.1

Annual changes in the value of stocks and work in progress
for over 1000 major UK companies
(£ millions)

Year	Changes in value against previous year
	Increases
1969	819
1970	817
1971	306
1972	763
1973	2694
1974	3846
1975	1620
1976	3732
1977	2710

Source: *Annual Abstract of Statistics*, HMSO

The sums of money invested in inventory are large. Table 3.1 shows the annual *movements* in stock and work in progress for over 1000 major companies in the UK, while Table 1.2 showed that, in 1977, stocks and work in progress represented 28 per cent of total assets and *some 47 per cent of*

27

capital employed. The adequacy of managerial control over this use of funds has a material effect upon profitability. This was clearly demonstrated in the comparative ratios of UK and US companies on page 22.

THE 'IDEAL' STOCK LEVEL

The ideal level of inventory would be the situation where materials, etc., are delivered into the factory, incorporated into the product, and delivered to the customer in one day. This 'ideal' situation cannot be achieved or may be undesirable for a number of reasons:

1. Materials and parts can be purchased more cheaply in large lots.
2. Reserve stocks would be required to avoid stoppages in production through interruptions in deliveries.
3. Production time cycles are longer than one day in most businesses.
4. The production flows from different manufacturing stages may not match, in which case the imbalance is adjusted through intermediate stock holdings.
5. The order pattern is not even. Orders arrive in irregular flows and to maintain customer goodwill quick deliveries are essential.
6. It is difficult to forecast future demand patterns.
7. The economies of scale may be lost.

While the 'ideal' stock level is impracticable, decisions on stock levels should only be taken with the knowledge that deviations from it may adversely affect profitability. Extensions of the time interval should be assessed in terms of the ultimate effect on the ROCE.

COSTS OF HOLDING STOCKS AND
WORK IN PROGRESS

Certain items of operating costs are clearly influenced by the level of stocks held. Space costs increase as additional warehousing is used; as items remain in the store longer, they are subject to additional deterioration and wastage; the risks of obsolescence and of changes in consumer tastes increase; the 'housekeeping' within the stores becomes more costly; insurance costs increase, etc. All of these may add up to a considerable mark-up on the actual material costs.

Risks

Stock level decisions must have some regard to the risks involved in committing funds in this way. The 'ideal' stock level has virtually no risk factor since the complete time cycle is one day. As that time cycle is stretched, the exposure to risk is automatically increased. Goods bought six months in advance of needs are much more at risk than those bought only one month in advance.

Obsolescence and changes in consumer tastes have already been mentioned. Other forces are at work the whole time which influence the firm's need for the materials, goods, etc., in question. Government economic or fiscal measures may reduce overall demand; a major customer may go out of business leaving no market for the products supplied, etc.

CAUSES OF DEVIATION FROM THE 'IDEAL'

Raw material and piece part stores

Inventory at this stage consists of materials and parts awaiting issue to manufacturing processes. Factors which induce management to move away from the 'ideal' stock position include those detailed below.

Avoiding interruptions to production. The lower the level of stocks maintained, the more susceptible is the business to interruptions to the manufacturing process by the cessation of outside supplies. This is evidenced most clearly in the motor industry in the UK, where strikes at suppliers quickly halt the assembly lines in the plants. This can be a costly factor which must be offset against the costs of holding reserve stocks.

Avoiding anticipated increases in material prices. Some materials such as wool and copper, are subject to substantial price fluctuations. It is quite rational of management, therefore, to overstock such materials at times when prices are likely to rise in the future.

This decision is not one, however, which is concerned basically with setting the right stock levels. It is one concerned with speculating in future material prices and the likely return on capital employed in this activity should be separately appraised together with the attendant risks.

Making the optimum use of purchasing power. The ability of the business to place substantial orders with suppliers may enable the buyer to win useful quantity discounts. When the orders are widely dispersed in small lots bargaining power may be diminished.

Sometimes, although large orders are placed, actual deliveries are spread to suit the requirements of the purchaser. Although the company may thus have off-loaded storage costs, the risks of stockholding remain since there is usually an enforceable contract to take the quantity ordered.

Work in progress

In the typical factory, production flow materials and parts pass through a number of manufacturing processes before finally emerging as a finished product. The time required for each of the manufacturing operations puts a minimum level to the value of work in progress to be carried. Moreover, it is frequently not possible exactly to match the capacity at each stage of production, and optimum batch sizes may differ. These factors can only be balanced by carrying the necessary buffers of work between each stage.

The task of management here is to weigh the benefits of optimum batch size at each manufacturing stage against the costs of carrying the buffer stocks required to even out product flows.

In some industries, it may be possible to reduce the burden of carrying stocks and work in progress by getting the customer to finance part of the cost. Typically, this is the case in the building and construction industry where the client makes progress payments based upon the value of work done. In any industry where individual orders are large and production cycles long, the possibility of financing work in progress in this way should be explored.

Finished stocks

Consumer demand requirements.   The ability to service customer requirements speedily is a part of the business's marketing strategy and will be offered as a major selling point in many cases. This is most clearly seen in retailing. The point of sale availability is the cornerstone of good retailing, and the more frequently a firm's lines are out of stock the less likely are customers to return. Since orders do not arrive, even in other industries, in a steady flow, it is in a firm's interests to maintain certain stock levels to avoid a 'stock out' situation.

This is not, however, a case for filling up shelves with stocks. Major supermarkets recognize this and introduce sophisticated forecasting techniques designed to balance supply and demand in individual shops. Some of these systems are computer based and take into account a range of information, the goal being to make a delivery to the shop just before stocks become exhausted. Attention can then be devoted to devising optimum delivery sizes and timings to link up with forecast demand levels.

Risks.   Finished products are often highly specific to an individual use and changes in demand can result in total or partial loss of value. While it may be possible to divert raw materials or processed parts to other uses, this is impossible with the end product.

Cyclical demand

Many industries are affected by cyclical patterns of demand for their products, or in the supply of raw materials. Ice-cream and toy manufacturers find that the requirement for their product changes with the seasons, whereas the canning industry is affected by the seasonal nature of the raw materials.

The choice facing management when the demand pattern is cyclical is whether to adjust the production levels to match the demand requirements, or to smooth production levels by building up and running down stocks. The former course of action will keep stock levels at a minimum but will have other disadvantages. The work force will have to be built up and run down each year causing problems with recruitment and training. Since there will be a peak production volume, plant and machinery will be maintained to support that level of activity, to be idle for the remainder of the year.

In the latter case, substantial stocks must be built up during the slack season to support the peak level of sales. This requires not only a high stock investment but also, since production occurs well in advance of demand, there is a much greater exposure to risk.

A similar situation exists where, although demand and supply need are not cyclical, the business has the opportunity of taking advantage of temporary low prices, whether due to seasonal or other influences, to stock up on forward material requirements. Whether or not it is worth while to do so depends upon an assessment of the differential between the savings and costs related to the decision, and the measurement of any expected increment of profit against the additional funds locked up.

SETTING OPTIMUM STOCK QUANTITIES

The determination of the optimum stock level is based upon the behaviour of the related costs. Some of the costs connected with the holding of stock increase as smaller lots are purchased or smaller production orders placed on the shop floor. The costs of placing orders in terms of buyer's time, clerical costs, etc., increase per given volume of purchases the smaller the individual order size that is adopted. Setting up costs, etc., increase the more frequently the product run is changed.

In trying to reach the minimum stock position, to save costs of carrying stock, there will come a point where the increased costs of small orders, etc., in trying to match goods in with goods out will more than offset the savings made. The optimum position is where the combined costs of carrying stock and costs associated with its acquisition and handling are at the minimum. This is the theoretical optimum, which, however, takes no account of risk. When management has considered this, it may find that a stock level somewhat less than the theoretical optimum may be more desirable.

Determining the economic order quantity (EOQ)

The basic factors which must be considered in setting the economic order quantity, whether from the point of view of orders placed upon outside suppliers or of orders placed on the shop floor, are:

1. The optimum cost position.
2. The related risk factors.
3. The consequences of being out of stock.

A useful formula for calculating the optimum order quantity is:

Let A equal the annual usage in units.
Let S equal the ordering and handling cost per order.
Let i equal the percentage cost of carrying stock.

Let C equal the unit cost of the stock item.
Then:

$$\text{Economic order quantity (EOQ)} = \sqrt{(2AS/iC)}$$

Example: Annual usage of BX 25 is 5000 tons at a cost of £20 per ton. It costs approximately £10 to place an order and process the receipt of material, and the overall cost of holding stock is estimated at 10 per cent p.a.

$$\begin{aligned} \text{EOQ} &= \sqrt{[(2 \times 5000 \times 10)/0.1(20)]} \\ &= \sqrt{(100\,000/2)} = \sqrt{(50\,000)} = \underline{222 \text{ tons}} \end{aligned}$$

The same problem in graphical form is shown in Fig. 3.1. There, the cost of carrying stock is based on the assumption that on average over the year one half of the order quantity is in stock. Note that it was only necessary to examine the lower range of possible order size. When the number of orders per year falls to about 5 or 6, the order costs begin to become a minimal figure and are far outweighed by the cost of holding stock. In the illustration, the largest order size is one tenth of the annual usage.

Figure 3.1

Determining economic order size

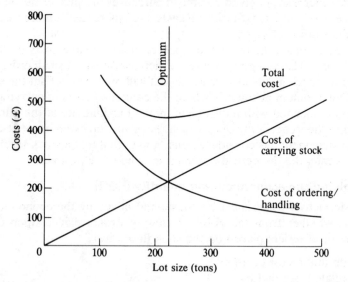

Determining the reorder point

One must consider not only the order size but also the point, in terms of remaining quantity in stock, at which a new order must be raised if a 'stock out' position is to be avoided. This should be based upon the time it takes between raising an order and the goods being delivered and the weekly usage in terms of quantity. For example, if 100 000 pressings are used each week, and it takes 4 weeks for an order raised now to be executed, then the reorder point is reached when the quantity in stock falls to 400 000 units, the order size being the EOQ.

This assumes that usage or customer demand can be forecast with accuracy, and that there is no risk of delay in deliveries. These factors can only be adequately considered in a simulation situation where probabilities can be assigned to forecast volume requirements and to delays in delivery.

4

Managing debtors

THE DETERMINANTS OF DEBTOR VALUES

The amount of the business's funds locked up in debtors at any time is determined by the volume of sales and the period of time it takes on average to collect the amounts due from customers. If credit sales are running at the rate of £1.2 million per annum and, on average, it is taking two months to collect debts, then the amount of debtors is £200 000. This indicates that control of debtors' investment is dependent upon the ability of management to set target collection periods, supervise the operation of cash collection procedures, and monitor the length of the achieved collection period. Allied to this will be the policy for the granting of credit and its implications for bad debt cost.

Volume of funds invested

The total volume of funds needed to finance debtors by over 1000 UK companies is shown in Table 1.2. In 1977, this amounted to nearly £20000 million. The *annual* call on finance for this use included in that table is shown in Table 4.1. In recent years, this has risen from under £1000 million to over £3000 million.

CONTROL OF DEBTORS

Overall management control

To effect close control of the funds invested, management must make a number of decisions relating to the credit period, the progressing of paper work leading to the collection of cash, and the procedures for slow payers. Management must also determine what information feedback it needs if it is to exercise full control.

Management control report. The information feedback that management needs is fairly simple to install and operate. The objective of the system is to ensure that the debtors do not increase at a faster rate than sales volume. If specific targets have been laid down for the reduction of the credit period, this becomes the interim objective until the new level is reached.

Table 4.1

New investment in debtors 1969–77
for over 1000 major UK companies

Year	Increase in trade debtors
	£ millions
1969	960
1970	820
1971	(164) decrease
1972	1112
1973	2480
1974	1690
1975	1217
1976	3177
1977	1880

Source: *Annual Abstract of Statistics*, HMSO

The indicator of the length of the collection period for this purpose is similar to the debtors' ratio discussed on page 21. Using the recent credit sales values (say over the last two or three months), the value of average daily sales over that period is calculated. This is divided into the latest debtors' value. Provided that these ratios are calculated every month or similar period, they can be collated on a report as shown in Fig. 4.1

$$\text{Days Sales Outstanding} = \frac{\text{DEBT VALUE}}{\text{AV DAILY SALES}} \quad (\text{DAYS})$$

Figure 4.1

Debtors' control report
Report on outstanding debtors at September 19x2

Month	19x1	19x2
	Days' sales outstanding	
Jan.	56	57
Feb.	58	57
March	57	59
April	60	58
May	62	61
June	61	60
July	58	57
Aug.	56	54
Sept.	57	53
Oct.	55	—
Nov.	54	—
Dec.	55	—

This control document enables the manager to see whether the trend in the collection period is moving in an adverse way or not, and how the achieved collection period compares with any standard laid down by management. Trends over periods of months can be compared and, to cope with the situation in which there are significant seasonal trends, last year's figures are included for comparison.

The effects of any breakdown in the collection system becomes immediately apparent in the days' sales outstanding. It is also a useful first indication that old debts which might prove to be uncollectable are beginning to accumulate. If current sales take the usual period to collect, then an accumulation of debts older than this period will soon show in the ratio.

Credit control. The granting of credit should not be automatic. Its control should be clearly specified as the responsibility of one manager, whether salesman or accountant, and the cost of bad debts should also be his responsibility. His standard of performance then becomes measurable.

Whether the accountant or the sales manager or some other executive is responsible depends largely on the business. Where sales are made to a very wide range of small customers by representatives calling at their place of business, and speed of delivery is a major selling point, it may be more practical to allow the representative to grant or withhold credit. The difficulty is that few representatives are likely to refuse credit since it reduces both sales and their income. With this approach, the cost of bad debts must be somehow reflected back in the salesman's income.

Where the value of orders increases and each becomes significant for the company, a more formal system for vetting customers is desirable. This should probably be done by the accounts department. As the individual amounts become more critical and are significant to the stability of the business if they become bad debts, it may be essential to insure against such loss.

The firm need not rely solely upon its own staff to appraise the creditworthiness of its customers. There are a number of agencies which specialize in providing such information, i.e., Messrs Dun and Bradstreet. Many trade organizations also deal with this type of work. Examination of liquidity and profitability trends shown in the accounts of client companies is another important source of information, together with bank and other references.

Invoicing and statements. A common cause of delay in collecting amounts due is slackness in rendering invoices to customers and delays in sending out statements, or not doing so at all. In the author's experience, it is quite common for invoices to be rendered several weeks after delivery of the goods. Such firms have no hope of collecting amounts due within a reasonable period, since the customer will not pay at the earliest until the invoice has been received, processed, and finally passed for payment.

Each day's delay in collection has repercussions on the overall need for funds and upon profitability. A firm with a turnover of £10 million per year adds almost £27 500 to debtors for every calendar day's delay in collection. Weeks must not pass before initiating the paperwork for collecting sums due.

The statement is often decried in the computer age as a rather extravagant piece of paper. Practical experience in collecting accounts suggests that this is not true. The statement performs two useful functions. Firstly, it ensures that the relevant accounts in both one's own and the customer's books remain in accord with each other. Secondly, it is the first step in the pressure on the customer to pay the account.

Overdue accounts.   When the customer has not paid his account within the allowed credit period, there should be an automatic follow-up procedure until it is paid. The statement forms the first step in this process, to be followed by a sequence of letters, personal calls, etc. Finally, at the end of this sequence of events, the account should be handed to solicitors or other agents for collection.

CASH DISCOUNTS

One method frequently adopted to secure the earlier payment of sums due is to offer a cash discount for prompt payment—say $2^{1}/_{2}$ per cent for payment within 30 days. Although this can effectively speed up average collection periods, the cost should be calculated.

In general, cash discounts should not be offered unless the cost has been allowed for when fixing the price of the product. This means that the person paying within the terms will be obtaining the goods at the normal price. Those taking longer will be surcharged for slow payment.

Unless the cost has been allowed for, it can more than wipe out profits. Consider the case in which the company is currently collecting accounts within two months and, by offering a $2^{1}/_{2}$ per cent cash discount for settlement within 30 days, it reduces the collection period for those customers using the scheme to one month. The effective cost of getting the use of the funds one month earlier is 30 per cent p.a., i.e., $2^{1}/_{2}$ per cent $\times$ 12.

DETERMINING THE CREDIT POLICY

The overall marketing strategy of the business should include some decisions as to the credit period to be adopted. The granting of long-term credit can be used as a key selling point, but the cost should be weighed against that of other forms of sales promotion. If the company is the market leader, then clearly the terms it offers may be matched by the other suppliers and it is, therefore, determining the normal market terms. As a result, all competitive firms have the same long collection period.

In the case of firms which do not have set collection periods, for example, in a specialized part of the market, full play can be made of credit terms. This policy should only be used after careful appraisal of the likely effect upon sales volume, and after ensuring that the additional profit generated more than compensates for the extra investment of funds.

At the other extreme, the firm could offer an ultra-short credit period, say seven days net, and use the advantages of increased capital availability to provide a competitive advantage in quality, price, etc., and by this means expand its market share. There are examples in the UK of individual firms having pursued such a policy effectively, even in industries in which credit periods are generally lengthy.

Blind adherence to the generally accepted trade practices is to be avoided at all costs. Management should devise the policy which it thinks will produce the best long-term effect upon the return on capital employed. This policy will be based squarely upon considerations of sales volume, profit margins, and the required investment of funds.

Use of trade credit to offset seasonal demand

For the company selling a product subject to seasonal fluctuations, the use of the credit period to smooth the production cycle and limit fluctuations in investment in stocks is a possible policy. Extended credit during the slack period is offered so that the customer advances his requirements by taking early delivery. Added to a small price inducement, this can be effective in translating an uneven demand pattern into a smooth production cycle.

Similar considerations arise where the income pattern of the customer dictates payment of his bills at specific periods. The farmer, for example, receives a large proportion of his annual income when the harvest is sold each year. The firm that is prepared to tailor the granting of credit to his needs has a competitive advantage. Similar is the scheme promoted by the oil companies for their domestic customers. An estimate of annual oil usage for heating requirements is made and the customer pays one twelfth each month, thus avoiding an uneven pattern of expense for the customer, to conform to his personal cash flow from salary.

The economics of extending credit

Quite apart from the special considerations outlined above, there may be more generally applicable arguments for extending credit to customers to promote the firm's sales. Important though it is, protection against risk of loss by bad debts may receive too much emphasis. It is necessary to take all reasonable precautions to prevent bad debts as far as possible, but at the same time the granting of credit terms should be based upon an assessment of the increased volume of sales, and consequently of earnings, that will be achieved and the amounts that will actually be at risk.

Taking the situation in which a firm has sufficient capacity to expand sales beyond the present volume, the problem should be considered under three headings:

1. The risk of losing the amount due.
2. The amount that is at risk.
3. The additional earnings that can be made from the increased sales volume.

Where sales are already at the limit of capacity, the avoidance of bad debts will have overriding consideration.

The risk of the customer's failure to pay is one to which management must put some range of probabilities. This will follow a study of the balance sheets of major customers, credit reports, etc. Trends in industry, economic conditions, and in the national economy can also have a bearing upon the incidence of business failure. Under credit-squeeze conditions, the number of bankruptcies and liquidations increases markedly.

The amount at risk is not the full value of the unpaid invoice since this represents the sale value to the customer. What is at risk is the cost of the goods to the business. Where the goods are of own manufacture and there are no capacity constraints, the real amount that is at risk is the *marginal cost* of production and selling. Assuming that extended credit is essential to obtain the order, then the effect is to increase production by x units, while only the variable costs rise in direct proportion.

Similarly, when considering the benefits of the additional sales accruing from the extension of credit, it is not the net profit that is relevant but the *contribution* that each unit makes towards fixed costs and profit.

Consider the following situation. Customer X requires delivery of £1000's worth of goods per month, but his credit-worthiness is suspect. Your business has spare capacity available, the variable costs representing 50 per cent of the selling price. You estimate that two months' deliveries would be unpaid at any one time. The amounts at risk and the contribution 'earned', e.g., in respect of goods actually paid for, is shown below:

Months	Sales value	Amounts at risk: Sales value	Variable cost	'Achieved' contribution to date*
	£	£	£	£
1	1000	1000	500	—
2	1000	2000	1000	—
3	1000	2000	1000	500
4	1000	2000	1000	1000
5	1000	2000	1000	1500

* Based upon payments being received two months after delivery.

The amount at risk increases to £1000 at the end of the second month with no 'achieved' contribution (no payments having been received from the customer). In the third month, deliveries of a further £1000 are matched by the receipt of cash for the first month's deliveries. As one month's sales have now been paid for there is an 'achieved' contribution of £500. Provided the customer keeps to the payment period of two months, the amount at risk remains at £1000 and the achieved contribution increases by £500 per month. After the fourth month, there can be no loss in real terms since achieved contribution now exceeds the amount at risk.

The danger in this sort of approach to the granting of credit is that before the customer finally fails there may be an increase in the number of months' sales owing. Obviously, if this grows to three or four months, the break-even point for risk is extended from the fourth to the fifth or sixth month. This indicates clearly that the control of creditors must include a continuous monitoring of individual customer's credit periods, both allowed and taken, and that when the period is exceeded the collection position and the supply position should be immediately reviewed.

Analysis of debtors and the recognition of bad debts

The appraisal of the *quality* of the outstanding debtors is just as important as an appraisal of their quantity. The speedier collection of more recent sales may obscure an increase in the number of old and doubtful debts. This can only be determined by an examination of the ageing of the outstanding debtors. Where the level of debtors is increasing, it is vitally important to know whether this increase is in respect of recent sales or whether it is an accumulation of long outstanding amounts which may never be collected.

Figure 4.2

Ageing analysis of debtors

	31/12/19x1		28/2/19x2		30/4/19x2	
	£000's	%	£000's	%	£000's	%
Debtors outstanding:						
Up to 30 days	146	72.5	155	70.5	159	68.8
Between 31 and 60 days	45	22.5	51	23.2	53	22.9
Between 61 and 90 days	9	4.5	11	5.0	14	6.1
Over 90 days	1	0.5	3	1.3	5	2.2
	201	100.0	220	100.0	231	100.0
Average daily sales	£4467		£5000		£5022	
Days sales outstanding	45 days		44 days		46 days	

An ageing analysis, such as that shown in Fig. 4.2, would establish adverse trends in the composition of the outstanding debtors. Although the trend in the collection period has hardly changed over the period covered, the proportion of debtors which have been outstanding between 60 and 90 days has risen from 4.5 to 6.1 per cent, and those outstanding over 90 days have risen from 0.5 to 2.2 per cent.

A rise in the overdue accounts of this size can be the early warning of a rise in the number of bad debts occurring in the future. Either the collection system is breaking down or customers are delaying payment of their accounts. It is important to find out the reasons as soon as possible. Is the granting of credit terms being carried out slackly? Is it a by-product of an economic squeeze? Are complaints being handled promptly? Is there something more sinister behind the rise, for example, invoices being raised for sales not made or goods not delivered?

Periodically, the analysis of debtors should include a full assessment of the real value of overdue accounts. Each individual item outstanding beyond laid-down periods should be appraised in terms of the customer's ability to pay, to ascertain particular reasons why he might be deliberately holding back payment.

Figure 4.3

Effect of investment in debtors upon return on capital employed

	All cash sales	3 months' credit	6 months' credit	12 months' credit
	£	£	£	£
Sales	1000	1000	1000	1000
Profit 10% of sales	100	100	100	100
Fixed assets (net):	400	400	400	400
Current assets:				
Stocks	200	200	200	200
Debtors	—	250	500	1000
Cash	100	100	100	100
	300	550	800	1300
	700	950	1200	1700
Creditors	300	300	300	300
Net assets/capital employed	£400	£650	£900	£1400
Return on capital employed	25%	15.4%	11.11%	7.1%

IMPACT OF CREDIT POLICY ON PROFITABILITY

Figure 4.3 illustrates the effects of a slowing down in the collection of debts on the ROCE. Starting with the case in which all sales are on a cash basis, the return on capital is compared with the corresponding rate when 3 months', 6 months', and 12 months' credit, respectively, are taken. Extending the credit period from 3 months to 12 months effectively halves the ROCE. While the change in the value of the net assets of the business exhibited in the example may enable a larger percentage of the capital employed to be borrowed and, therefore, affect the financing decision, the differences are too large to be ignored.

5

Managing cash and near cash

The carrying of funds in the form of cash in hand or at the bank, or in a form near cash, such as short-term investments, is just as much an employment of those funds as if they were locked up in stocks or debtors. Such a use will add little or nothing to profit. Only if the liquid funds are invested will a small return be earned. The objective of management should, therefore, be to minimize the amount of funds so used. One could visualize the 'ideal' position being where the cash coming in exactly matches the cash being paid out, with no cash being kept in hand.

Figure 5.1

Holdings of cash and near-cash balances

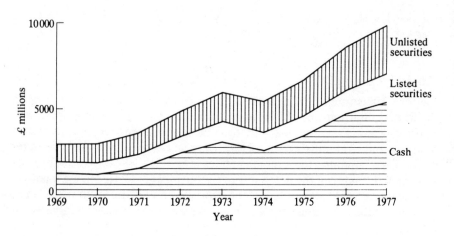

Source: *Annual Abstract of Statistics*, HMSO

This chapter examines some of the factors requiring a departure from the 'ideal' and some of the policies that kept the departure to the minimum consistent with the smooth servicing of the business's day-to-day cash needs.

Cash holdings of companies

The volume of funds in the form of certificates of tax deposit, marketable securities, and cash held by over 1000 listed companies is shown in Fig. 5.1. It can be seen that the *total* holdings of highly liquid assets has increased from under £3000 million to over £9500 million during the period covered. This increase no doubt reflects the impact of inflation as Table 1.2 shows that there has been no substantial change in the percentage of total assets held as cash or near cash.

CLASSES OF CASH AND NEAR CASH

Currency

Bank notes, coins, etc., normally form only a relatively small part of liquid funds. Problems of security dictate the prudent policy of using currency for only immediate petty cash requirements, with bank or giro transfer systems for most payments.

Bank current account

This represents cash which is immediately available to the business against which cheques can be drawn, the bank merely acting as the custodian of the firm's funds. Funds kept in this form do not usually earn any return in the usual sense. The bank frequently permits the firm to make a certain use of its transfer facilities free of cost thereby producing some cost saving.

Deposit accounts

Cash in excess of the immediate day-to-day requirements may be placed upon deposit with a bank or other institution or lent on the interbank market. The terms of the deposit usually require that a period of notice be given before funds are withdrawn.

The rate of interest paid depends upon the current minimum lending rate, the type of institution the funds are deposited with, and the repayment notice that is required. Deposits with the clearing banks pay less than the other institutions (usually at 2 per cent below minimum lending rate). In non-inflationary times, the longer the period of deposit and the repayment notice the higher the rate of interest. In times of inflation the position is often reversed if current interest rates are high and are expected to fall in the near future. For example, on 11 September 1979 the rates offered by local authorities at two days' notice were 14 per cent and 13 per cent for one year; money deposited for one month with finance houses earned $14^1/2$ per cent, for 3 months $14^1/2$ per cent, and for one year $13^1/4$ per cent.

Local authority loans

Many local authorities receive money on deposit for short periods, such as the two-day period quoted above. Mostly, however, they receive deposits for fixed periods of one or two years. There is a specialized broker service now operating in the placement of funds in this area.

Fixed interest securities

Government loans, company debentures, and other forms of loan stock may be purchased and sold in the usual way through the Stock Exchange. Here, there are dealing costs to consider. The return earned will be the going rate at the time of the investment. In addition, there will be the possibility of making capital gains or losses on the investment, which in the case of UK government stocks are tax free if held for more than one year.

Funds on deposit maintain the same value in terms of units of currency. If one deposits £1000 one gets back £1000 plus interest. There is no such guarantee in investment in fixed interest securities. If interest rates change during the currency of the investment, its capital value changes—a factor to be considered when deciding how to place surplus funds.

Equities

Funds invested for some time may best be put in equities. The major objective is to place the funds where they are protected against inflation. The movement of prices is much more volatile than that for fixed interest securities and is subject to dealing costs in the same way.

Certificates of tax deposit

Possibly the largest single payment that a company makes in the normal course of business is the annual payment of tax. A company may have anything between 9 and 21 months' delay after the end of the accounting year before it pays the tax based upon that year's profits. There is a similar delay for individuals and partnerships.

To encourage taxpayers to have the cash to meet this commitment, taxpayers are offered certificates of tax deposit purchasable with a view to surrendering them in settlement of the tax liability. The certificates entitle the purchaser to interest when used for the purpose of paying tax. If surrendered for cash, the rate is reduced.

DETERMINING POLICY ON CASH HOLDINGS

Reasons for holding cash resources

The credit-worthiness of a business is one of its most valuable assets. Management should, therefore, ensure that there are no serious hold-ups in the payment of amounts due which could give the business the name of a bad payer or, even more importantly, cause creditors to resort to litigation.

Receipts and payments of cash do not follow smooth patterns, but fluctuate from day to day. Some payments, e.g., for tax, are on an annual payment basis, others at shorter intervals of time. Peaks of receipts and of payments will not necessarily coincide in time.

One situation in which liquid funds of some magnitude are often retained is that of a takeover bid. The ability to offer a cash alternative in the bid struggle can often be decisive and reduces the dilution of earnings on the existing capital.

COSTS, RISKS, AND CONTROL OF CASH HOLDINGS

The cost of holding cash

The cost of holding cash is the profit that could have been earned had the funds been put to another use. If a business is able to earn 20 per cent on the investment of funds internally, then this is the effective cost of maintaining large cash balances. This cost may be ameliorated to some extent by investing those funds in short-term securities, but the return earned in such uses is unlikely to match what could be earned if used in the operations of the business. Unless there are special reasons for so doing, maintaining excess holdings of liquid resources is as much a sign of bad financial management as a lack of ready cash.

Risks of holding cash

Cash holdings are not subject to physical deterioration as are holdings of manufactured goods or raw materials, nor are they at risk through changes in consumer demand. But, without exception, cash is at risk for quite other reasons, the chief being its decline in real value and, with foreign currency, the possibility of exchange rate adjustments.

When governments consider that a 'gentle' inflation is good in itself, the degree of inflation each year is a cost of holding funds—a cost so certain that it falls outside the scope of risk. The real danger lies in the government's losing control of events and inflation becoming uncontrollable. Cash and short-term securities can then rapidly lose much of their value.

When funds are in the form of marketable securities, movements in the market price can create losses as well as profits, although there is some possibility of at least maintaining their real value when the investments are in equities. Funds placed out on deposit are not entirely risk free, as the collapse of some finance houses and building societies has demonstrated.

Control of cash resources

The control of cash and near-cash resources will rest upon adequate and accurate short-term cash forecasts. This will help determine the minimum and maximum cash demands during the period under review.

Where there is a fluctuation due to seasonal or other factors, the forecast pattern of cash requirements might approximate that represented in Fig. 5.2. Curve AA represents the pattern of cash needs over the period. If permanent finance is raised to more than the level indicated by line BB, it will be idle during the whole year to the extent of the excess over B. If permanent finance is raised to cover the requirement CB, the funds will find employment only for part of the year, lying idle or earning only a meagre return for the remainder.

Figure 5.2

Profile of cash needs

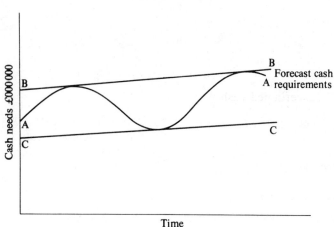

If long-term funds do not support the requirement at least to the extent of C, then short-term funds are being used to supply a long-term need, which may cause liquidity problems. The ideal financing policy would be to finance the cash needs up to C with long-term funds, covering the needs in the band CB by short-term borrowing.

Management's choice may be much more restricted than the above presentation indicates, because of two factors:

1. Long-term funds are usually raised in large tranches at infrequent intervals, perhaps only once every several years.
2. It is necessary to time the raising of long-term funds to minimize their cost.

In considering at what point on the scale of cash requirements to enter the market for long-term funds, management will base its decisions upon these factors:

1. Changes in the percentage taken by issue costs. Where long-term capital requirements are satisfied by more issues of smaller amounts to bring funds

raising in line with funds requirements, this may impose a higher cost burden.

2. The potential benefits of timing fund raising when the cost of long-term funds is historically low.
3. The relative costs and availability of short-term and long-term funds.
4. The loss of income due to reinvesting long-term funds short term at lower rates of interest.
5. The liquidity risk if short-term funds are used for long-term needs.
6. The volatility of the industry in which the business operates.
7. The effect of high short-term funds usage on the credit rating of the business.

The objective of management policy is to optimize the balance between these factors, rationalizing to some extent the attitude to risk bearing. The issue is that rational decisions cannot be made unless the cash requirements of operating decisions are known and, based on that knowledge, policies devised to meet the ascertained cash need within known cost/risk characteristics. This cash strategy can then be used as the basis of a cash budget to control cash movements and initiate corrective action.

CASH HOLDINGS OVERSEAS

Obligations expressed in other currencies

Many companies engage in some way in overseas transactions. This introduces a major problem into the management of the related cash flows since the parity between the home and foreign currencies may change substantially, with loss to the firm.

If a currency is floating there can be significant changes in the rate of exchange over the period of a transaction. Even when a currency has relatively fixed parities, in schemes such as the European Monetary System, there is room for movement on either side of parity as well as changes in the parity itself. Such movements may more than eliminate the profit on the transaction. In such cases it would be logical for management to pay overseas liabilities if there is a possibility of the home currency weakening, even if this means advancing normal payment dates. If sales are denominated in the home currency the exchange risk is borne by the customer. If they are denominated in a strong overseas currency then the later the sales proceeds are received the greater may be the sterling equivalent. If, however, many firms do this, the resulting pressure on the balance of payments makes that decline more certain.

In the author's view, directors have an overriding obligation to protect the shareholders' interests in any legal way. Governments, who are mainly responsible for the state of the economy, have failed in their job if the currency weakens. Without this threat firms would not want to anticipate payments. If governments cannot manage the economy effectively they should not expect individual firms to stand the cost of their failure. However, managers must come to their own conclusions on this question.

One of the attributes required of management in its dealings with foreign obligations is a continuing awareness of trends in the international monetary market and trade balances. This awareness should signal decision points at which the firm's obligations in total or in a specified area should be reviewed and necessary action taken. The major areas in which policy decisions should be taken which have a more general effect include the following:

Receivables from overseas sales.   Sales to countries which have a stronger underlying trend in trade balances can be expressed in units of the overseas currency. Thus, if the value of the home currency declines the real value of the debt is maintained. Sales to countries with chronic balance-of-payments problems should be expressed in the home currency. If this is not possible, urgent measures should be taken to collect such debts if devaluation by the external government seems likely.

Obligations payable overseas.   The same objective applies, namely to keep the obligations payable in the stronger currency to a minimum. As the firm has greater control over its payments, it can influence its risks here quite considerably.

Covering obligations, etc., by forward exchange dealings.   Where there are no exchange control restrictions, the risks of holding overseas obligations is reducible by purchasing the foreign currencies needed to effect payment at the time the obligation is incurred. This is held and utilized to make the payment to the overseas creditor.

Cash held by group companies overseas.   Companies operating internationally frequently hold liquid resources in overseas territories. In this case, they will have an established branch or subsidiary company abroad. Management should consider the interests of the group as a whole and mobilize (if exchange control requirements permit) all liquid resources in the territory with the stronger country, leaving only essential working funds in areas exposed to risk.

Apart from the restrictions imposed by exchange control regulations, management would also consider the relative earning capacity of funds in different territories. Possibly, earnings differentials make up for the differences in risk.

Other assets held overseas.   Changes in exchange rates usually reflect differing rates of inflation in various countries. Whenever possible, funds should be invested in assets which retain their real value, and obligations to third parties be expressed in terms of the depreciating currency. For example, if one has the choice between buying a new factory overseas for £1 million, part of which is financed by a local loan of 60 per cent of the value at 15 per cent interest, or of renting it for £120 000 per year, and the economy in the local territory is inflating at the rate of about 10 per cent per year, there are clear advantages in ownership, as is shown in Table 5.1.

Table 5.1

Effects of inflation on the real costs as between ownership and rental of properties
Inflation assumed of 10% compound
Values in local currency:

	Building cost	Loan 60% of cost	Equity in building	Interest on loan	Rent (assumed rent adjustment at 5-yearly intervals)
Present value at date of acquisition	1 000 000	600 000	400 000	90 000	120 000
Value in 10 years' time in units of currency at that time	2 360 000	600 000	1 760 000	90 000	283 000
Real values in 10 years' time	1 000 000	254 000	746 000	38 100	120 000

MONEY TRANSMISSION SYSTEMS

The different media by which money transfers between individuals and firms are made can have an impact upon the level of cash and near cash held by the firm. In the UK, the introduction of the National Giro and the upgrading of the clearing banks traders' credit system to a full giro provide a choice in how funds are transferred between two parties.

For management, the choice of transfer methods is based upon the cost factors involved in the preparation of the paperwork and the charges made by the operators of each transfer system. Also, the speed with which the funds are extracted from the firm's cash resources bears on the cash it needs to retain for servicing day-to-day payments. This latter point is often overlooked in debating the merits of the different transfer systems.

The giro payment systems available today are 'sold' on the basis that they cost the customer nothing, as well as the paperwork being more simple. They are not free, however. The giro obtains the deposit of funds as soon as the transfer is put into the system and it enjoys the use of those funds until the other party's account is credited. This contrasts with the cheque payment system whereby the funds remain in one's own account until sometime after the payee's account has been credited. The time differential between the two systems with the present standard of postal service is likely to be between one and two weeks. This is a time differential with an important bearing upon relative costs.

6

Investment in long-term assets

Management decisions on the commitment of funds to long-term uses within the business are among the most critical for its continued success, while also being among the most difficult to make.

Such decisions are critical because they deal with large amounts of funds over long periods and there is little chance of reversing the decision once made and put into effect. The commitment of £1 million to highly specialized machinery, for the manufacture of a product which loses popular favour shortly afterwards, cannot be reversed quickly. Capital investment decisions, therefore, have lasting influence for good or evil on the profitability of the business.

The success or otherwise of management in *generating* and *selecting* the right uses for the company's funds has a decisive influence on the growth of the business. Through its long-term effect upon the level of profitability, it determines the capacity of the business to attract funds needed for expansion. Businesses compete with each other and with alternative uses for the funds offered by investors. Those businesses which can offer a better-than-average return are able to attract new funds, whether from shareholders or lenders, whereas those offering less than average are unlikely to attract new funds at all.

The investment decision is a difficult one because it requires an assessment of future events. The longer ahead that it is necessary to forecast, the more difficult the process becomes. The uncertainties surrounding the future are caused by technological, economic, and social changes, competitive forces, and the actions of governments. The latter, at least as far as the UK is concerned, instead of striving to achieve a stable framework within which business can operate, has added considerable new areas of uncertainty. Frequent and rapid changes in economic objectives, fiscal legislation, investment incentives, etc., have added major uncertainties to the investment decision.

THE PLACE OF THE INVESTMENT DECISION IN THE MANAGEMENT PROCESS

Funds become available to the business internally by the release of funds from existing projects in the form of depreciation and profit. To these funds accruing from inside the business, other funds may be added from new shareholder's funds and new borrowing. Together, these form a pool of funds available for investment. Management's function is then to decide the particular uses to which these funds are to be put. Over a period of time, these decisions determine the composition of the capital employed in terms of type of assets and products, thereby defining how the return on capital employed is determined.

Fixed assets will not be the only form of asset affected by the decision. By determining the fixed asset and product framework for the business, management limits the extent to which it can influence the investment in stock and work in progress, and debtors.

Technique v. policy

Methods of investment project selection are techniques which can be used to assist management; they are not substitutes for management. Unless the techniques are set within the proper framework of management decisions and policy, disappointment in the outcome is certain.

The major management policy decisions necessary before any capital investment appraisal technique can be fully effective are:

1. Setting the objective and long-term goals of the business.
2. Deciding on the balance to be maintained between shareholders' funds and borrowed funds in the capital structure.
3. Setting parameters for risk and profitability which will be acceptable.

Objectives and long-term goals

This decision area is more fully discussed in Chapter 16. It is effectively the starting point for all the decision-making processes within the business. By setting targets for the business for a period of years, management determines the framework within which all other decisions must be made and courses of action inhibiting the achievement of the company's goals are rejected.

In the larger business where many, if not all, investment proposals are generated by line management, this element of a common goal is essential. Without it, managers are primarily concerned with their own area of responsibility rather than with the whole business. There may, therefore, be a dispersion of effort as each ploughs his own furrow.

Setting objectives and specific goals, and *making them known* to all levels of management coordinates activities leading them towards that common goal. The critical nature of the capital investment decision becomes more evident when considered in this light. Only if management knows what kind of business it wants in, say, 10 years can it have a rational policy of acquiring fixed assets which it may hold for 10 or 15 years. To operate a capital investment system that is to be effective and conducive towards the achievement of higher profitability, without setting long-term goals, is to put it at the mercy of the winds of change, rather than shaping the course of events.

The balance between shareholders' and borrowed funds

This balance should form a part of the underlying policy on which the long-term growth is based. It is an important decision area in its own right and is dealt with in depth in Chapter 13. Its importance for the capital investment decision is in helping to determine the cost of capital. The latter has an important role to play. It forms a critical lower limit to rates of return on new investment that will be acceptable to management.

Setting parameters of risk and return

If management has included in its long-term goals the achievement of an after-tax rate of return on capital employed of 15 per cent, there is little merit in accepting new investment proposals which yield only 8 per cent, even though this may be more than the cost of capital. In such a case, management should set the minimum target return that will be approved after considering the likely mix of projects and returns that would provide the required 15 per cent.

Most firms are obliged to invest a part of their capital in uses which provide no return, or one too intangible to measure. The provision of recreational facilities for staff, and expenditure on fire and burglary prevention required by the insurance company, fall into this category. Since the cost of capital has to be exceeded by new investment as a whole, it is necessary for the earning projects to make up the deficiency.

In setting the parameters, the board should also consider inflation, and risk and uncertainty. Inflation seems to be approved by most governments with little chance of its being arrested in the foreseeable future. Management fails in its duty to shareholders if it does not take inflation into account in its financing and investment decisions.

Risks and uncertainty are always present in the investment decision, more so in some investments than in others. When the risks are high, management may well set a higher minimum rate of return than for when they are low. This may be formalized by classifying investments by degree of risk or type, and setting different minimum rate of return criteria for each. Typical categories could include:

Cost saving investment	Low risk
Financing decisions	Low risk
Leasing or buying	Low risk
Replacement machines	Medium risk
Extension of existing capacity	Medium risk
Marketing new products	High risk

APPRAISAL SYSTEMS

Requirements of a capital appraisal system

The effectiveness of an appraisal system depends upon its ability to take a range of competing investment proposals and assess them against two requirements:

1. To provide the means of selecting projects by ranking them in order of profitability.
2. To ensure that investments are not made in projects which earn less than the cost of capital, or the appropriate minimum or cut-off rate of return.

An appraisal system not performing both functions adequately will at best make only a limited contribution to the management process and at worst lead to wrong decisions.

The accounting rate of return

Investment appraisal has been taking place for many centuries and since the beginning of the Industrial Revolution the problems have been similar in nature to present-day ones. The most commonly used basis of appraisal has been centred upon expressing the likely level of average annual profits as a percentage of the cost of the project, e.g:

Investment	£10 000	
Profits:		
Year 1	4 000	⎫
Year 2	3 000	⎬ 'Life' of project 4 years
Year 3	2 000	⎪
Year 4	1 000	⎭
Total expected profit	10 000	
Average annual profit	2 500	
Average profit as percentage of initial investment	25%	⎫ These can also be
Average profit as percentage of average investment	50%	⎬ expressed after tax

There are problems in defining the measures to be used, as can be seen from the alternative ways shown of calculating the rate of return. These, however, could be overcome by the adoption of a common standard.

How well does the method measure up to the two requirements above? Assume that the previous example is only one of three projects and that the firm has only £10 000 to spend. Does it give the right ranking to enable a selection to be made?

The data in respect of each of the investment projects is shown in Table 6.1, and the accounting rate of return for all three is the same. Management would, therefore, be indifferent as to the choice of project since they are equally profitable. But is this really true?

Consider first projects A and B. From an inspection of the pattern of profit flows, A is shown to earn its profits much earlier in its life than B and since those profits can be put to use to earn further profits they are more valuable. A is, therefore, more profitable than B.

Table 6.1

Comparison of three investment projects by the accounting rate of return

Project	A	B	C
Investment	£10 000	£10 000	£10 000
Profits:			
Year 1	4 000	1 000	2 500
Year 2	3 000	2 000	2 500
Year 3	2 000	3 000	2 500
Year 4	1 000	4 000	2 500
Year 5	—	—	2 500
Total profit	10 000	10 000	12 500
Average annual profit	2 500	2 500	2 500
Accounting rate of return	25%	25%	25%

This choice was fairly easy since the relative earning patterns could be seen by inspection. But how does one choose between projects A and C? Project C has an extra year's earnings in the fifth year. How does this compare with the higher receipt of earnings by A in the first two years? There is no simple answer. A solution can only be worked out by measuring the value of the timing differences of the profit flows.

The weakness of the accounting rate of return is that it does not take into account differences in *timing* of profit flows or *differing lives* of projects. To the extent that these two aspects are present in the projects being compared, the results will be deficient.

Payback period

Because of the risks the future holds, it could be considered that the earlier the capital invested is recovered the more desirable is the project. The payback method of appraisal is based upon measuring the time it takes to recoup the original expenditure and selecting projects from those with the shortest payback period.

Once timing is introduced as a major factor in the assessment of a project, the question arises as to whether profit is the right measure to use. Profits and cash do not flow at the same time, e.g., tax on profits is paid some time after the end of the accounting period. Original outlay can, therefore, only be considered as being recouped when the *cash* is received, and payback has commonly been computed on this basis.

Cash flow in this context can be defined as the *after-tax profits arising plus depreciation*. The components of the cash flows are allocated to the actual years in which they are received or paid, rather than those in which they are recorded in the books of account.

How effective is this technique in satisfying the two requirements of an appraisal system? Assume that a choice has to be made between two projects as shown in Table 6.2. On the basis of the payback measurement, project A is the most desirable since the payback period is only four years against six and a half years for project B.

A little consideration of the two projects shows, however, that this would be the wrong choice. The rate of return on A is zero since it does nothing more than recoup the original outlay. Project B, however, earns a positive rate of return since the cash receipts exceed the original outlay. From the profitability point of view, B is preferable to A.

Table 6.2
Comparing two projects by the payback method

	Project A	Project B
Investment	£10 000	£10 000
Cash flows:		
Year 1	4 000	1 000
Year 2	3 000	1 000
Year 3	2 000	1 000
Year 4	1 000	2 000
Year 5	—	2 000
Year 6	—	2 000
Year 7	—	2 000
Year 8	—	3 000
Payback period	4 years	6¹/₂ years

This technique does not attempt to measure profitability since it takes no account of any cash flows which arise after the payback period. It should, therefore, only be used for the purpose which its title indicates and not to measure profitability.

Discounted cash flow (DCF)

This technique is also based upon the concept of cash flow. It is, however, much more rigorous in its approach. *All* cash flows related to the project must be taken into account and a definite time scale for the project set out. These cash flows are brought together in a single appraisal situation to determine the rate of return or the relative ranking or profitability for each project.

The pattern of cash flows

The pattern of cash flows associated with a project consists of an initial outlay on the acquisition of assets, followed by inward cash flows from profits, depreciation, and residual values. Each component of the cash flow is allocated to the time period during which the movement is expected to take place.

The basis of the DCF technique is to bring together all of the cash flows on to a common time basis. It does not matter what base period is chosen for this purpose, but for convenience it is usual to select the year of investment, e.g., the 'present time' or, if there is more than one year of investment, the last. This means that the following year will be the one in which the first inward cash flows from operations occur.

The DCF rate of return method (Internal rate of return, internal earning power, etc.)

To establish the rate of return by the DCF method, it is necessary to find a rate of discount which, when used to discount the future cash flows back to their *present value* at the base period, makes the sum of those present values equal to the original investment (or over the whole period of the project the present value of all the cash flows is zero). This rate of discount is the rate of return on the project.

The present value method

This method of using DCF is based upon the same factors as the rate of return method. However, instead of searching for an interest rate that provides the solution, the appropriate cut-off or criterion rate of return is used. This means that the sum of the present values may be greater or less than the original investment. If they are greater, the return exceeds the criterion rate; if they are less, the project does not meet that rate.

This has only met the second of the two requirements of an appraisal system, that is whether it meets the cost of capital or other minimum rate of return requirements. It is now necessary to rank by order of profitability so that a process of selection can be carried out. This is done by calculating the *profitability index*, which is ascertained by dividing the original investment into the sum of the present values of the future cash flows. The profitability index shows, therefore, the proportionate increase in present value after taking into account the criterion rate.

DISCOUNTING

Discounting is a reflection of compound interest. Using compound interest, one takes a sum invested at the present time and calculates the value to which it will have grown over a series of years at a specified rate of interest. Discounting takes the same series of values but looks at the future sum, calculating its present value (i.e., what sum would have to be invested now to reach the value of that future sum).

This relationship is illustrated in Fig. 6.1. Taking a compound interest rate of 10 per cent, £100 invested now will have a value of £110 after one year and £121 after two years. This is the same as saying that £110 receivable after one year at 10 per cent has a present value of £100, and £121 receivable after two years also has a present value of £100. To provide a common factor employable for any value of cash flow, the present values can be expressed as the amount invested now which will provide £1 at the end of the specified number of years. This is commonly called the *present value (PV) factor*.

Figure 6.1

Relationship of future and present values
Interest rate 10 per cent

	Now	1 year	2 years
Compound interest	£100 ──────→£110 ──────→£121		
Discounting	£100◄────────£110		
	£100◄──────────────────────£121		
Present value factors	$\frac{100}{110}$ ◄─────── £1		
	=£0.909		
	$\frac{100}{121}$ ◄──────────────────── £1		
	=£0.826		

To find the present value of any sum receivable in the future it now need only be multiplied by the appropriate PV factor (a selection of which are given in Appendices B and C). Let us assume that one holds a fully paid-up insurance policy which it is estimated will produce £3500 in 15 years' time. It has a present surrender value of £1500. If one estimates that one could earn 6 per cent net on money invested personally, then the choice between surrendering the policy now or leaving it to maturity can be solved by comparing the two present values, the highest present value being the most desirable.

The sum of £3500 receivable in 15 years is multiplied by the PV factor of 0.417 (being the PV factor for 6 per cent over 15 years). That is to say £3500 × 0.417 = £1459.50. This compares with the present surrender value of £1500. Judged solely on these factors it would be preferable to surrender the policy now and invest the proceeds oneself, since this would produce more than £3500 in 15 years' time.

However, in common with other investment decisions, there may be other relevant factors. How certain can one be of being able to earn 6 per cent net? What probability is there of one dying before the expiry of 15 years and the insurance monies being received that much earlier? The estimates and the uncertainties are a part of the hazards of looking into the future and will be present in practically every investment problem.

APPLYING DISCOUNTING TECHNIQUES TO INVESTMENT PROBLEMS

Assume that one of the projects for appraisal is the investment of £1000 now, followed by three years' cash flows of £500, £500, and £177. To calculate the rate of return it is necessary to find the rate of discount which, when used in the discounting process, equates the cash flows with the value of the original investment. This is a process of trial and error. Using the data set out in Table 6.3, assume that the first rate chosen was 8 per cent. Applying the PV factors for 8 per cent to the cash flows produces a total present value of £1032. This is higher than the value of the original investment, therefore that rate is *too low* and a rate higher than 8 per cent must be tried.

Table 6.3

Finding the rate of return by the DCF method

Investment £1000
Operating cash flows:

Year	Cash flow	PV factor 8%	PV	PV factor 12%	PV	PV factor 10%	PV
	£		£		£		£
1	500	0.926	463	0.893	446	0.909	454
2	500	0.857	428	0.797	399	0.826	413
3	177	0.794	141	0.712	126	0.751	133
			£1 032		£971		£1 000

If the 12 per cent rate is tried next, following the same process, the total present value of the cash flows is £971, which is less than the original investment. A rate of 12 per cent is, therefore, *too high*.

The rate that just fits the problem is 10 per cent. Using that rate, the sum of the present values just equals the original investment. The DCF rate of return on the project is, therefore, 10 per cent. That is to say: *'The project earns sufficient cash flows to repay the original investment and provide a return of 10 per cent on the funds invested in the project in each year of its life.'*

To shorten the process of arriving at the solution rate, once the actual rate has been bracketed, as was the case after the 8 and 12 per cent rate had been calculated, the solution rate can be found by interpolation. In the example in Table 6.3, the rate is calculable as follows:

$$8 \text{ per cent} + 4 \times 32/61 = 10 \text{ per cent}$$

Meaning of the DCF rate of return

An appreciation of what the DCF rate of return represents is critical for the proper understanding of its part in the capital investment system. In the definition of the rate of return given above, there were two basic elements:

1. The cash flows must be adequate to repay the original investment.
2. In addition, they must provide for the appropriate rate of interest on the outstanding capital each year.

The cash flows in an investment project can be resolved into their interest and capital repayment elements in the same way as the repayments to a building society. Taking the example in Table 6.3 and resolving the cash flows into the two elements, Table 6.4 shows that, after providing for the interest each year on the amount of capital outstanding at the beginning of the year, the balance of the cash flows is sufficient to repay the original investment of £1000.

Table 6.4

Resolution of cash flows into interest and capital

Repayment elements

Year	Opening balance of investment	Cash flow	Interest at 10% on opening balance	Capital repayment	Closing balance
	£	£	£	£	£
1	1000	500	100	400	600
2	600	500	60	440	160
3	160	177	16	161	(1)
Total	—	1177	176	1001	—

Considering the business as a whole, it might be said that the project has borrowed £1000 from the capital employed. What the rate of return measures is the 'interest' rate that the pattern of cash repayments provides for, in addition to the capital repayments. It is as truly the earning rate for the capital employed as the interest rate is for the building society.

The use of the rate of return method of DCF outlined enables management to rank projects directly in order of profitability. Those showing a rate of return lower than the criterion rate can be discarded.

The present value method

The criterion rate discussed on page 52 will be used as the discounting rate with this method instead of searching for a solution rate (where there is more than one criterion rate, the one selected should be appropriate to the risk category of the project). The sum of the present values calculated in this way is then compared with the amount originally invested.

Taking the example in Table 6.3 and assuming the criterion rate of return is 8 per cent, the present value of the future cash flows would be £1032. As this present value exceeds the amount originally invested, the project meets the criterion rate of return. This satisfies the second of the two requirements of an appraisal system. So far, however, it has not provided the facility for ranking projects by order of profitability. This can be achieved by calculating the *profitability index* as follows:

$$£1032/1000 = 1.032$$

FORECASTING CASH FLOWS

If the DCF technique is to be used effectively, there must be a much greater discipline within the firm in its forecasting techniques. As will be appreciated, there are two basic elements in the capital investment appraisal system. First, there is the process of forecasting values for such things as sales revenue, costs, life of the project, residual values, tax rates, and allowances, etc. The results of the appraisal system will be critically dependent upon the adequacy of this forecasting. The second element in the system is taking the values which are the result of the forecasts made, and using them to provide a profitability ranking.

The forecasting of sales revenue, operating costs, etc., is not dealt with in this chapter, being described adequately elsewhere. Instead, those special aspects, particularly of taxation, which affect the amount and timing of the cash flows are considered, under two headings:

1. The effect that the tax system and investment incentives may have upon the amount and timing of the cash flows.
2. The application of the incremental principle.

Taxation and investment incentives

The firm must take into account the proportion of its earnings taken in taxation. In most countries the rate exceeds 50 per cent. Only the amount left after tax contributes to the net cash flows.

Since timing is of the essence in calculating the rate of return, tax payments must be included in the years in which they actually take place. In many countries companies pay tax on earnings on a 'pay-as-you-earn' basis, paying a high proportion of the tax on estimated current year earnings in quarterly instalments during that year. In the UK, the *payment* of corporation tax by companies is not made until some time after the end of the accounting period. In the case of companies in existence at 5 April 1965, payment will not be made until between 9 and 21 months after the end of the accounting period. For companies formed after 5 April 1965, there is a uniform delay of 9 months.

As well as removing earnings in the form of tax, the state may also provide subsidies and other incentives to encourage firms to invest in new productive assets or to settle in a particular geographical area. These may take the form of cash grants, accelerated capital allowances, and ordinary depreciation allowances. The rates of capital allowances given in the UK in 1980 are shown in Table 6.5.

Table 6.5

Capital allowances in the UK

	Initial allowance	Annual writing-down allowance
Industrial buildings	50%	4% straight line on cost
Hotels	20%	4% straight line on cost
	First-year allowance	
Machinery, plant, office equipment, vehicles, etc. (excluding private motor cars)	100%	25% on the reducing balance in second and subsequent years if not all 100% taken
Motor cars	nil	25% on reducing balance from first year
Scientific research	100%	—
Patent rights and know-how	—	$^1/_{17}$ of the cost of patent over 17 years and $^1/_6$ cost of know-how over 6 years
Ships	100%	—

The treatment of depreciation should be carefully noted. The basic rule in the UK is that depreciation is not an allowable expense for tax purposes. The depreciation charge is, therefore, added back to the net profit to arrive at the taxable profit. Against this taxable profit is offset the total of the capital allowances due for that year under the tax codes. In some countries (e.g., the US), such allowances are those provided by the firm in its own records within certain limits.

Where one disposes of assets related to a project this may entail adjustment to depreciation or capital allowances already given. Under most tax regimes the total depreciation allowances are adjusted to the actual cost of ownership, i.e., cost of the assets less any amount received on their disposal. Thus, if an asset has a written-down value for tax purposes of £10 000 and it is sold for £15 000, £5000 of the allowances given are then taken back. In the UK, where companies almost invariably claim 100 per cent first-year allowances for plant and machinery, the proceeds of any sale of such assets are deducted from the pool account which shows the total of expenditures for which capital allowances have not yet been claimed. If this balance on the pool account becomes negative, it is deducted from the capital allowances claimed for the year. Otherwise it simply reduces the future claims for annual writing-down allowances.

Application of DCF to a typical investment project

Description of project.   To replace an ageing product 'XL' with 'Super XL'.

Part of the existing plant, which has a written-down value for tax purposes of zero will be sold and is expected to realize £1000. The new plant will cost £125 000 and the firm intends to claim 100 per cent first-year allowances. The life of the new product is estimated at 10 years, at the end of which the plant is expected to realize £5000.

The new product will require a higher level of investment in working capital and it is expected that this will amount to £16 000 in the year in which the plant is replaced and a further £10 000 in the first year of operations.

No increase in profit is expected in the changeover year, but in the year following the investment profits are expected to increase by £20 000 and £30 000 per year subsequently. The tax rate is 50 per cent.

Calculate the DCF rate of return so that this project can be ranked with other projects. The cut-off rate for risk projects such as this is 15 per cent after tax.

Net cash investment

		£
Purchase of new plant and machinery (Year 0)		(125 000)
Disposal of old plant: Sale value (Year 0)	1 000	
Less adjustment to capital allowances		
1 000 @ 50% × 0.970 (Year 1)	(435)	
	——	9 565
		(115 435)
Increase in working capital Year 0	(16 000)	
Year 1 10 000 × 0.870	(8 700)	
	——	(24 700)
TOTAL		(140 135)

Annual and residual cash flows

Year	Increase in profit before depreciation (a)	Tax at 50%[2] (b)	Capital allowances (c)	Tax saved by capital allowances[3] (d)	Cash flow[4] (e)	PV factor for 15% (f)	Present value[5] (g)
	£	£	£	£	£		£
1	20 000	—	125 000	62 500	82 500	0.870	71 775
2	30 000	(10 000)			20 000	0.756	15 120
3	30 000	(15 000)			15 000		
4	30 000	(15 000)			15 000		
5	30 000	(15 000)			15 000		
6	30 000	(15 000)			15 000	3.393[1]	50 090
7	30 000	(15 000)			15 000		
8	30 000	(15 000)			15 000		
9	30 000	(15 000)			15 000		
10	30 000	(15 000)			15 000		
11	—	(15 000)			(15 000)	0.215	(3 225)
	290 000	(145 000)	125 000	62 500	207 500		133 760

Annual and residual cash flows (contd)

Residual values:					
Working capital[6] (year 10)			26 000	0.247	6 422
Sale of plant (year 11)			5 000	0.215	1 075
Claw-back of capital allowances (one year later than sale of plant)	(5 000)	(2 500)	(2 500)	0.187	(467)
	120 000	60 000	236 000		140 790

Notes

[1] PV factor from Appendix C. Factors for 15 per cent years 1 to 10 is 5.019, less factors for years 1 and 2 not required: 0.870 and 0.756 = 3.393.

[2] Assuming tax paid one year later than profits earned.

[3] Assuming profits elsewhere in the business against which allowances can be set.

[4] Cash flow (e) made up of (a) − (b) + (d) = (e).

[5] Present value = (e) × (f) = (g).

[6] Working capital run down in last operating year.

At a discounting rate of 15 per cent, the present values of the future cash flows almost exactly match the present value of the net cash investment. The rate of return is, therefore, 15 per cent and this equals the cut-off rate. The project is, therefore, acceptable, but whether it receives final approval depends upon what returns other projects offer and the volume of funds available. If other projects earning more than 15 per cent would absorb all the funds available, this project would not be approved at present.

Risk and uncertainty

It could quite properly be pointed out that the data upon which the solution to the above problem was based are only estimates of the expected values. Where management has the analytical facilities available, and this includes the use of a computer, a further analysis of the problem could be made to provide some idea of the effect on the forecast return of the uncertainties present in the project. This aspect will be dealt with further in Chapter 17.

7

The use of financial data in decision making

The task of management in organizing the resources of the business to meet profitability targets is assisted by the correct interpretation and use of cost and other information. Proposed courses of action being considered for the firm's activities should be tested against two criteria:

1. Will the proposed course of action increase or decrease profit?
2. If, additionally, the proposal requires a further investment in fixed assets or working capital, there must be a further appraisal to see whether the return on investment it offers meets the investment criteria set by management.

The organization of this data system is based upon the analysis and accumulation of operating data. While this is the purpose of a costing system, the information provided by such a system may be used for a number of different purposes, the basic uses being to:

1. Provide a means of controlling the operations of the business.
2. Provide the information upon which management decisions can be taken, the most important relating to pricing and product strategy.

The second function is based on an understanding of how costs vary in the various decision situations and is dealt with in this chapter, while the price/product strategy is covered in Chapter 8.

ELEMENTS OF COST

An examination of the manufacturing and profit and loss account of a business (or the trading account in appropriate cases) will reveal the costs of all categories incurred. These can be analysed under the headings of:

1. Expenses identifiable directly with units of product or service rendered.
2. Expenses incurred in manufacturing operations, but not identifiable directly with units of product as in 1 above.

3. Expenses concerned with the selling and distribution of the company's products.
4. Expenses incurred in administering the business as a whole.

Direct costs

Direct materials.   Materials used in the manufacturing process directly identifiable with each unit of product or service provided. Usually incorporated in the product itself.

Direct labour.   That part of the cost of people directly engaged on manufacturing operations identifiable with each unit of product or service. Staff are generally divided into 'direct' and 'indirect'. 'Direct' staff are those performing operations such as operating a power press, assembling motor cars. Indirect staff are those whose efforts, while contributing to manufacturing operations generally, cannot be identified with the unit of product.

Direct expenses.   In some types of business, expenses can be attributed to individual contracts, e.g., where the business consists of a relatively few large value contracts. Costs associated solely with a contract can be treated as direct.

Indirect manufacturing expenses (overheads, burden, etc.)

Included here are all those expenses related to manufacturing not classifiable as direct. Such expenses include:

Indirect labour, i.e., supervision, storekeeping, planning, etc.
Expenses of occupying premises, i.e., rent, rates, repairs.
Providing and maintaining plant and machinery.
Provision of ancillary services and supplies.

While the above classification of costs is appropriate to a manufacturing activity, the same principles apply in other activities. For example, if one is appraising the performance of a number of retail outlets or classes of insurance, some costs can be directly attributable to each activity being assessed, while others will be indirect.

BEHAVIOUR OF COSTS

Management is not only concerned with the level of cost of products at a particular time, it is also concerned with the way in which costs may vary, e.g., when volume changes. This section is concerned with how costs change in relation to volume *within a given plant capacity*. This condition cannot be emphasized too strongly. If one is considering a change going beyond plant capacity, some costs formerly considered 'fixed' will begin to change.

The first stage in considering cost behaviour is to examine each cost item to see whether it will vary with the volume of production/sales or whether it will tend to remain the same whatever the level of activity.

Variable costs will include the direct costs, consumption of power, repairs and maintenance, indirect labour costs such as waiting time, overtime premiums, etc.

Fixed costs will include rents and rates, depreciation, supervision, etc.

Cost, revenue, volume relationships

Over a range of volume, not only do costs change but so does revenue from sales. These concepts can be brought together in the form of a break-even chart, or profitograph. One is shown in Fig. 7.1. The vertical axis of the chart is a measure of the total costs (variable plus fixed equal total) and of total revenue from sales. The horizontal axis is a measure of volume in terms of units of product, resources, or sales.

Let us take the example illustrated in Fig. 7.1. Rayco Ltd manufactures a specialized valve with an annual capacity of 40 000 valves. Its accountant estimates that the fixed costs amount to £80 000 p.a., the variable costs being £6 per valve. The valves sell at £9 each.

Taking first of all the fixed costs of £80 000. As they will be the same at all levels of production, the curve representing this cost is a straight line horizontal to the base line. Variable costs are zero when output is zero, while at capacity the total variable amounts to 40 000 × £6 = £240 000. The variable cost curve connects these two points. The total cost over all output is found by adding the fixed and variable cost curves together.

Figure 7.1

The break-even chart

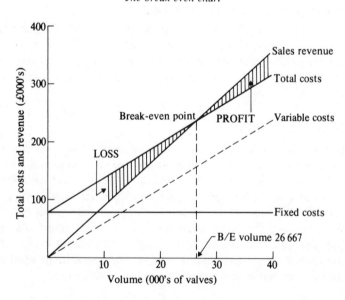

Each unit of sales adds £9 to revenue, therefore at the capacity of 40 000 units total revenue is £360 000. This reduces to zero at zero production, the sales revenue curve reflecting this change.

The point at which total cost and total revenue curves cross is the 'break-even' point. At the volume of activity that this point represents, the business makes neither a profit or a loss. As volume expands above this volume, profit increases, the amount at each volume being represented by the difference between the two curves. If volume is less than the break-even volume, the firm makes a loss measured by the difference between the two curves in exactly the same way.

The break-even volume can also be obtained by using the following formula:

Break-even volume = Fixed costs/(Selling price − Variable cost)
    £80 000/(9 − 6) = £80 000/3 = 26 667 break-even volume

Use of break-even analysis

The break-even chart shows in a very simplified form the basic operational data for the business. In considering steps that might be taken to improve operating profit, management can gain an appreciation of the range of volume or other changes to be considered and some consequences of each.

Increased volume. This can only be considered within the limits of capacity beyond which fixed costs would go up. Increasing the volume raises profit by the increase in number sold × (SP − VC). In Fig. 7.1, every extra unit sold increases profit (or reduces loss) by the difference between SP and VC (or the *contribution* that each unit makes towards fixed costs and profits).

Increased selling price. An increase in the SP steepens the slope of the sales revenue curve. This means that it crosses the total costs curve at a lower volume. One major consequence of the change is that break-even volume is lower than previously.

Decreased fixed costs. A decrease in the fixed costs lowers both the FC and TC curves, the new TC curve being parallel with the old (this is so since the cost reduction is the same at all levels of volume). The reduction in the break-even volume is greater than was the case with the increase in selling price since the benefits of the latter taper off to zero at zero production.

Decreased variable costs. A decrease in variable costs reduces the slope of the TC curve. As its effect on contribution is the same as an increase in price of the same magnitude, it has the same effect upon break-even volume.

This method of analysis enables the broad implications of some aspects of management policy to be examined and the consequences evaluated. It can also be used to assess the *practicability* of possible courses of action. The percentage changes in selling price, variable costs, etc., required to achieve a given increase in profit can be determined and an appraisal made on whether the percentage change is one within management's capacity.

Among these considerations is the effect of any proposed change upon the *margin of safety*, i.e., the amount by which the currently achieved volume can shrink before break-even volume is reached.

The final decision may consist of a combination of two or more of the alternatives examined. Each detailed proposal can be tested against the framework of the break-even analysis.

Alternative presentation

The foregoing examination of the break-even volume was made upon an examination of *total* costs, etc. The presentation is equally possible on the basis of fixed and variable costs and sales revenue *per unit*. Here, the SP and VC curves are straight horizontal lines, and the FC curve will decline with increases in volume. Using the data for Fig. 7.1, the break-even chart appears as in Fig. 7.2. In this case, the gap between the SP and TC curves shows the profit or loss per unit or product.

Figure 7.2

Break-even chart showing costs and revenue per unit

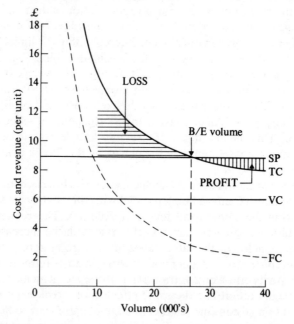

Contribution

The difference between selling price and variable cost represents a contribution to fixed costs and profit. Up to the break-even volume, all the contribution goes towards fixed costs, and when fixed costs have been covered, which occurs at the break-even volume, the contribution from each additional unit sold adds directly to profit.

This concept of contribution is very important in analysing cost and financial information relating to decisions. If one finds a solution maximizing contribution, then that is the solution which maximizes profit. This flows from the nature of the fixed cost element. As this remains constant at all levels of volume, the balance left for profit must be at its greatest when the total contribution is greatest.

INCREMENTAL COSTS

This level of analysis goes beyond the concept of working within a limited capacity. It is essentially dealing with problems of choice and examining the difference in cost between alternative courses of action. To ascertain those differences it is necessary to know what relevant costs will vary.

Assume that one owns a motor car and has taken the trouble to analyse the costs of running the vehicle, as follows:

	Budgeted cost per year	
Petrol and oil	£450	Average annual
Replacement tyres	25	mileage
Maintenance	125	10 000 miles
Insurance	100	
Tax	50	
Depreciation	500	
	£1250	= 12.5 p per mile

The car owner faces a number of decisions regarding the use of his car, as set out below.

The decision whether or not to use the car for a particular journey. The costs that are relevant to this decision are those that will change if the decision to use the car changes. In the situation shown above, this will be the group of costs that change with the mileage covered or 6.0p per mile. In deciding, the user compares this level of cost with that of other means of transport.

Note that the cost differential is not the only difference between the two alternatives. Factors of comfort, convenience, time, etc., are all relevant to the decision and must be considered in making it. Aspects of a problem not quantifiable are present in many decisions encountered in practice.

The decision whether or not to use the car for a period of time. In choosing whether or not to lay up the car for the winter, for example, the motorist would consider the costs of running the car during that period against those that would be incurred if it were laid up. These include all of the running costs, and much of the costs of taxing and insuring the car for the period.

The decision whether or not to own a car. Here, the whole of the costs of car ownership are variable and can be avoided if other means of transport are used. This total cost will be compared with the cost of using other means of transport after taking into account the aspects of time, comfort, etc.

In this decision, however, there is a further relevant dimension. Do the benefits of car ownership provide a large enough return on the capital invested in purchase to make the investment worth while?

The above example shows that, instead of being concerned with how costs are allocated and controlled, as with the cost system, in decision taking one is concerned with identifying those costs that change as between the alternative courses of action being considered.

The 'make or buy' decision

This problem centres on decisions whether or not parts and manufactured items should be bought out or made within the business. This choice must be assessed in terms of:

1. To what extent the choice made will increase or decrease income.
2. Whether the increase in income represents an adequate return on any additional investment required.
3. The relevant non-financial factors.

Note that it is the *incremental* change in costs that is relevant.

Example: Makebuy Ltd currently purchases its entire annual requirement of 50 000 units of assembly 135J at a unit cost of £1.50. The works manager has proposed that in future these assemblies should be manufactured internally, putting forward the arguments that:

1. Most of the manufacturing operations could be accommodated on existing machines.
2. Manufacture internally would produce greater flexibility in design changes.
3. It should produce cost savings.

At the request of the managing director, the cost accountant has produced the following information: material cost per unit—60p, labour cost per unit—40p. The overhead rate for the department is 200 per cent of direct labour.

From information obtained, the managing director has estimated that the additional costs in the department would comprise:

Additional supervision	£3500
Additional storekeeper	1800

Additional maintenance	1500
Additional power	1000
Additional depreciation	1500
Sundry expenses	800

The solution to the problem can be carried out in three stages:

Stage I   Compare the cost differentials

Costs of purchase		Additional cost of manufacturing	
	£		£
50 000 units		Materials 50 000 × 60p	30 000
@ £1.50	75 000	Labour 50 000 × 40p	20 000
		Additional overheads listed above	10 100
			£60 100

On the basis of cost factors alone, a decision to manufacture would add £14 900 to profit.

Note that the present departmental overhead rate is not relevant in this context. The present overheads of the department do not change as a result of the decision to manufacture. Only those overheads bearing extra costs if manufacture is carried out should be considered in the appraisal.

Stage II   Non-financial implications

(a) At present, management has only to control the assemblies from the point of purchase. Manufacture will entail carrying material stocks and work in progress, with the attendant costs and risks.

(b) On the other hand, production of assemblies may be phased so as to reduce the need to carry substantial stocks since the risk of interruption of supplies is confined to one firm only.

(c) The convenience in making design changes when the whole of the manufacturing operation is carried out by one organization.

(d) The loss of flexibility due to locking up machine time, etc.

Stage III   Return on investment criteria

The inclusion of additional depreciation in the extra overheads indicates that some further machines would be required. The cost of such additions, plus the additional working capital that might be required, should be assessed so that the return on investment can be calculated.

Adding or deleting a product line

The question of product-line profitability is one that is frequently encountered. The individual product looked at on its own may appear to be unprofitable. The real test of profitability is, however, only measurable in terms of the effect on overall profit that dropping the product would have.

What costs can be avoided if the product is no longer made and sold? The direct costs could be avoided, while some indirect costs would no longer be incurred. Some of the overheads would, however, continue whether the product is made or not. For example, the allocated overheads will include a proportion of directors' salaries, accounting costs, personnel costs, factory management, planning, etc., much of which is unaffected by the decision.
Example: Multiprod Ltd sells a range of five different products and, in response to management requirements of improved profitability, an analysis has been carried out by the finance staff producing the following breakdown of profit per product:

	A	B	Products C	D	E
	£	£	£	£	£
Materials	10.2	4.6	3.9	8.7	6.4
Labour	8.4	4.0	3.6	6.2	4.2
Overheads					
(150% of direct labour)	12.6	6.0	5.4	9.3	6.3
Total cost	31.2	14.6	12.9	24.2	16.9
Profit	3.1	1.2	1.5	(2.2)	1.7
Selling price	34.3	15.8	14.4	22.0	18.6
Annual sales volume (units)	1800	18 500	16 200	12 700	8800

As a result of this analysis, the accountant has proposed 'that the company drop product D. By eliminating the loss of £27 940 (£2.2 × 12 700) made on this product profits would be increased by a similar amount.'

If, however, it is ascertained that approximately 40 per cent of the overheads are fixed, such a decision would lead to a reduction in profits rather than an increase, i.e.:

Loss of revenue £22.0 × 12 700	£279 400
Costs saved Materials £8.7 × 12 700	110 490
Labour £6.2 × 12 700	78 740
Overheads 60% × £9.3 × 12 700	70 866
	£260 096
Loss	£19 304

While it is making a loss in total cost terms, the product is in fact making a positive contribution towards fixed costs.

Again, a number of other factors would need to be taken into account. Could capital released through dropping product D be put to more profitable use elsewhere? Are we required to sell a complete product range? How certain are we of the split between the variable and non-variable overheads? And so on.

Management must maintain a clear distinction between the purposes for which it requires cost information. That required to control the operations of the business comprises a complete analysis of all the costs incurred and is basically oriented to the concept of apportioning total cost. That used in the decision-making process is highly selective, being concerned to identify the cost differentials between alternative courses of action.

The non-financial aspects are important, frequently having serious implications for the business. And, finally, the cost appraisal in the decision-making situation is often only the first stage of a capital investment appraisal decision.

8

Costing and the price/marketing strategy

THE IDENTIFICATION OF PROFIT AREAS

The market

In many cases the business sells its products in competition with others. Few businesses are monopolies in that the needs that they satisfy cannot be met by some other means. As business has become more multinational, international competition has limited some monopolistic tendencies.

In the market, the seller's costs are normally known only to himself and he is faced with the market price set by the interaction of the activities of the various firms who make up the market and the demand for their products. The profitability of different products, customers, sales outlets, etc., to the firm is determined by the differences between the market price and 'cost'. The question at issue is the right measure of cost to be used.

In other types of business, individual quotations are made for each job and competitive quotations may or may not be submitted. In such circumstances, management needs to assess what the customer is prepared to pay and the level of likely competitive quotation, in relation to the firm's costs.

In this chapter, the competitive market is examined first, followed by the situation in which individual quotations are given.

Traditional pricing policies

In the past, the most common basis for pricing a product has been to estimate 'the cost' of the product, i.e., the total manufacturing or purchase cost, and to add a percentage for selling and administrative costs together with profit. Viewed in this way, the practice has superficial attractions. 'The cost' is calculated and a price fixed which should cover total costs and provide a profit. Total costs are covered, and unless in the long run this is so the firm will go out of business.

The practice assumes, however, that it is possible to calculate 'the cost' of a product accurately. This is unrewarding since many costs of manufacture are not directly attributable to products, let alone units of products. If there are four companies operating in the same market and *each company has exactly the same cost structure*, all making the same range of products, what are their relative competitive positions for individual products? Assume that the range of products includes BX 135 with the following direct cost values:

	£ *per unit*
Direct materials	120
Direct labour	194 (representing 103 labour hours)
Machine time 82 hrs	

If each company in the market sets its selling price by reference to 'the cost', plus a mark-up of 30 per cent on cost for other overheads and profit, but selects a different basis for allocating indirect manufacturing costs, each company's quotation for BX 135 might appear as follows, assuming the overhead recovery bases shown[1]:

	Company A	Company B	Company C	Company D
			(£'s per unit)	
Direct materials	120	120	120	120
Direct labour	194	194	194	194
Overheads	136 (70% of direct labour)	78 (65% of materials)	62 (60p. per direct labour hour)	33 (40p. per machine hour)
Total manu-facturing cost	450	392	376	347
Mark-up 30%	135	118	113	104
Selling price	585	510	489	451

Each company manufacturing BX 135 derives a different selling price *solely on account of the method used to attribute total overheads to products*. The implications for the individual companies and for the industry as a whole should be clearly understood. Company D is most likely to receive orders for BX 135 since its quotation is well below those of its competitors. This may appear satisfactory for that company, if not for its competitors. But is it necessarily so?

[1] Overhead recovery based upon the following data which is common to each company:
Materials £144 649
Direct labour £134 360 (156 754 hours' work)
Overheads (manufacturing) £94 052
Machine hours worked 235 130
Overhead as a percentage of direct labour 70%
Overhead as a percentage of direct materials 65%
Overhead as an amount per labour hour 60p.
Overhead as an amount per machine hour 40p.

Each competing company will be manufacturing a range of products and, given that each has the same cost structure, if one product is underpriced relative to the competition, other products must be overpriced. Taking the company as an economic unit, the overheads of the business will have been apportioned to products as a whole, but the allocation basis used will considerably affect the individual product cost and hence the price.

Company D will, therefore, attract business from its competitors for product BX 135 and by hypothesis lose custom for other products which are relatively overpriced. What are the likely results of this trend if it is allowed to proceed unchecked? The expansion of sales for each business lies in products which tend to bear less than their due proportion of overheads, and which, therefore, in real terms are likely to be less profitable than other products.

A typical example of a product not bearing its due proportion of the overheads is one in which it makes more use of automated equipment than other products. In extreme cases, therefore, the expansion in turnover for a business is likely to be in capital intensive products. The end result of the policy can be an expansion in low-profit-margin products at the expense of higher-profit-margin products. Further, if this goes unchecked, the expansion may call for the further investment of funds in capital equipment to keep up with sales volume.

Response of mark-up method to market stimuli

The mark-up method of pricing must also be tested in terms of the decision indicators it provides for management. To provide a viable pricing technique, it should furnish the correct decision indications at the right time.

Consider C.D. Ltd which manufactures a product of which it is estimated 100 000 units will be sold next year. The company's practice is to add a mark-up of 20 per cent to the total cost of manufacturing to derive the selling price. The price build-up for the product is as follows:

	£	
Direct materials	6.5	
Direct labour	4.0	
Variable overheads	3.2	
Fixed overheads	3.8	(£380 000/100 000 units)
Total manufacturing cost	17.5	
Mark-up 20%	3.5	
Selling price	£21.0	

If the prices quoted by companies making the same product range from £19 to £22, then C.D. Ltd will tend to lose business to its competitors who quote lower prices. The change in volume of products sold indicates to management that its selling/pricing policy should be reviewed. When forecasting the volume of activity for the next year, it is found that the likely volume of sales for the product is only 60 000 units. Using the mark-up method, the price for that trading period will be set at £24.04, i.e.:

	£	
Direct materials	6.50	
Direct labour	4.00	
Variable overheads	3.20	
Fixed overheads	6.33	(£380 000/60 000 units)
Total manufacturing cost	20.03	
Mark-up 20%	4.01	
Selling price	£24.04	

The use of the mark-up method indicates to management that *a price should be increased, even though the company is already losing business to its competitors because the product is overpriced.* The attempt to recover total costs through the cost plus mark-up method may well in such circumstances result in the wrong corrective action being taken.

The accidental underpricing of the product may present similar problems. If the original selling price of £21 set by C.D. Ltd had proved to be the lowest price of all the firms in the business, C.D. Ltd would tend to expand its share of the market for the product. If by the end of the year it had expanded output by 50 per cent, a price of £19.48 is indicated for the next year, made up as follows:

	£	
Direct materials	6.50	
Direct labour	4.00	
Variable overheads	3.20	
Fixed overheads	2.53	(£380 000/150 000)
Total manufacturing cost	16.23	
Mark-up 20%	3.25	
Selling price	£19.48	

Here, the signal given by the mark-up method is that *although the company is gaining business from its competitors because its price is already undercut-*

ting them, the company should still further cut its price. This is not to say that that policy is necessarily wrong, but it does raise two quite fundamental questions. Firstly, if the company is already winning additional business at its present price why should it reduce profit margins to win even more business? The additional volume will add to profit but not necessarily to the extent that could be achieved by expanding the volume of other products.

The policy outlined might be appropriate, but should not be implemented solely on the information provided so far. The firm would be embarking on a policy of expanding its output without a firm appraisal of that product's profitability relative to other products. Moreover, it should be appraised from the point of view of the impact the expansion will have upon the firm's overall return on capital employed, after the additional investment of funds is considered.

This leads to the second point regarding this decision. The indicator given by the pricing process is to further lower the price. The company may, therefore, embark upon a policy of continually reducing the price and expanding volume and drawing in the capital resources of the business to support a product which is relatively unprofitable. As mentioned previously, this will be reinforced by the fact that this situation probably arises with capital-intensive products. The end result of the policy may well be a condition of unprofitable expansion.

The effects of this approach to pricing would not be limited to the individual firm. Where various firms compete across a range of similar products, the result may be that each firm attracts to itself the major volume of business in those products which are relatively underpriced, losing business in relatively overpriced products. The effect is a continuous decline of profit margins in the industry.

DEVISING AN ACCEPTABLE MEASURE OF PROFIT

One of the difficulties in the application of the mark-up method lies in the treatment of the fixed-overhead element in the manufacturing cost. It was the attempt to allocate this cost to individual products which caused the variations in price. This leads to consideration of whether the attempt to do so should be abandoned and the concept of contribution used instead.

Measurement of product profitability

The basic assessment of product profitability lies in the profit it contributes as a percentage of sales. The different results obtainable by using contribution rather than profit are shown in Fig. 8.1. On the basis of profit, it appears that the two products are equally profitable, the percentage profit to sales being $12\frac{1}{2}$ per cent in each case.

The further analysis of the two products on the basis of contribution shows that, due to the different methods of manufacture, the relative contributions of each product are quite distinct. Product A had a contribution/sales ratio of 50 per cent, that for product B being only 28.1 per cent.

THE CONTRIBUTION/SALES RATIO (CSR)

The contribution/sales ratio is a much more meaningful measure of relative profitability. This is because it measures the increased cost incurred in producing additional volume against the increase in sales revenue. The total cost basis does not do this, since some of the costs included are fixed, not increasing if volume increases.

Figure 8.1

Comparative profitability of products

Measured by profit to sales:

	Product A	Product B
	£	£
Direct materials	4	8
Direct labour	8	16
Variable and fixed overheads	16	32
Total cost	28	56
Profit	4	8
Selling price	32	64
Profit as a percentage of sales	12.5%	12.5%

Measured by contribution to sales:

	Product A	Product B
	£	£
Direct materials	4	8
Direct labour	8	16
Variable overheads	4	22
	16	46
Contribution	16	18
Selling price	32	64
Contribution as a percentage of sales	50%	28.1%

Every additional £1 sales of product A makes a contribution of 50p towards fixed overheads and profit, whereas each additional £1 of product B contributes only 28p.

In considering its selling policy, management requires from cost data an indicator of the relative desirability of different products in its range, to direct selling efforts to the more profitable lines rather than less profitable ones. The contribution/sales ratio in the case illustrated shows that selling effort should be directed towards product A rather than B, or that steps should be taken to bring the two CSR's more into line with each other by adjusting prices. By using the CSR, management can rank the products of a business in order of desirability, establishing priorities for its use of resources in marketing the product range.

Example: Contro Ltd markets a range of six products, all competing with similar products of other companies. It is currently working at a loss, and management is trying to devise a selling policy to restore the business to profitable operations. Because of past losses, management has set a limiting factor by ruling that the capital employed is not to be increased beyond its present level. This rules out a straightforward volume increase since this would add to working capital and, therefore, to capital employed. Also, it is not considered possible in view of the company's competitive position to raise prices.

The current cost, price, and volume data for the products are as follows:

				Product			
	1	2	3	4	5	6	Total
	£	£	£	£	£	£	£
Direct materials	2.1	2.7	4.7	3.1	6.4	2.8	489 300
Direct labour	2.3	3.8	5.2	4.8	7.2	3.0	578 200
Variable overheads	1.8	3.6	3.2	4.2	5.1	2.2	408 100
Fixed overheads	3.0	4.2	1.0	1.5	2.3	4.2	180 100
	9.2	14.3	14.1	13.6	21.0	12.2	1 655 700
Profit/(Loss)	(1.1)	(0.5)	0.1	(0.1)	—	(0.2)	(2 500)
Selling price	8.1	13.8	14.2	13.5	21.0	12.0	1 653 200
Volume (units)	2 000	5 000	50 000	22 000	25 000	3 000	

The initial aim of management is to produce a profit of £100 000 p.a. within the overall sales volume of £1.6 million.

The first step towards a viable policy here is to assess the relative profitability of the products sold. The profit or loss per unit shown in the cost structure previously is not the proper one to use since it does not show the effect on profit of expanding or contracting sales of each of the six product groups. The comparative profitability should be assessed on the basis of the relative contribution/sales ratio as follows:

			Product			
	1	2	3	4	5	6
Sales price	8.1	13.8	14.2	13.5	21.0	12.0
Total variable cost	6.2	10.1	13.1	12.1	18.7	8.0
Contribution	1.9	3.7	1.1	1.4	2.3	4.0
CSR	23.5%	26.8%	7.7%	10.4%	11.0%	33.3%
Profitability ranking	3	2	6	5	4	1

Although product 3 alone was previously shown to make a profit, it comes last in the ranking process when the CSR is used. Management should now consider how they are going to reorient the selling and marketing effort for the range of products, recalling that the resources for this purpose are limited. Clearly, in the circumstances, priority in selling effort should be given to product 6, closely followed by products 2 and 1. Selling effort related to products 3, 4 and 5 should be limited to release resources the other products require, the objective being to alter the balance in the product mix.

If this policy is successful, it *may* result in the following or a similar pattern of sales and profit. Bear in mind, however, that although the illustrative solution keeps within the constraint of the overall sales volume, it should be tested to see whether the changed sales mix results in different capital needs elsewhere.

			Product				
	1	2	3	4	5	6	Total
Selling price	8.1	13.8	14.2	13.5	21.0	12.0	
Variable costs	6.2	10.1	13.1	12.1	18.7	8.0	
Contribution	1.9	3.7	1.1	1.4	2.3	4.0	
Volume	8 000	25 000	30 000	15 000	15 000	25 000	
Sales value	64 800	345 000	426 000	202 500	315 000	300 000	1 653 300
Total contribution	15 200	92 500	33 000	21 000	34 500	100 000	296 200
Fixed overheads							180 100
Profit							£116 100

USE OF CONTRIBUTION WHERE THERE IS NO FIXED MARKET PRICE

Where individual quotations are given for each job, the use of the total cost for price fixing may result in loss of orders which could have made a contribution to profit. If the firm has spare capacity, any order that can be secured at a price greater than variable cost is desirable.

Controlling the use of contribution

While contribution is a useful method of assessing the desirability of individual orders, it is still true that in the long run total costs must be recovered if the business is to make a profit. The discipline of the mark-up method ensures that this is done since, in one way or another, total costs are built into the pricing structure.

Where contribution is used the assessment of profitability is based upon the relationship between total variable costs and selling price. The danger, in practice, is that as it becomes widely known in the business that as long as a product covers its variable costs it adds to profit, there will be a tendency to quote lower prices to obtain business. This is a natural tendency since the salesman's performance is assessed in sales volume rather than profit.

The adoption of CSR as a pricing tool frees management from building fixed costs into the selling price, but the need remains to provide sufficient total contribution to cover fixed costs and the required volume of profit. Within that contribution level, it no longer tries to ensure that *all* products achieve the desired CSR, but only that the product range *as a whole* achieves it. Some may earn a higher rate and others a lower rate, thus putting a much more flexible tool into the hands of the sales force.

To prevent abuse of CSR, it is necessary that management:

1. Sets a target contribution figure based upon the known or forecast level of fixed costs and the desired profit.
2. Monitors the contribution earned and the CSR continuously during the trading period and compares the result with the target set.

Target CSR

Setting the target CSR should form a major part of the control system. Starting with the basic data of capital employed and the required ROCE set by management, the target average CSR can be established. The total contribution required is the amount of profit providing the target ROCE plus the budgeted fixed costs. This can then be expressed as a percentage of the forecast sales volume.

Example: CSR Ltd has a capital employed of £1.5 million and the board has set as the target ROCE 15 per cent before tax. The budgeted fixed costs amount to £600 000 and forecast sales £5.2 million.

			£
Required contribution:	Profit 15% of £1.5m	=	225 000
	Fixed costs		600 000
	Total contribution		£825 000

Target CSR 825 000 × 100/5 200 000   =   16%

If at the year end the average CSR is above 16 per cent, the sales volume is as forecast, and fixed costs do not exceed budget then the ROCE will be more than 15 per cent before tax.

CONTROLLING CSR

The process of control can be achieved by logging incoming orders (normally done in any case) and adding to the recorded information the contribution from each order. On a daily, weekly, or monthly basis, as is appropriate, the contribution and sales value can be compared to see whether they match up to the standard set. This recording operation could be carried out in a form similar to that in Fig. 8.2.

Figure 8.2

Record of CSR on actual sales

Order number	Customer	Address	Item	Value	Contribution

As an overall management control, the progress of the actual contribution earned to date in the year is plotted on a graph as in Fig. 8.3. The curve OA shows the planned build-up of contribution over the year. If there are seasonal fluctuations, this line is not straight but reflects the seasonal pattern. The actual contribution for the period is plotted on line OB. Additionally, it may be useful to show the level of fixed costs to be covered. This will indicate to management the point at which each additional order will add directly to profit.

If the actual contribution falls below target, either the sales volume is less than forecast, or the achieved CSR is less than target. The latter will be evident from the control information. If it is due to small sales volume, management must make a decision as to whether or not to reduce the CSR target to improve volume. The course chosen is the one which management believes, given the circumstances, will maximize total contribution.

Figure 8.3

Contribution control chart

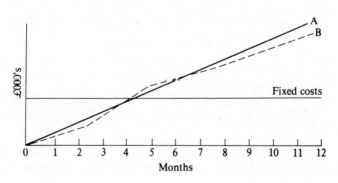

Controlling CSR on large contracts

Where business consists of a small number of large contracts, the process set out in the previous paragraphs might not be appropriate. Each major contract commits a proportion of the resources of the firm. Management's task, therefore, is to ensure that by the time the available resources are fully committed the required level of contribution has been secured.

Each contract should be analysed on receipt and the units of each major resource required for each month of the contract ascertained. This process is likely to be carried out in any case in the process of production planning. In addition, the estimated level of contribution earned in each month must be calculated. The utilization of resources and the earning of contribution will then be plotted on graphs similar to Fig. 8.4. The required contribution is calculated as previously.

Figure 8.4

Control of contribution on contracts

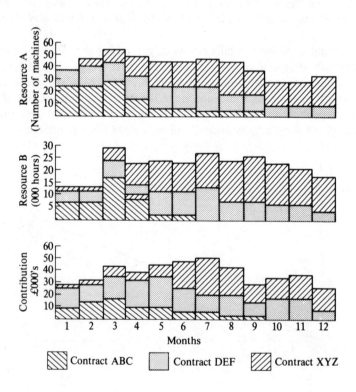

The two resources illustrated could be any the business uses which might impose a constraint upon the volume of business that could be undertaken. The target contribution shown is at the rate of £60 000 per month or £720 000 per year.

USE OF CONTRIBUTION IN OTHER SITUATIONS

The use of contribution to identify sources of profit for the business need not be confined to the simple use of the CSR in assessing product profitability. Distribution methods, classes of customer, quantity discounts, etc., can all be appraised in the same way. To illustrate possible techniques two situations will be explored: one in which a business is considering giving quantity discounts, and one in which the limiting factor on volume is not the ability to sell the firm's products but a restriction on its ability to make them.

Use of quantity discounts

Granting quantity discounts can significantly affect the CSR and the class of business the firm wins. The possible implications should be thoroughly explored before the decision to grant them is finalized.
Example: The sales manager of Disco Ltd has been investigating the possibility of setting a range of quantity discounts for Hyfo 35. Quantity discounts have been given in the past on an *ad hoc* basis and it is felt that this should be regularized. One competitor gives discounts on the following scale on the basic price of £10:

Orders for 100+	10%
Orders for 1000+	20%
Orders for 10 000+	30%

To gain an edge on this competition, the sales manager proposes discounts of 10 per cent on orders of 100 upwards, 22½ per cent for 1000 upwards, and 35 per cent for 10 000 and more. These will be on the firm's basic price of £10.2. It is estimated that a 5 per cent saving in the labour cost and variable overheads can be made for 1000 plus orders and savings of 10 per cent on orders for 10 000 plus. The cost of the product is as follows:

	Per Unit
	£
Direct materials	3.0
Direct labour	2.0
Variable overheads	2.0
Fixed overheads	2.0
Profit	1.2
Selling price	£10.2

What would be the possible consequences of this policy? The first step in the process is to assess the likely effects of the policy upon the CSR as below:

Quan-tity	Competi-tor's price	Own proposed price	Vari-able cost	Selling price	Variable cost	Contri-bution	CSR
	←– – – –£s per unit – – – –→			←– – – £s per order – – –→			
1	10	10.2	7.0	10.2	7.0	3.2	31.3 %
100	9	9.18	7.0	918.0	700.0	218.0	23.7 %
1 000	8	7.905	6.8	7 905.0	6 800.0	1 105.0	13.98%
10 000	7	6.63	6.6	66 300.0	66 000.0	300.0	0.45%

From this analysis of the problem the manager obtains an objective assessment of the likely outcome of the proposal if approved as it stood. The reduction in the contribution/sales ratio at the 1000 order size is substantial, and at an order size of 10 000 units it becomes dangerously low. If the company were to obtain a balanced mix of order sizes, this *might* be an acceptable proposition. But there is a further hazard in the proposal as it stands. At one end of the scale, the prices are above those of competitors, e.g., at the 1 and 100 unit order size, whereas at the other end of the scale the prices would undercut competitors. A likely outcome of the policy would, therefore, be for the competition to capture a major share of the market in the smaller order size, Disco Ltd becoming composed more and more of the larger order size, which we know to have an exceedingly low CSR.

In the long run, the balance of the business obtained would become tilted decisively in the direction of low CSR orders which, because of the volume of business probably following that trend, could lead to substantial further investments of capital in plant to keep up with demand. This investment is unlikely to be rewarding.

USE OF CSR WHERE THERE ARE SCARCE RESOURCES

The analysis of profitability of products, etc. made so far has assumed that sales volume is the limiting factor, the company's marketing strategy having been discussed on that basis. While this may often be true, it is not always so. Some companies may find that other factors exercise a constraint on the possible volume of business. The production resources may be limited in some way, funds may only be sufficient to finance a limited level of activity, and so on. Here, management is faced with a different problem.

The objective of the marketing strategy is as before, i.e., to maximize profit. Whereas when sales capacity was the limiting factor the contribution was related to sales in the CSR ratio, when other limiting factors are present the contribution is related to that limiting factor in an attempt to maximize total contribution.

In deciding the marketing strategy here the desirability of products is determined by the relative contribution each makes *in terms of units of the limiting factor*. For example, if capacity is limited by the availability of skilled labour of a particular kind, the key factor in deciding sales priorities should be the contribution that each product or service yields per man hour.

Example: Limito Ltd sells five products, each of which is manufactured upon a bank of 50 power presses all usable for any of the products. Each press can produce approximately 160 hours of effective work per month. The fixed costs of the factory are £20 000 per month. The cost and potential sales volume of the five products are:

Product	Selling price	Total costs	Variable costs	Press hours per unit	Potential sales volume
	← — — — — — — per unit — — — — — — — →				
	£	£	£	Hours	Units per month
N	20	18	15	2	1200
O	20	13	10	3	1500
P	10	9	7	1	5000
Q	22	19	14	2	1600
R	34	31	24	6	1800

The first stage in the analysis of a situation such as this is to determine the relative desirability of each product in terms of its contribution per press hour. Neither the total cost nor the fixed costs are relevant since we need to maximize the total contribution. This relative ranking would appear as follows:

Product	Selling price	Variable cost	Contri-bution	Number of press hours	Contribu-tion per press hour	Ranking
	← — — — — -per unit - — — — —→					
	£	£	£		£	
N	20	15	5	2	2.5	4
O	20	10	10	3	3.33	2
P	10	7	3	1	3.0	3
Q	22	14	8	2	4.0	1
R	34	24	10	6	1.67	5

The optimum mix can now be ascertained by filling up the available capacity first with product Q, and working through the ranking order until the available capacity has been absorbed, e.g.:

Product	Units	Hours per unit	Total hours	Contribution per unit	Total contribution
				£	£
Q	1600	2	3200	8	12 800
O	1500	3	4500	10	15 000
P	300	1	300	3	900
			8000		28 700
				Fixed costs	20 000
				Profit	£8 700

This will not necessarily be the sales mix achieved. Other factors may override the considerations that have been taken into account. For long-term reasons it may be necessary to continue marketing the complete range of products. What it has indicated is that, within the constraints that may be present, the marketing strategy should be oriented so as to concentrate selling effort on products Q and O, and to a lesser extent product P. What must be borne in mind is that the more the sales mix achieved deviates from the above optimum, the lower will be the achieved profit. The substitution of units of any other product for those shown will lock up limited production capacity in work making a lower contribution per press hour.

In a situation such as the above management may look to ways of making more intensive use of the limited resource. One possibility might be to consider taking on an evening shift which would increase the capacity of the plant by 50 per cent. Because of the increased supervision and other costs it is estimated that this would add approximately £8000 to fixed overheads. (Note that fixed overheads vary as capacity is increased.)

The optimal solution to this question follows on from the previous example. Whether it will be worth while or not to put on the extra capacity will depend upon whether the additional contribution that can be earned will be greater or less than the addition that will be made to the fixed overheads, viz.:

Product	Units	Hours per unit	Total press hours	Contribution per unit	Total contribution
				£	£
P	4000	1	4000	3	12 000

The additional contribution of £12 000 is greater than the addition that would be made to fixed overheads; therefore, on the considerations taken into account so far, the proposal would increase profit by £4000. Other considerations already noted may prohibit full optimization. Additionally, the increased level of activity that the proposal implies would probably add to working capital requirements. This would require further analysis and appraisal to determine whether the return on capital is acceptable in accordance with the considerations outlined in Chapter 6.

CONCLUSIONS

This chapter merely outlines some of the major considerations which apply when setting the marketing and pricing strategy of the business. Such a strategy rests squarely upon the identification of the sources from which the business derives its profit, so that the marketing and other resources can be concentrated in those areas and not upon less favourable ones.

9

Control of contract investment

PROBLEMS OF LONG-TERM CONTRACTS

Where the business is engaged in winning a limited number of large contracts, each with a life cycle lasting many months or years, the control of investment in work in progress is particularly difficult. Each contract is often large enough to affect the overall return to the business significantly. Even with the best managed companies operating in this field, one reads regularly of individual contracts having badly affected the company's profitability in a given year, or even produced a loss.

Here, the overall control of investment in work in progress cannot be left to the kind of turnover ratio dealt with on page 20. Much more positive control must be introduced if management is to master the situation. Rationally, this control should be concentrated upon the individual contract—in fact, treating the contract as a separate business.

The industries popularly identified with this type of operation are the construction industry, heavy engineering, shipbuilding, etc. Other industries often have sectors with similar operations, e.g., the electronics industry, particularly that part centred upon government contracts.

Typically, the work such industries carry out is in single contracts, tenders being submitted in competition with others, either on an open or restricted basis. With such large contracts, the contractor usually receives progress payments as work proceeds. Finally, there is an agreement as to the total value of the work done and the balance due, including any retentions, paid to the contractor. Such contracts are usually highly specific, each being related to an individual client's needs, although occasionally a sequence of contracts is taken for what is virtually the same product.

Characteristically, a very high proportion of the total costs of the business are directly attributable and charged to individual contracts. Even items of plant and machinery, in other industries considered fixed assets, are often purchased for or allocated to the contract and charged as a part of the direct costs. This is most evident in the construction industry, where all operations connected with a contract are concentrated on a separate site.

A high proportion of the total funds of the business are, therefore, directly related to the contracts in hand, rather than to fixed assets serving a range of products. The return on investment of the individual contracts undertaken effectively determines the return on capital employed for the whole business.

In addition to the type of contract outlined above, there are also major long-term contracts entered into by various industries to supply a quantity of units of a product over a period. This type of contract is classifiable as a 'long-term contract with multi-unit deliveries', as against the first type, classifiable as a 'single end-of-contract delivery contract'.

The multi-unit delivery contract may also call for the purchase of items of plant and machinery specific to that contract and not added to the fixed assets of the business. Part of the contract may be financed by the customer and various arrangements prevail, some almost amounting to a joint venture between the parties.

Significance of contract investment

The importance of the role of contract investment lies in two factors:

1. The large proportion of the company's funds locked up directly or indirectly in the contract.
2. The long period of time the funds are so committed with little or no option of reversing the decision until completion, or changing the negotiated terms of the contract.

Volume of funds committed to the contract

The size of funds locked up in a contract is determined by the balance between the monies laid out on the contract to date and the amounts recovered from the customer at any point in time. The day-by-day or month-by-month relationship between the cumulative totals of cash expended and cash received is the indicator of funds committed for that contract.

Time scale of contracts

Not only will the *volume* of funds locked up influence the overall contract performance, but also the *length of time* that the funds are invested. Say, for example, a company is looking at two current tender situations. Tender A would require the investment of £20 000 over a 12-month period, showing an estimated profit of £2000. The prospective contract would, therefore, show a return on investment of 10 per cent (2000 × 100/20 000). If tender B involves the same average investment and the same anticipated profit, but a contract lasting 18 months, it would show a return on investment of only $6^2/_3$ per cent [(2000 × 100/20 000) × 12/18].

Actions taken to shorten the time span of a contract, therefore, directly contribute to improved profitability, and the dire consequences of allowing the time span of a contract to 'stretch' can be easily seen.

Typical cash flow profile

For most contracts, the outlays of cash relate to paying for wages, materials, supplies, subcontractors, etc., and for additional overheads incurred and fixed assets acquired as a result of taking on that contract. The cash receipts arise from the periodic delivery of goods and payment by the customer or, in the case of single end-of-contract delivery contracts, progress payments.

Typically, the pattern of cash flows has an appearance similar to that in Fig. 9.1. In the early months of the contract, there are the cash outlays on site preparation, manufacture of prototypes, etc. As this early preparation period is completed, the cash outlays start to build up rapidly as materials are purchased, labour is brought on to the job, etc.

Near the end of the contract, these outlays fall off until only those connected with rectifying last-minute faults, etc., are incurred.

Figure 9.1

Cash flow profile of long-term contract

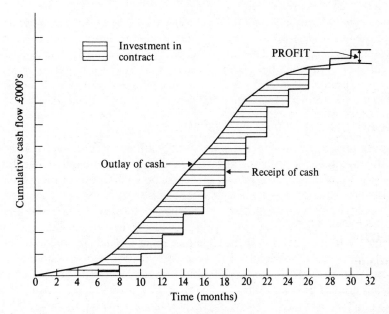

The cash receipts from the contract depend on the class of contract and the precise arrangements made with the client for financing the work in progress. With multi-delivery contracts, the solution is for the customer to pay for units as delivered. With the single delivery type of contract, the customer may make no contribution towards financing. In some countries, for example, the building contractor frequently finances the construction, the client only paying on delivery of the completed building.

Most common in such contracts, however, is for progress payments to be made on the value of work done to date. In the building industry, this is based upon a measurement of work agreed with the client's surveyor; in others, it is more usually based upon costs expended. The customer safeguards his position by retaining a percentage of the monies due, releasing them only on satisfactory completion.

The net inflow or outflow of cash each period depends upon the precise timing of the payments for materials, etc. This timing is determined by the company's policy on the payment of creditors, subcontractors, etc., and by the effectiveness of the control exercised over the collection of amounts due. Some companies attempt to make the utmost use of the credit extended by suppliers. The longer the period taken, the more likely that the time gap before outlays are reimbursed will be cut to the minimum or be non-existent.

The contract conditions may limit the business's ability to use suppliers' credit. HM Government, for example, inserts clauses in many contracts that progress payments will only be made *after* the relevant suppliers' and subcontractors' accounts are settled.

The cash commitment can also be reduced by more effective methods of collecting cash due from customers. This is just as important in relation to contracts as to any other type of business. The procedures dealing with the recording of costs, making claims, invoicing part deliveries, and securing the cash due are aspects which management must plan and control with the aim of restricting the time cycle as much as possible.

RETURN ON CONTRACT INVESTMENT

The cash flow profile in Fig. 9.1 is not greatly different from that for a capital investment project, the chief difference being that the capital investment project generally covers a period of years, and the contract investment a period of months. As was seen in Chapter 6, it is the amount of the investment and the pattern of return cash flows which help determine the rate of return on a project. The same holds true in respect of the investment of funds in a long-term contract. To assess the right pattern of projects in which to invest, i.e., the most profitable pattern of contracts, it should be possible to rank contract returns in order of profitability so as to choose from among the differing possibilities on offer.

OBJECTIVES OF CONTRACT CONTROL

Profitability maximization

The basic objective of a system of appraising contracts and controlling performance is to select, where there is a choice, those contracts earning high returns on the funds invested, rather than those with lower returns. A further objective is to see that funds so used earn at least as high a rate of return as can be earned in any other way in the business. One must not, therefore, concentrate exclusively on the *amount* of profit a contract may earn, but more particularly whether it meets the rate of return criteria that has been set by management.

To provide effective management control of contracting companies, the information system to be developed should include techniques for:

1. Measuring contract profitability.
2. Setting contract profitability targets.
3. Measuring performance against targets and identifying significant variables.

Management's attention is thus focused on the *profitability* of the work undertaken rather than solely on profit margins.

Attention to profit margins is most clearly evidenced in the building and construction industry. One frequently meets contracts surveyors who deliberately undervalue work done in the early months so as 'to leave more freedom of manoeuvre in settling the final claim'. The volatile horse of profitability has escaped before the stable door of margins can be shut. A further instance is the manager who, for whatever reason, fails or delays to carry out the rectification work and other items needed to obtain settlement of the final bill and the release of retentions. Such managers are clearly unaware of the way in which profitability can be lowered while funds continue to be locked up in the contract.

MEASURING CONTRACT PROFITABILITY

What is investment in the contract?

As with most manufacturing operations, the major part of the investment in work in progress consists of wages paid and materials purchased for the job. In contrast with other types of businesses, however, the costs directly identifiable with the contract are much higher. In the construction industry, in addition to direct labour and materials, there is the cost of site supervision, storekeeping, etc. In the large contract, there may even be an element of self-accounting on site. Apart from purely head office functions, all such costs are properly identified with the contract.

It is, of course, not only a question of what costs can be identified with contracts, but also whether they will vary with the level of work on hand. If the contract manager and site agent are to be kept on by the firm irrespective of whether there is any work for them, their cost cannot be considered as a part of contract investment. This is because these costs are incurred whether or not the contract is obtained. In a sense, one is once again looking for the *differential* costs rather than absolute costs.

In many cases, specialized equipment is required specifically for a contract, e.g., for testing to Ministry of Defence requirements products manufactured under contract to ministry specifications. Since such equipment is specialized for one contract only, it should be considered as part of the investment on it.

To the extent that overheads vary with the volume of work in hand, their cost also counts as part of the cost of investment. This may be particularly true of some government contracts. Frequently, the specialized nature of such work requires exceptional control over the whole of the manufacturing process from the raw materials to the finished product, e.g., to AID requirements. In appraising government work, this aspect should be carefully weighed, especially as to its implications for the overall level of investment in work in progress.

Where assets are purchased for a series of contracts, a formula must be devised enabling a value to be assigned to each of the contracts in turn. The cash-flow measurement approach is most suitable here. Using this as a basis, the investment in each contract could be measured as follows:

	Input to contract	Credit to contract
First contract	Cost of asset to the firm	Saleable value at end in its then state
Second contract	Value credited to first contract plus value of work done on reconditioning	Saleable value at end in its then state
Third contract	Value credited to second contract plus value of work done on reconditioning	Saleable value at end in its then state

While the above basis of allocation may seem a little inequitable, since the first contract bears a high proportion of total costs, it is basically logical. At the time of purchase of the asset, there may be no certainty of further work for it after the present contract. When it is released from the first contract, management has the opportunity of realizing its cash value or of retaining it for further use. Each investment can, therefore, be seen as a result of various independent decisions.

Where plant, etc. is held centrally by a subsidiary company and hired out to the remainder of the group, the plant-hire company should include in its charges to others a reasonable return on the capital locked up in its stock of plant. The hire charges then properly form part of the contract investment in so far as they have not been reimbursed.

Average investment

To calculate the return on investment, the profit earned over the period of the contract is adjusted to an annual basis and related to the average amount invested.

Let us take the pattern of cash flows for a contract like that in Table 9.1. In each of the 10 months of the contract, outlays are incurred in respect of contract costs. Additionally, there is a measure of the investment of plant and equipment.

Table 9.1

Measuring contract investment

	Months										
	1	2	3	4	5	6	7	8	9	10	11
Cash outlays:						£000's					
Wages	10	11	11	12	13	10	8	4	3	2	—
Purchases	16	15	32	40	20	16	10	4	2	1	—
Site overheads	3	3	4	4	4	3	3	3	3	3	—
Investment in plant	20	5	5	—	—	—	—	—	—	—	—
Total	49	34	52	56	37	29	21	11	8	6	—
Receipts											
From client	—	24	30	45	46	34	28	25	26	25	27
Plant disposals	—	—	—	—	2	3	8	2	1	1	1
Total	—	24	30	45	48	37	36	27	27	26	28
Net monthly (investment) or disinvestment	(49)	(10)	(22)	(11)	11	8	15	16	19	20	28
Cumulative investment		(59)	(81)	(92)	(81)	(73)	(58)	(42)	(23)	(3)	25
Average investment to date	(49)	(54)	(63)	(70)	(72)	(72.5)	(70.4)	(67)	(62)	(56.1)	

The projected cash flows are then totalled for each of the months during which the contract will be operating. Offset against this commitment of funds will be the receipts in cash from customers in respect of part deliveries or progress payments. In addition, the investment in the contract may be reduced by the release of capital equipment, either by sale or by reabsorption into the general stock of assets held.

The net difference between outlays and cash receipts anticipated for the contract represents the absorption or release of funds for that month. At the end of month 1, this investment amounts to £49 000. At the end of month 2, it has risen to £59 000 with the average investment over the two months of £54 000 [(49 000 + 59 000)/2]. By the end of month 3, the total investment increases to £81 000 and for the three months the average investment has been £63 000.

Over the whole contract period, the average amount locked up is £56 100.

Measuring return on investment

The overall profit on the contract illustrated in Table 9.1 is estimated as £25 000, being the forecast excess of cash receipts over cash payments. The salient factors about the contract for management are:

1. The overall contract price   £310 000

2. The overall contract costs:
   Wages   £84 000
   Materials   £156 000
   Overheads   £33 000
   Consumption of
     capital equipment
     £30 000 less
     £18 000   £12 000
                                                                   ─────────
                                                                   £285 000
                                                                   ─────────

3. Average investment of funds:
   £56 100 over 10 months

4. Return on funds invested in the contract:

$$\frac{25\,000 \times 100}{56\,100} \times \frac{12}{10} = 53.4 \text{ per cent}$$

This percentage return is not, of course, an assessment of the 'net' return, no attention having been paid so far to the overheads of the business as a whole. Rather, it would be an assessment of the contribution percentage earned on that investment. It provides the correct profit ranking for projects since, as was noted in Chapter 7, when contribution is maximized so is profit.

An acceptable level of contribution/investment percentage has to be determined by management, taking into account the likely volume of work carried out over the next year, the profit required to provide the target return on capital employed, and the forecast level of company overheads.

CONTROLLING CONTRACT PROFITABILITY

What is the right rate of return?

Contract profitability is not directly comparable with return on capital employed, for two reasons. As already mentioned, the return on contract measurement takes no account of company overheads. Secondly, in addition to the capital invested in this and similar contracts, the business has part of its capital invested in fixed assets and working capital which are common to the whole business and not specific to one contract.

The approach to defining the desired level of contract contribution should follow the lines laid down for setting the CSR. Management should determine the target return on capital employed it wants to earn in that budget period. In conjunction with the forecast volume of funds to be employed, this determines the profit target for the period.

The operating budget sets a target for spending upon overheads not specific to contracts, together with some idea of the potential sales volume. These provide the basis for calculating the 'target' return on contract investment for the period.

Assume that C.L. Ltd has a capital employed of £3.6 million, £2.4 million being attributed to contract investment; the remainder is tied up in investment not directly identifiable with individual contracts. If management has set as its target a return on capital employed of 15 per cent before tax, the profit target can be set as follows:

Total profit target £3.6 million × 15% = £540 000

Now, assume further that the budgets for the period show that the spending on overheads that cannot be directly allocated to contracts is £375 000. The total contribution required from contracts is:

Total profit target	£540 000
Overheads	375 000
Target contribution	£915 000

The target return on investment, i.e., that which must be achieved on average if the target profit is to be earned, can now be set as follows:

Target contribution	£915 000
Investment in contracts	£2.4 million
Required return on contract investment	38.1 per cent

The required return on investment is the minimum average return on contract investment that should be earned on the total funds invested in contracts over the budget period. Individual contracts may be accepted which provide lower returns, provided that over the period the average return is maintained.

Management now has two financial measures with which to assess its attitude to potential contracts. The contribution/sales ratio dealt with on page 79 will have provided an assessment of the mark-up required to provide the target profit level. This measure can now be looked at alongside the measure of return on contract investment. The latter should be the determining factor, since it combines the return on sales factor with the investment of funds.

Build-up to target profitability

As with other control functions within the business, the reporting time scale should be adjusted to the time within which management intervention can be effective. With contracts, it is clearly undesirable to set a contract return-on-investment target and then only compare the actual return achieved at the end of the contract when any hope of influencing the result has gone. To exercise the control function adequately demands continuous comparison of achieved contract profitability against the target, at intervals during the duration of the contract. The interval of reporting should be short enough to enable management to intervene at the earliest possible time should serious divergencies emerge between target and actual returns.

Table 9.1 shows the average investment at monthly stages throughout the contract. The profit attributable to the contract can also be spread over its life in relation to the amount of work done at each stage or, if there are special factors which affect the contract, in conformity with those special factors.

With multi-delivery contracts, this is assessed on the number of units delivered to date as a proportion of the whole, i.e., units delivered/total units × total contract profit. In the single end-of-contract delivery contract, the build-up of claims on the client usually includes the profit element in the work carried out to date or, if the bill is divided into activities, the profit element in each activity completed.

In either case, the contract planning should include the planned profit accumulation over the life of the contract, which is then matched against the average investment at any point of the contract. When the profit figure is adjusted to an annual basis, the rate of return on investment to that point of time can be calculated.

Assume that the planned profit build-up for the contract illustrated in Table 9.1 is as follows:

Month	Profit for the month	Cumulative contract profit
	£000's	£000's
1	0.2	0.2
2	1.1	1.3
3	1.2	2.5
4	2.9	5.4
5	2.6	8.0
6	3.7	11.7
7	3.6	15.3
8	4.7	20.0
9	3.5	23.5
10	1.5	25.0

The calculation of the return on contract investment over its life can now be set out as shown in Table 9.2.

Taking the figures for the first month, there is a target profit of £200 which is an annual rate of £200 × 12 or £2400. Expressed as a percentage of the contract investment to date, £2400 represents a return of 5 per cent. This process is repeated for each month, the profit to date being adjusted first to the annual rate.

Table 9.2

Build-up of return on contract investment

| | Months | | | | | | | | | |
	1	2	3	4	5	6	7	8	9	10
Average investment to date (£000's)	49	54	63	70	72	72.5	70.4	67	62	56.1
Target profit to date (£000's)	0.2	1.3	2.5	5.4	8.0	11.7	15.3	20.0	23.5	25.0
Return on contract investment on an annual basis	5%	14%	16%	23%	27%	32%	37%	45%	51%	53%

Controlling contract performance

Having established the target performance, the next requirement is a reporting system providing values for actual contract investment and profit at each stage during the contract. From these, the performance to date can be calculated and compared with the forecast performance.

Figure 9.2

Control chart—return on contract investment

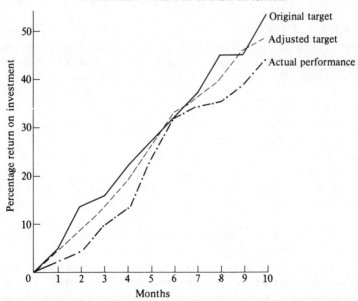

A useful visual method of setting out the comparison between planned and actual performance is the graph in Fig. 9.2. On this is plotted the build-up to the target return on investment which can be adjusted for any major variations in the terms of the contract agreed between the parties. Against this is plotted the actual returns achieved month by month. Where significant deviations occur from the planned or adjusted planned performance, the causes should be investigated and performance brought back on target where possible.

CAUSES OF DIVERGENCE FROM TARGET PROFITABILITY

The time 'stretch'

One of the major reasons for profit performance falling below that forecast is that the time scale of the project exceeds that forecast. For example, taking the figures used in Table 9.2, if total contract profit remained the same but the contract was not completed for 12 months, the final return on investment would be £25 000 × 100/£56 000 = 45 per cent, as against the planned 53 per cent. The consequences of the contract time being exceeded in terms of return on investment should be appreciated at all levels.

There are techniques available to management which, though outside the scope of this book, are used to control the 'time budget' for the contract, e.g., critical path analysis, line of balance, etc. The impact of cost and profit performance should be linked to the critical path performance to which management works.

Incurring costs too early

The earlier costs are incurred and paid for, the greater the level of contract investment. Management should consider these implications when working out the purchasing schedule and the terms on which suppliers are paid.

Obtaining early payment from the customer

The object here is to influence two factors—the *amount* that is claimed and the *time* it takes to obtain payment.

Consideration should be given to all factors influencing the amount that can be claimed from the customer at all stages during the contract. The holding over of amounts until final settlement of the contract is clearly one which should be discouraged. Where there is uncertainty as to the amount of overheads chargeable in the interim claims, the highest permissible figure should be used, any overcharging being cleared up at the final settlement.

There is an unfortunate tendency, once a claim has been submitted to the customer, to think that that is the end of the matter. As shown on page 41, the amount tied up in debtors considerably influences profitability. An adequate follow-up system for amounts due should be instituted to collect them with minimum delay.

Delivery/inspection/acceptance procedures of customer

The customer may have rigid rules governing the acceptance and payment for goods received. Deliveries not conforming to these requirements may be subject to considerable delays in payment. Care will ensure that all requirements are met to obviate such delays.

Movement of capital equipment

The longer capital equipment is on site or committed to a production contract, the higher is the average investment. The contract planning should take into account the need for the minimum commitment of fixed assets. During operations, such assets should be released from the contract as early as possible to reduce contract investment.

Part 2
Managing sources of funds

10

Controlling liquidity

ROLE OF LIQUIDITY IN FINANCIAL MANAGEMENT

What is its importance?

The liquidity of a business is one of the key factors determining its propensity to success or failure. Making provision for the cash needs and the sources that are drawn upon to satisfy those needs help determine how far the company is put at risk. Among these risk factors can be distinguished those concerned with the balance between long- and short-term funds, and those concerned with the relationship between shareholders' and borrowed funds at the long-term end. The former element is dealt with in this chapter, the latter in Chapters 13 and 14.

One quite basic rule can be set out at once: long-term assets should be financed by long-term funds. To use short-term funds for this purpose courts disaster. This rule may seem self-evident to most people, but surprisingly it is one often ignored in practice, as many business failures testify.

Like most rules, there are exceptions. Banks and building societies operate almost exclusively upon short-term funds, but most of those funds are committed to what are essentially long-term loans. There is the fiction that bank overdrafts are recallable on demand, but the banks' ability to realize funds loaned out to customers is severely limited in practice. Their ability to operate in this way depends upon two things.

Firstly, lending to such institutions has become an acceptable way of holding liquid funds in a secure form, at the same time possibly earning interest since banks have learned always to keep adequate cash resources available to meet sudden demands from depositors. Secondly, the funds are invested in a relatively risk-free way. There is a wide spread of loans or investments which in total are not likely to be much affected by the success or failure of an individual borrower. British banks learned the lesson the hard way in the nineteenth century, but some overseas banks can still be affected by a run on funds by depositors.

The critical factor which enables financial institutions to borrow short and lend long is confidence. As long as depositors have confidence that they can withdraw their deposits on demand or within the terms of their agreement, such institutions can survive. If that confidence is lost even they can be in trouble, as was demonstrated in the secondary banking crisis in the UK in 1973–74. Manufacturing and trading companies cannot show the liquidity and spread of risks of a financial institution and the golden rule should be to cover all long-term uses with long-term funds.

The leasing of equipment in high capital cost industries, e.g., airlines, poses very similar problems. Here, the relatively high value of continually accruing lease payments is a constant drain on liquid resources. At the same time, the lease payments may set a high level of fixed costs and, therefore, a high percentage of capacity as the break-even point with a small margin of safety. Moreover, with leased equipment there is no cash flow related to depreciation since the assets are not owned.

One is frequently surprised by the number of quite senior businessmen who fail to distinguish between profitability and liquidity, thinking that profits should emerge as cash in the till. Yet a moment's thought indicates that this is not necessarily so. The company which is profitable and expanding rapidly is in need of additional liquid funds as the increasing level of investment in fixed assets, stocks, and debtors more than absorbs the new funds generated through retained profits and depreciation. One of the prime tasks of management is to assess their forward operating plans in terms of cash requirements, ensuring that the business has cash available to meet these commitments.

MEASUREMENT OF LIQUIDITY

In the analysis of financial reports, there are two principal ratios used to distinguish trends in the liquidity of a business over time, and to assess the current ability of the business to meet its commitments. Being based upon historical data, they must, of course, be treated with some caution but may, nevertheless, provide useful data for management decisions. Their use may also be affected by differences in industry practices.

Current ratio

This ratio measures the number of times that current assets cover current liabilities as shown in the balance sheet. Taking the figures for Incognito Ltd on page 112, the current ratio would be:

$$\frac{\text{Current assets}}{\text{Current liabilities}} = \frac{4\,619\,798}{1\,286\,032} = \underline{3.6{:}1}$$

It was generally considered that this ratio should be at least 2:1. Table 10.1 shows that, while this view was adhered to until the mid 'sixties, it has stabilized over recent years at about 1.5:1. The lower level of liquidity may well be due to the pressures of inflation. It could also be the early expression of a change in the underlying attitude as to what is the 'right' ratio.

The weakness of this ratio as an indicator of liquidity lies in the size of the stock and work in progress value it includes. If a high proportion of current assets consists of this item, the 1.5:1 ratio might not be adequate. (Again, much will depend upon what each industry is prepared to accept as standards of behaviour as they affect liquidity.) Retailers with no debtors and some industries, e.g., the construction industry, may be able to operate with much lower ratios.

Quick (or acid test) ratio

Recognizing that inventory might not be very liquid, this ratio takes the quickly realizable assets and measures them against current liabilities. Basically, this means omitting the stock and work in progress items from the calculation. Taking the figures for Incognito Ltd, the quick ratio is:

$$\frac{\text{Quick assets}}{\text{Current liabilities}} = \frac{2\,320\,828}{1\,286\,032} = \underline{1.8:1}$$

The conventional 'normal' ratio is 1:1. For British industry, the trend is shown in Table 10.1. From an average of just over 1.1:1 up to the mid 'sixties, the ratio has dropped gradually to around .9:1 in 1977.

DETERMINANTS OF LIQUIDITY

The *measurement* of liquidity was accomplished by comparing current assets and current liabilities, but what factors actually *determine* the ratio? Unless management is aware of these, it is not able to institute the controls required.

Table 10.1

Current and quick ratios for over 1000 major UK companies 1969–76

Year	Current ratio	Quick ratio
1969	1.59:1	.92:1
1970	1.53:1	.88:1
1971	1.57:1	.91:1
1972	1.57:1	.94:1
1973	1.50:1	.89:1
1974	1.45:1	.78:1
1975	1.50:1	.82:1
1976	1.53:1	.84.1
1977	1.65:1	.91:1

Source: *Annual Abstract of Statistics*, HMSO

The determinants to be considered fall under three headings:

1. The level of investment in fixed assets in relation to total long-term funds.

2. The volume of business.
3. The adequacy of control over current assets.

Investment in fixed assets.   The absorption of funds by fixed assets is one of the major causes of illiquidity. As more and more of the firm's funds are absorbed in this way, there is less left to finance short-term needs and, therefore, liquidity ratios fall. This fall is only avoidable by the provision of more *long-term* funds to cover the increased requirements of the fixed assets. Its effect is illustrated in the last column of Table 10.2.

The volume of business.   The increasing volume of business raises the funds required to finance current assets. Part of this requirement is met by a corresponding increase in creditors but, other things being equal, the invest-

Table 10.2

The effect upon liquidity of changing volume of activity and increased investment in fixed assets

	Balance sheet before change		Doubled activity: no change in fixed assets		Doubled activity: double fixed assets	
	← – – – – – – – – – –£000's– – – – – – – – – –→					
USES OF FUNDS						
FIXED ASSETS						
Plant and machinery (net)		500		500		1000
CURRENT ASSETS						
Stock and work in progress	300		600		600	
Debtors	200		400		400	
Cash	20		–		–	
	—	520	—	1000	—	1000
		1020		1500		2000
Less:						
CURRENT LIABILITIES						
Bank overdraft	–		170		670	
Taxation	20		40		40	
Creditors	200		400		400	
Dividends	30		60		60	
	—	250	—	670	—	1170
NET ASSETS		770		830		830
SOURCES OF FUNDS						
Share capital		300		300		300
Capital reserve		120		120		120
Retained profit		250		310		310
		670		730		730
8% debentures 19x2/x5		100		100		100
		770		830		830

ment of long-term funds to finance its share of the increased working capital is necessary to maintain the ratios.

Adequacy of control over current assets. If poor control over the investment of funds in stocks and debtors leads to a level of investment considerably higher than it should be, then the ratios again sharply decline unless more long-term funds are made available. The corollary of this is that improved performance in controlling such investments improves liquidity ratios.

The effects of the above factors upon the liquidity ratios are illustrated in Table 10.2. Before expansion, the company had a good liquid position showing the following ratios:

Current ratio   520/250 = 2.1:1
Quick ratio   220/250 = 0.9:1

The second column shows that when the level of activity changed, even with no change in the investment of fixed assets and after allowing for an increase of £60 000 in retained profits, the ratios have fallen to:

Current ratio   1000/670 = 1.5:1
Quick ratio   400/670 = 0.6:1

The change in the two ratios may not then have reached a critical stage, despite a considerable decline. If one now adds the doubled investment in plant and machinery shown in the last column, the liquidity ratios become:

Current ratio 1000/1170 = 0.9:1
Quick ratio   400/1170 = 0.3:1

The significant points of the comparison are:

1. The funds required for the expansion of current assets are partly provided by the related expansion of current liabilities. The demand on long-term funds is confined to the net expansion in working capital required to maintain the desired ratio.
2. The whole of any expenditure on fixed assets is an immediate drain upon liquid resources.
3. Borrowing from the bank, being a short-term source of funds, merely increases current liabilities. (It may, of course, provide a temporary alleviation to the problem.)
4. The limits to the use of creditors as a source of funds are set by the effect that the increasing level could have upon the liquidity ratios.
5. Correction of a poor liquid position can only be accomplished by:
   (a) raising more long-term funds, whether from shareholders or by borrowing, or
   (b) reversing the trend of investment by selling off some of the fixed assets, or
   (c) managing the current asset investment more efficiently.

The effect that improved management of investment in current assets can have upon the ratios is shown in Table 10.3. The turnover of stock and work in

progress improves from twice to three times per year and the collection period
of debtors reduces from 90 to 60 days. These changes improve the current
ratio from 1.35:1 to 1.62:1 and the quick ratio from 0.6:1 to 0.73:1. Management of stocks and debtors has, therefore, a twofold effect upon the business.
By improving turnover of capital employed it aids profitability and by reducing the demand for working capital it improves liquidity.

Table 10.3

Effect on liquidity ratios of more effective use of debtors and stocks
(Based upon constant working capital of £560)

		£			£
Stock and work in progress					
(Turned over twice p.a.)		1200	(Turned over three times p.a.)		800
Debtors (90 day collection)		900	(60 day collection)		600
Cash		60			60
Total current assets		2160			1460
Current liabilities:					
Bank overdraft	500			—	
Creditors	800			600	
Tax	200			200	
Dividend	100			100	
	—	1600		—	900
Working capital		£560			£560
Current ratio	2160/1600	1.35:1	1460/900		1.62:1
Quick ratio	960/1600	0.1:1	660/900		0.73:1

SOURCES AND USES OF FUNDS

The balance sheet and profit and loss account of the business can be used to
obtain an overall appreciation of the funds flows of the business over periods
of time. The funds flows which concern us here are:

1. What activities have absorbed funds during the period under review?
2. From what sources did the business provide the overall funds required in 1?

Because of the dual aspect of transactions and the method of recording
them in the balance sheet, there is always an equality between the assets and
liabilities. Items 1 and 2 above are, therefore, always equal for any period.

Funds flows are generated in one of the following ways:

1. By earning a profit or incurring a loss.
2. By funds absorbed or released by reason of changes in the current asset and
   current liability items.
3. By expenditure of funds on new fixed assets and the release of funds from
   such investments through the operation of depreciation and plant sales.
4. By distribution of profits earned.
5. By raising new capital or repaying existing capital.

The balancing account affected by all of the above changes is that recording the cash balance. If more funds are being absorbed in other uses than are being generated or released from other sources, the cash balance will decline, and vice versa.

If one looks at a set of published accounts, such as that shown in Fig. 10.1 for Incognito Ltd, an analysis of the changes in the balance sheet items during the year provides a schedule of those items which have contributed funds and those which have absorbed funds.

The basic rules of determining whether a change is a source or a use of funds are as follows:

Uses of funds comprise:
  Increases in asset values
  Decreases in liability values
  Decreases in the value of shareholders' funds.
Sources of funds comprise:
  Decreases in asset values
  Increases in liability values
  Increases in the value of shareholders' funds.

Applying the above rules to Incognito Ltd's accounts for the year to 31 December 19x1, the following first statement of sources and uses for the period 1 January to 31 December 19x1 can be obtained.

Figure 10.1

Incognito Limited and subsidiary companies

Consolidated profit and loss account for the year to
31 December 19x1

19x0			£
372 900	Profit from trading (after charging the following items)		593 818
	84 220 Directors' emoluments	90 820	
	6 000 Auditors' remuneration	7 000	
	224 430 Depreciation	275 782	
111 840	*Add:* Interest receivable		113 960
484 740	Profit before taxation		707 778
90 000	*Less:* Corporation tax on profit for year		277 300
394 740	Profit after taxation		430 478
	Less: Dividends:		
	58 200 Interim paid 10 October 19x1	61 014	
	124 000 Proposed final	145 480	
182 200			206 494
212 540	Retained profit for year		223 984

Figure 10.1

Incognito Limited and subsidiary companies

Balance sheet as at 31 December 19x1

	19x1 £	19x1 £	19x1 £	19x0 £	19x0 £
Authorized and issued share capital[4]	1 265 000		2 530 000		
Capital reserves	868 948		868 948		
Revenue reserves[3]	3 534 060		2 676 520		
Total shareholders' funds	5 668 008		6 075 468		
Deferred taxation	637 722		654 680		
Current liabilities					
Trade creditors		923 470	1 140 552		
Proposed final dividend		124 244	145 480		
		1 047 714	1 286 032		
		7 353 444	8 016 180		

	19x1 £	19x1 £	19x0 £	19x0 £
Fixed assets				
Land and buildings[1]		1 633 722		1 686 410
Plant and equipment[2]		1 604 014		1 709 972
		3 237 736		3 396 382
Current assets				
Stocks and WIP	1 885 350		2 298 970	
Trade debtors and payments in advance	1 109 940		1 117 748	
Money on deposit at call	1 022 768		1 051 992	
Tax recoverable	16 730		31 174	
Cash at bank and in hand	80 920		119 914	
		4 115 708		4 619 798
		7 353 444		8 016 180

Figure 10.1

Notes to the Accounts

¹ *Land and buildings*

	£
Balance at 1 January 19x1	1 633 722
Additions during year at cost	52 688
Balance at 31 December 19x1	1 686 410

² *Plant and equipment*

	At cost	Accumulated depreciation		Net book value
	£		£	£
Balance at 1 January 19x1	3 239 014		1 635 000	1 604 014
Additions less sales for the year	(13) 377 412			377 412
Adjustments re disposals		(14)	(4 328)	4 328
Depreciation charge for year		(15)	275 782	(275 782)
	3 616 426		1 906 454	1 709 972

³ *Movements in revenue reserves*

	19x1
Balance at 1 January 19x1	3 534 060
Add: Undistributed profit for year	223 984
Deferred tax written back	183 476
Less: Applied to increase share capital	(1 265 000)
Balance at 31 December 19x1	2 676 520

⁴ *Issued share capital*

	£
At 1 January 19x1 2 530 000 ordinary shares of 50p	1 265 000
Add: Capitalization issue from reserves 2 530 000 ordinary shares	1 265 000
At 31 December 19x1 5 060 000 ordinary shares of 50p	2 530 000

Sources of funds			*Uses of funds*		
Share capital	1 265 000	(1)	Revenue reserves	857 540	(5)
Deferred taxation	16 958	(2)	Land and buildings	52 688	(6)
Trade creditors	217 082	(3)	Plant and equipment	105 958	(7)
Final dividend	21 236	(4)	Stock	413 620	(8)
			Debtors	7 808	(9)
			Money at call	29 224	(10)
			Cash at bank	38 994	(11)
			Tax repayable	14 444	(12)
	1 520 276			1 520 276	

Once this preliminary assessment of the scale of changes has been prepared, more underlying detail can be derived by studying the notes to the accounts which are included in the report. Some of the more complex items included above can now be analysed as follows:

A *Fixed assets*

	£	
Plant and equipment		
Additions	377 412	(13)
Adjustment on disposals to		
depreciation	4 328	(14)
Additional depreciation	(275 782)	(15)
	105 958	

B *Changes in reserves*

Profit before tax	707 778	(16)
Less: charge for tax	277 300	(17)
	430 478	
Less: provision for dividends	206 494	(18)
Undistributed profit for year	223 984	
Deferred tax written back	183 476	(19)
	407 460	
Less: Applied to increase		
share capital	1 265 000	(1)
Decrease	(857 540)	(20)

C *Taxation*

Deferred tax change	(16 958)	(2)
Change in tax repayable	14 444	(12)
Tax charge	277 300	(17)
Deferred tax written back	(183 476)	(19)
	91 310	(21)

The data from the original sources and uses statement, together with the subsidiary information from the detailed analyses, can now be assembled in a detailed statement as in Table 10.4. There are various ways of presenting the information, the trend being to group the sources and uses by the part they play in the overall business activity.

The Accounting Standards Committee issued in 1975 a Statement of Standard Accounting Practice No. 10, entitled 'Statements of Source and Application of Funds' which illustrates the favoured layouts.

Table 10.4 is divided into three sections only. The first shows the volume of new funds generated by the current operations of the business. These consist of those profits retained in the business after provision for taxation. The detail management wishes to incorporate depends on the purposes to which the statement is put. If it is required to show how the gross revenue from sales has been disposed of, this part of the statement could well start with the sales

Table 10.4

Statement of sources and application of funds

Incognito Limited 19x1

Source		
Profit before tax	707 778 (16)	
Adjustment for items not involving the movement of funds:		
depreciation	275 782 (15)	
		983 560
Application		
Capital expenditure:		
Additions to premises	52 688 (6)	
Acquisitions of plant, machinery, etc., less receipts on disposals	381 740 (13) (14)	
		434 428
Increase in working capital:		
Increase in stocks	413 620 (8)	
Increase in debtors and payments in advance	7 808 (9)	
Increase in creditors	(217 082) (3)	
		204 346
Tax paid		91 310 (21)
Dividends paid	(21 236) (4)	
	206 494 (18)	185 258
		915 342
Increase in liquid funds as shown below		68 218
Increase in net liquid funds		
Increase in money on deposit at call		29 224 (10)
Increase in cash at bank and in hand		38 994 (11)
		68 218

revenue and the major items of cost to arrive at the value for operating profit. In any case, this detail should include the depreciation charge since it is a major contributor to the cash flows.

The second section of the statement deals with those changes in balance sheet values under the headings of capital expenditure and working capital. It also deals with the actual movement of funds in respect of tax and dividends actually paid.

The final section sets out how the changes outlined above have contributed to or used up the funds of the business in the year under review. The aggregate of the net changes in funds under those headings represents the change in the cash balances.

THE NEED FOR FORECASTING FUTURE CASH REQUIREMENTS

As noted in Chapter 5, the financial manager requires a detailed assessment of the future cash needs of the business. In that chapter, the forecasting requirement was concerned with the advance information needed to enable the manager to make the best use of cash and near-cash funds. Upon this advanced forecasting would be based a policy for the investment of surplus funds and the financing of short-term cash needs.

In addition to this use, the forecasting of future cash needs should be directed towards controlling the liquidity of the business, the crucial test of liquidity being the ability or otherwise of the business to meet cash commitments as they arise. Cash forecasting must, therefore, take into account all the following requirements:

1. Maximize the return (or minimize the cost) of funds locked up in liquid form.
2. Forecast short and long-term cash requirements for the purpose of maintaining the ongoing liquidity status.
3. Provide a control tool for management which will assist the planning of future cash needs and monitor the performance against that plan.
4. Ensure that proposals for future operations of the business are within the financial resources available.

Forecasting techniques

Cash planning can only be meaningful when it is based upon adequate assessments of operating requirements. A first step in the process is to ascertain the long-term objectives set by the board. This indicates the long-term resources likely to be needed, together with an assessment of profit performance.

The more immediate cash forecasting is based upon the short-term operating budgets which most businesses set each year. This budget sets standards of performance for all business activities during a period of time, usually a year. These comprise the expected sales volume, the levels of manufacturing expenses, and other expenses of operating the business. To these are allied forecasts of changes in investment, e.g., in stock levels, in debtors, and new machinery needed to provide the necessary productive resources.

The projected balance sheet method. This method of forecasting cash needs rests on a projection of the balance sheet as it will appear at the end of the period. When the values of all the other assets and liabilities and net worth have been forecast at that date, the balancing item will be the cash in hand or cash deficiency.

The projections of asset and liability values are based on the operating budget values for each item, e.g.:

1. Value of goods manufactured and sold, collection period for debtors, payment period for creditors, etc., between them determine the value of debtors and creditors at the end of the period.
2. Requirements for new investment in buildings, plant, and machinery, and in the levels of stocks and work in progress, determine the values of fixed assets and inventory.
3. Forecast operating profit, taxation rates, and dividend policy determine the value of the owner's funds and the provisions for future tax and dividends.
4. Non-operating changes, e.g., loan repayments, expected receipts from disposal of non-operating assets, etc. determine other changes.

An example of a projected balance sheet is shown on page 120.

The cash forecast.   The serious disadvantage of using the projected balance sheet method of forecasting cash needs is that it only shows the cash balance/deficit at one point in time, e.g., the end of a year. Where the business is seasonal, or the whole level of activities is changing, or there are other factors which affect the timing of cash flows, this will not indicate the cash needs at intermediate points. These needs can be substantially different from the year-end figure.

The cash forecast is based upon a detailed assessment of individual cash movements at monthly or other intervals during the year so that the extent and duration of cash needs is known. The operating budget itself should be divided up into monthly or other units of time for control purposes. Starting with the individual items of income and costs, the associated cash flows are scheduled in the months in which they are paid or received.

Cash flows from items other than those included in the operating budgets are similarly scheduled. These include not only the scheduled purchases of new plant and equipment, repayment of loans, etc., but also items which are derived from the operating profit but which may not be included in the operating budgets themselves, i.e., tax payments or dividend payments.

The method employed in preparing and presenting cash forecasts is shown in the example for Cashneed Ltd *(a)* on page 118.

The operating budget *(b)* on page 118 for the following year (19x2) has been prepared, together with schedules of sales by month and planned purchases. The firm's suppliers allow one month's credit and the firm itself manages to collect accounts receivable approximately 60 days after sale.

The company maintains two months' stocks of materials at all levels, the purchases schedule being based upon buying goods two months ahead of forecast sales volume. (It is assumed for simplicity that no work in progress or finished stocks are held.)

(a) Balance sheet for Cashneed Ltd as at 31 December 19x1

	£000's	£000's
Uses of funds		
Fixed assets:		
Premises, fixtures, and vehicles at cost	150	
Less: Depreciation	66	
	—	84
Current assets:		
Stocks of materials	21	
Debtors	55	
Prepayments	8	
Loan to suppliers	5	
Cash at bank	36	
	—	125
Less		209
Current liabilities:		
Creditors	8	
Tax (payable 1 January 19x2)	15	
Dividend (payable 25 March)	15	
	—	38
		£171
Sources of funds:		
Share capital		50
Capital reserve		27
Retained profits		78
Total shareholders' funds		155
Tax provision (payable 1 January 19x3)		16
		£171

(b) Operating budget for the year 19x2

	£000's	
Sales	600	
Cost of goods sold	420	
	—	
Gross profit	180	
Operating expenses:		
Rent	20	(payable ¹/₂ yearly March/September)
Wages	72	(equal monthly)
Light and power	12	(payable quarterly March/June, etc.)
Rates	6	(half-yearly January/July)
Sundry	24	(equal monthly)
Depreciation	6	
	— 140	
Operating profit	40	
Tax	17	
	—	
Profit after tax	23	
Dividend	15	
	—	
Retained profit	8	

Sales and purchase schedule

£000's	J	F	M	A	M	J	J	A	S	O	N	D	Total
Sales	20	10	30	50	80	100	80	80	70	30	30	20	600
Purchases	21	35	56	70	56	56	49	21	21	14	14	7	420

It is estimated that equipment worth £8000 will be purchased in March and an additional delivery van costing £2000 in June. The supplier has intimated that he will repay his loan, probably in September.

Taking the above information, the forecast month-by-month cash movements would be as follows:

Cash forecast for the year 19x2

	J	F	M	A	M	J	J	A	S	O	N	D	Total
Payments out:													
Purchases	8*	21	35	56	70	56	56	49	21	21	14	14	421
Rent			10						10				20
Wages	6	6	6	6	6	6	6	6	6	6	6	6	72
Light/Power			3			3			3			3	12
Rates	3						3						6
Sundry	2	2	2	2	2	2	2	2	2	2	2	2	24
New plant				8									8
Dividend			15*										15
New van						2							2
Tax	15*												15
Total	34	29	71	72	78	69	67	57	42	29	22	25	595
Receipts:													
Sales	30*	25*	20	10	30	50	80	100	80	80	70	30	605
Loan									5				5
Total	30	25	20	10	30	50	80	100	85	80	70	30	610
Net inflow/ (outflow)	(4)	(4)	(51)	(62)	(48)	(19)	13	43	43	51	48	5	
Opening cash balance	36*												
End of month surplus/ (deficiency)	32	28	(23)	(85)	(133)	(152)	(139)	(96)	(53)	(2)	46	51	

* From 19x1 balance sheet.

The balance sheet as it would appear at the end of the budget period is shown on page 120.

Note that there is a direct link-up between the operating budget, the cash budget, and the projected balance sheet. Changes in the values for balance sheet items between the opening and closing of the budget period are represented by differences in the values for that item between the operating budget and the cash budget.

To illustrate this, take the value for debtors. At 31 December 19x1 this item was in the balance sheet at £55 000, and at 31 December 19x2 at £50 000, a decrease of £5000. This decrease is accounted for by the difference between the sales value of £600 000 in the operating budget and the value of £605 000 included in the cash budget for receipts from sales.

Depreciation.   A further difference in treatment is in respect of depreciation. It follows from the above rules that the increase in the cumulative depreciation in the balance sheet results from the charging of £6000 depreciation in the operating budget, there being no outlay for the expense in the cash budget. (Depreciation being solely a book entry, there is no cash flow ensuing.) This latter point is often overlooked when providing for the cash outlays in respect of overheads.

Long-range forecasts.   Such forecasts cover a number of years' operations. The number of years chosen will depend upon the nature of the firm's business. Retail operations, for example, are likely to have a much shorter forecasting cycle than a firm building heavy electrical equipment.

The objective of the forecast is to provide management with an assessment of the long-term demand for funds that is implicit in the objectives, targets, and goals set for company performance over the planning period. When these global sums have been calculated, together with the likely timing of the requirements, financial management is charged with ascertaining whether, given the profit performance of the business, it will have the capacity to raise the volume of funds the plans would require.

Projected balance sheet at 31 December 19x2

	£000's £	£000's £
Uses of funds		
Fixed assets:		
Premises, fixtures, and vehicles at cost	160	
Less: Depreciation	72	
	—	88
Current assets:		
Stocks (last 2 months' purchases)	21	
Debtors (last 2 months' sales)	50	
Prepayments	8	
Cash (as per cash forecast)	51	
	—	130
		218
Less		
Current liabilities:		
Trade creditors (last months' purchases)	7	
Tax (long-term provision in last B/S)	16	
Dividend (provision in operating budget)	15	
	—	38
		£180
Sources of funds		
Share capital		50
Capital reserves		27
Retained profits (£78 last B/S plus £8 retained this year)		86
		163
Tax provision (forecast provision on year's profits)		17
		£180

11

Sources of short- and medium-term funds

Uses of short-term funds

The financing requirements of a business consist of those which are permanent in character and not released for many years or, as in the case of shareholders' funds, until the business is wound up, and those which are needed to fund part of the short-term uses and to cover temporary uses. Such temporary uses arise from exceptional non-recurring work loads, seasonal fluctuations, bridging gaps in financing needs, etc.

Volume of short-term funds used

The extent to which short-term funds are used is shown in Table 11.1. Until the early 'sixties, the proportion of total assets financed by short-term funds had remained fairly constant at just under 20 per cent. During the period covered by the table the proportion rose to reach the 40 per cent level.

TRADE CREDIT

The capital needs of the business

The use of credit from suppliers should not be ignored when deciding how to meet the overall capital requirements of the business. The availability and cost of medium and long-term funds should be compared with the costs of making the maximum use of trade credit, e.g., in the loss of suppliers' goodwill and cash discounts. Many companies and small businesses may have little alternative but to 'lean' on suppliers during periods of early growth when capital from normal sources is virtually unobtainable, or when such sources are barred through government action.

The average payment period can be extended by a careful selection of suppliers. The buyer should place orders as far as possible with those suppliers with the longer credit periods. When making payments to suppliers, priority is given to those whose supplies are critical or which have a tough collection policy, not to those rather unconcerned about payment. This policy can be further extended by 'rotating' orders among different suppliers, and on a rotating basis clearing up individual accounts to a 'paid-up' basis.

Table 11.1

Use made of short-term funds in the UK 1969–77

Year	Bank overdraft	Trade credit	Other current items	Total short-term funds	Total assets	Total assets financed by short-term funds (%)
1969	2505	6 895	2479	11 879	33 228	35.7
1970	3001	8 131	2309	13 441	35 895	37.4
1971	2911	8 415	2288	13 614	38 043	35.8
1972	3251	9 736	2716	15 703	43 472	36.1
1973	4611	13 126	2920	20 657	52 738	39.2
1974	6360	15 858	2385	24 603	60 522	40.7
1975	6227	17 941	2229	26 397	67 104	39.3
1976	7449	21 357	2721	31 527	78 444	40.2
1977	8151	23 387	3060	34 598	86 730	39.9

Source: *Annual Abstract of Statistics*, HMSO

If trade credit is considered as 'cost-free' capital, then, within the constraints of liquidity requirements, financial policy dictates that the fullest use possible be made of this source. This source, however, is frequently not in fact 'cost-free', e.g., the supplier might stop deliveries or put up the price, and this, together with the liquidity requirement, considerably constrains its use.

Balance between amounts owing and liquid resources

As with any other use of other people's money, the use of trade credit must not be expanded beyond the capacity of the firm's cash flow to service the payment requirements. The higher the level of creditors in relation to the cash flow, the greater the risk that a creditor may take steps to recover an amount due by taking legal proceedings—a process which may trigger off widespread claims by other creditors which the firm cannot meet.

The proper relationship between trade credit outstanding and the cash flow varies between industries. In the construction industry, for example, the amount owing to subcontractors and suppliers is very high in relation to the cash flow, whereas in most retailing it is very low. What is acceptable in one industry may not be in another.

The 'credit image' and the supplier

The reputation as a slow payer can very soon become widespread among suppliers. Credit reporting agencies realize the situation through their corresponding companies and through enquiries. This can have a twofold effect. Those suppliers who apply effective credit-control techniques may stop or delay supplies, giving priority to good payers. This may be particularly so where the materials, etc. are not in plentiful supply or a monopoly of supply exists, e.g., the supply of electricity and gas.

Where prices are subject to individual negotiations, prices to the slow payer may be increased to compensate for the expected delays in payment, or provisions inserted in the contract for the charging of interest on overdue accounts.

Such factors make the use of such funds no longer 'cost free'. They may, in effect, incur substantial additional costs, such as increased material prices, additional waiting time in the factory, and additional labour costs in fending off importunate creditors.

Value of cash discounts

In Chapter 4, the high cost of granting cash discounts was discussed. The reciprocal aspect of this cost is the earning of cash discounts for prompt payment.

The precise balance between the desirability or otherwise of taking advantage of cash discounts depends upon the rate of discount offered, the additional time payment could be delayed without incurring further costs, and the cost of raising funds from other sources. For example, if a creditor's terms are $2^1/_2$ per cent cash discount for payment within one month, the cost of foregoing the discount can be calculated as follows:

1. Payment can be stretched to one month beyond discount period: effective annual cost 30 per cent.
2. Payment can be stretched to two months beyond discount period: effective annual cost 15 per cent.
3. Payment can be stretched to three months beyond discount period: effective annual cost 10 per cent.
4. Payment can be stretched to four months beyond discount period: effective annual cost $7^1/_2$ per cent.

If alternative sources of funds cost 10 per cent, the break-even point is three months beyond the discount period. If the supplier's credit can be extended to four months in all without incurring any other costs or disadvantages, it would pay to use trade credit. Otherwise, advantage should be taken of the cash discount terms and the funds needed to finance the payments to be made obtained from elsewhere.

BANK CREDIT

The banks are in business among other things to lend money. They earn a major part of their income from the margin between the interest rate paid to depositors and that charged to borrowers.

The role of the bank is only appreciated by managers if they understand the real differences of return and risk as between the extender of trade credit and the lender of bank money. The return that the lender of money earns is confined to the interest charges made. This should be compared with the potential return to the giver of trade credit outlined on page 39. Not only does the bank receive *only* the stated rate of interest, but additionally the whole of the amount of the loan outstanding is at risk, whereas in many cases the trade creditor has at risk only the marginal cost of producing and selling the goods not paid for and not the nominal sum outstanding.

What sometimes seems to be an ultra-cautious approach to lending by bank managers can be better appreciated when it is put into this context of risk and return. Again, it is not the bank's own money that is at risk, but deposits from its customers.

Objectives of the bank

The ideal loan from the bank's point of view is one which is short-term, self-liquidating, and well secured. Short-term because the banker does not see himself as a provider of long-term funds, since he would then be borrowing 'short' himself and lending 'long'. This is not so in every country; for instance, in Germany and Japan, commercial banks provide extensive long-term funds for industry. This is also true of other countries where the market for long-term funds is not developed to any extent.

In Britain, commercial banks operate almost entirely as providers of short-term funds through the negotiation of overdraft limits for periods of 12 months or less at a time, requiring specific renewal at the end. In the US, the overdraft is almost unknown, bank lending being in the form of specific amounts borrowed for specific periods of time on promissory notes (usually styled in the balance sheet as 'bank notes').

Bankers must be sure that the business to which they lend will generate sufficient liquid funds to repay the loan within the agreed time. Ideally, the purpose for which the loan is made automatically makes liquid resources available at the right time. In a seasonal business, loans to finance seasonal stocks are automatically liquidated by the run-down of stocks, loans to finance a major contract from the sales proceeds of that contract, etc. When this self-liquidating property is absent, the borrower is normally required to demonstrate his ability to repay from other maturing cash resources.

The perfect short-term self-liquidating loan can often turn sour. The market for the firm's products collapses, strikes hit the plant, government action curtails or makes illegal the activities of the business, technical problems bedevil the development stage of a large contract, etc. The effect is to make impossible repayment of the loan as planned. How then is the banker to ensure that the sum owing will eventually be recovered? This is usually done by requiring the borrower to provide some security, separate from the activity being financed, which the bank can realize to recoup the loan.

Security

The financial standing or the personal qualities of the customer may sometimes be an adequate criterion for lending money. The banker usually, however, requires something more tangible than this. Ideal are readily realizable assets such as shares and bonds, insurance policies, etc., all easily convertible into cash.

Less satisfactory forms of security are charges upon the assets of the business or upon those of its directors. Almost any of the assets of the business can be charged in this way, e.g., fixed assets, stocks, and work in progress, debtors, etc. Although together these may represent a value considerably in excess of the amount borrowed, the security can only be enforced by the sale of those assets. A forced sale in such circumstances may realize values far below the recorded book values.

The chief danger for the bank is that it will get 'locked in' a lending situation. When things become difficult for the borrower, the bank is unwilling to force liquidation to realize the security, and with a very plausible client the danger may not be readily apparent.

The alternative for the bank is to support its client over the period of danger, frequently with a further injection of funds to keep other creditors quiet. This leaves the bank with much more at risk and, due to incurred operating losses, the asset backing for the loan is frequently eroded. The decision whether to cut losses by an immediate enforcement of security at the first signs of danger, or to hope that the whole loan can be recovered through providing additional lending to see the customer through a sticky period is one of the most difficult that the banker has to make.

The protection of limited liability may prove to be illusory as far as the directors of the smaller company are concerned when it comes to bank borrowing. They are usually required to provide personal guarantees to the bank indemnifying it against loss up to the amount of the loan. Their private fortunes are then at risk should the business fail up to the amount of the guarantees they have provided.

Making the best use of bank credit

Negotiating the overdraft. To obtain a view of the loan proposition, the bank manager calls upon the customer to provide a range of information about the company and the loan proposition. Before approaching the bank, the manager should make sure that he can place before it in easily understood and in quantified terms:

1. Why the business requires funds at the present time.
2. What size of loan is needed to cover the above requirements.
3. How, when, and from what source the loan will be repaid.

The above requirements are minimal ones and the loan application is greatly helped if supplemented by cash forecasts supporting the data submitted. In the discussions which no doubt follow the preliminary request, the following matters are likely to arise:

1. Information, probably from balance sheets and profit and loss accounts, of the financial state of the business.
2. What security can be offered.
3. What are the possibilities of the business meeting difficulties and not being able to meet the repayment timetable from the planned sources?

Relations with the bank. The firm's relationship with the bank can prove to be of inestimable value and management should endeavour as far as possible to cultivate it. When considering a loan request, the bank tries to supplement its information requirements with an assessment of the nature of the business of its customer, the quality and character of its managers, and their record of ability as managers. If the bank has had virtually no contact with the firm over the years, all this will be largely an unknown quantity at the time the loan is being considered. At best, therefore, these factors have merely a neutral effect on the decision, at worst a decisively negative one.

The moral is that management should formulate a continuing programme of contact with the bank. This should include showing bank officials the manufacturing set-up and how it is organized; discussing with the bank manager changes in the firm's range of activities; providing him with current financial statements; and generally keeping him informed as to what is happening.

As a result of such contacts, the bank is able to fit the loan request within an already known and established framework of personalities and activities, and the battle is already partly won.

Loans, etc., from finance houses and merchant banks

Short- and medium-term finance may be arranged from merchant banks or finance houses, such as Lombard and UDT, to fill short-term needs when normal bank facilities are not available for any reason. The loan is usually for a specific amount for a specific period.

LEASING, HIRE PURCHASE, AND OTHER SOURCES

Hire purchase

The use of hire purchase for the acquisition of assets is quite common and follows the pattern of domestic hire purchase. The asset belongs to the hire company until the final instalment is paid, when it becomes the hirer's property. For tax purposes, the asset is usually treated as having been owned from the beginning of the HP agreement. For businesses, the charge made by the finance house is an allowable expense.

Instalment credit

Similar in effect to the HP agreement as far as financing is concerned is the instalment credit purchase. The major point of difference between this and the HP agreement is that the property in the asset passes to the purchaser immediately. The purchase consideration, together with the interest and other charges, is then paid by instalments.

The total outstanding HP debt is shown in Table 11.2.

Table 11.2

The use made of hire purchase and instalment credit finance, and leasing

Year	HP and credit instalments:[1] New credit extended	Total outstanding	Leasing:[2] Leased assets acquired	Total assets owned
1972	2466	2106	130	516
1973	2846	2550	288	761
1974	2508	2386	321	1078
1975	2981	2373	340	1428
1976	3586	2716	421	1669
1977	4392	3341	675	2378
1978	5515	4300	1214	3407

[1] For finance houses only. Includes durable goods shops, department stores, and instalment credit retailers. Approx. $1/2$ new credit.
Source: *Annual Abstract of Statistics*, HMSO

[2] By members of the Equipment Leasing Association.
Source: *Midland Bank Review*

Leasing

Although not strictly a source of funds, leasing effectively avoids the need for funds. This is achieved by the business obtaining the use of assets, not by purchase, but by paying an annual rental charge, never becoming the owner.

Since ownership is never accomplished, one effect of the use of leasing to obtain assets is to limit the expansion of the borrowing base. This aspect has important implications and should not be lost sight of. The extensive use of this source of finance may prejudice existing loans through reducing the asset backing. At the same time, the need to finance growing annual lease payments reduces the profit cover for interest payments on loans should poor trading conditions be encountered. For these reasons, the terms on which long-term loans are made may prohibit the use of this source. The total funds devoted to leasing are shown in Table 11.2.

Borrowing on the security of debtors

Quite apart from the use of debtors as a basic security for bank or other loans, debtors can be used in more specific ways to provide short-term funds.

Bills of exchange.   Although common in overseas trade, this form is not encountered very often in internal trade. Effectively, the seller draws a bill of exchange which is accepted by the customer or by a bank acting on his behalf, payable at a specified date in the future. The bill, together with the documents of title to the goods, are then discounted by the bank through the bill market, i.e., the amount of the bill, less an interest charge, is advanced to the seller immediately.

The amount of interest depends on the standing of the acceptor of the bill, since it is to him that the bank will look first for payment. Thus, the bill is usually accepted by a bank or by *accepting houses* who specialize in this activity. The well-known name will mean that the interest rate charged is low, usually a little over minimum lending rate.

Discounting debtors.   The company borrows against the security of the debtors, either in whole or against a selection of customers only. The discounting house advances a percentage, say 80 per cent, of the face value of the debts, the advance being repaid out of the collection of debtors. The company is usually still responsible for invoicing and collecting amounts due.

Factoring debtors.   Where this method is used the business no longer retains title to the amounts owing to it. The company providing the finance sets up a sales company which it controls, and through it the sales are invoiced. The name of the sales company is that of the firm whose debtors are being factored with the word 'sales' included as a part of the title. All invoices are raised and issued in the name of the sales company which collects the amounts due. Each week, or other period, 75 or 80 per cent of the invoiced value for that period is advanced to the business, the balance of the invoice value being paid only after the amount due has been collected from the customer.

Although the invoices and related amounts due are the property of the discounting house, there are usually recourse provisions whereby the value of invoices which prove uncollectable are charged back to the business. The need for this becomes obvious since it is possible for the business to draw invoices for goods not in fact sold and discount them in the usual way. Although this comes to light in time, the firm can supplement its funds in the interim.

Although in some conditions the last two methods of raising short-term funds can be of great benefit, the cost of using them should not be underestimated. There is a commission to pay and the costs of running the sales company to be met. The argument that the firm will save the cost of collecting amounts due is frequently met with, but also frequently proves to be illusory. Since the finance house is receiving a substantial rate of interest on the amounts outstanding, it has no real incentive to chase the debtors.

If the firm decides to make use of this source of funds, management should make sure there is a sufficient feedback of information from the sales company to enable the firm to put pressure on customers, without the need to maintain a full set of records of debtors, duplicating that kept by the sales company.

Using the customer

The customer should not be neglected as a potential source of short-term funds. As was seen in Chapter 9, the provision of progress payments is quite normal in many types of long-term contract.

Where such provisions are not normal, it may nevertheless be possible to persuade the substantial customer to put up some of the finance needed to support his contract, even to the extent of sometimes providing the fixed assets that are required. Bearing in mind the effect that such advances would have upon contract profitability, it can be seen that they provide the additional advantage of providing a source of short-term funds.

12

Sources of long-term funds

In the previous chapter, consideration was given to the use of short-term funds in a business. Attention must now be given to those funds committed to the business permanently or over long periods of time. One characteristic of short-term funds was that fundamentally they should not be used for the purpose of financing the business as a whole, but only for a very specific function. Even those funds bordering on long term, e.g., HP finance, are not committed with the intention of financing the business as an entity, but solely to finance the acquisition of specific assets for specific periods of time.

The providers of such funds would not be looking to the financial probity of the business and its continuing profitability for their security. Instead, they seek specific guarantees which are enforceable without regard to the business's profitability or interference with the ability of the company to carry on after the security has been realized.

With long-term funds, one is looking at sources of finance which the owners will commit to a business for some years and which, even with collateral security, look primarily to continuing profitability as the guarantee of eventual repayment.

Basic long-term fund types

Long-term funds fall mainly into two classes. They may be funds provided by the *owners* of the business, whatever its legal framework, or they may be funds provided by people who *lend* money. In the one case, the providers of funds exercise the function of ownership and, with companies, are members of that company. Otherwise, they are only creditors of the business and exercise none of the rights of ownership in relation to the business's affairs.

In addition to the above basic types of long-term funds provided by original subscription, there are profits and other increases in value which the owners have left in the business rather than withdrawing them for personal use. These include the capital and revenue reserves shown in the balance sheet.

VOLUME OF LONG-TERM FUNDS

The value of new funds raised by British companies during the period

1967–1977 is shown in Table 12.1. This shows that the companies covered came to the market for sums ranging from just under £200 million in 1974 to over £1500 million in 1975. The chief point is the change in the balance between shareholders' funds and borrowed funds which occurred from 1967 onwards. The high proportion of debt in the early years reflects the effect of the 1965 Finance Act. After that period the tax changes in 1973 and the financial crisis of 1974 brought the percentage down.

Table 12.1

New Issues made by UK companies 1967–77

Year	Debt				Preference		Ordinary		Total issues
	Convertible debt £m	Other debt £m	Total debt £m	Percentage of total issues	£m	Percentage of total issues	£m	Percentage of total issues	£m
1967	29.7	313.8	343.5	*81.5*	5.7	*1.4*	72.6	*17.2*	421.9
1968	128.3	161.3	289.6	*44.1*	3.1	*0.5*	363.7	*55.4*	656.4
1969	231.7	144.8	376.5	*65.9*	—	—	195.0	*34.1*	571.5
1970	101.3	183.0	284.3	*80.4*	17.2	*4.9*	51.9	*14.7*	353.4
1971	96.7	243.7	340.4	*51.3*	12.8	*1.9*	310.4	*46.8*	663.6
1972	96.4	199.2	295.6	*30.9*	10.9	*1.1*	649.9	*68.0*	956.4
1973	21.6	21.3	42.9	*20.4*	14.0	*6.7*	153.6	*73.0*	210.5
1974	25.6	17.2	42.8	*26.4*	—	—	119.3	*73.6*	162.1
1975	117.0	95.8	212.8	*13.5*	44.9	*2.8*	1320.7	*83.7*	1578.4
1976	14.8	77.7	92.5	*8.0*	44.5	*3.8*	1023.9	*88.2*	1160.9
1977	2.0	91.8	93.8	*9.9*	33.9	*3.6*	819.6	*86.5*	947.3

Source: *Midland Bank Review*

The pattern exhibited in Table 12.1 shows, in addition to this once-and-for-all change, a cyclical pattern which superficially at least appears to follow the pattern of the trade cycle. The percentage of new capital raised from shareholders peaks in the years 1972 and 1975–76 which were years of 'squeeze' and credit restraint. The underlying economic and financing forces influencing these trends are factors which management must consider in appraising financing alternatives. The market values of quoted securities are shown in Table 12.2.

Table 12.2

Market value of securities listed on the London Stock Exchange (March 1979)

	Market value £ millions
British government and government-guaranteed stocks	54 805
Other government and corporation stocks and bonds	11 712
Corporate loan capital	4 709
Preference capital	1 580
Ordinary and deferred capital	254 064
	326 870

OWNERS' FUNDS

Who are the owners?

In a modern society one tends to think of business as being carried out mainly by large corporations, whether state owned or publicly quoted. In terms of separate business units, these are far outnumbered by the small privately owned business, irrespective of whether this ownership is exercised through the medium of the corporate structure or not.

Sole proprietor or partnership

The funds provided by the proprietors of a business are recorded in the balance sheet under the heading of 'capital account'. This account is a comprehensive ownership account. It includes not only the original capital put into the business by the proprietor(s), but also the profits earned whether of a revenue or capital nature, less amounts drawn out of the business by the owner(s) for private use.

With the sole proprietorship, the business is nothing more than an extension of the legal identity of the owner. Similarly, the partnership as a business has no independent legal existence outside its members.

Corporate bodies (private sector)

The provision of a large volume of funds can usually only be made by a large group of people. This creates problems in regulating the exercise of ownership rights as between the members. In the partnership form, the entity of the business changes with each change of partners. This can be accommodated where the numbers are few and changes infrequent, but would be impracticable where large numbers of people are involved. The corporate form of legal framework overcomes this difficulty.

The regulation of affairs between the owners is carried out in the form of a company registered under the Companies Acts, so that its capital can be divided into a large number of 'shares' held by different persons. Changes in the composition of shareholders do not then interfere with the continuity of the corporation. There are other forms of incorporation, e.g., by Royal Charter, which provide for a similar division of the capital into shares. Unless otherwise stated, references to companies imply companies incorporated with limited liability under the Companies Acts 1948, 1967, 1976 and 1980.

In these forms, the company itself has a legal identity quite separate from that of its owners. This continues even though effectively the ownership is vested in a single individual. [Salomon v. Salomon & Co. Ltd (1897) A.C.22.]

The state-owned corporation

The corporation has a separate legal existence in the same way as the company incorporated under the Companies Acts. Ownership is, however, vested in the State.

Powers of owners

The basic powers of the owners are concerned with two major aspects:
1. Their ability to control the activities of the body corporate or other business form.
2. Their right to profits (or liability for losses).

The sole proprietorship. In this simplest legal framework, there is no problem at all in dealing with these two requirements. Since there is no intervening corporate structure, the control of the business is directly exercised by the owner and is circumscribed solely by legal and competitive requirements. The profits accruing to the business directly benefit the owner and all his personal wealth is at risk to cover liabilities.

The only modifications which might be made to the ownership rights are those needed to modify claims on assets and income where the owner borrows money on behalf of the business. The lender wants specific claims upon the assets and income to be recorded in the loan instrument.

The partnership. In addition to the modification of rights due to the borrowing of funds, the partners must provide for the regulation of the rights and duties in relation to the business as between the individual partners. These will include *inter alia* how control is exercised, and how profits and losses are to be shared (although there is a joint and several liability for the whole of the firm's liabilities).

A class of 'limited partner' is provided for in the Partnership Act 1890. The limited partner has no further liability for the debts of the partnership provided that he takes no part in running the affairs of the partnership.

The corporation

The modification of ownership rights is usually much more sophisticated in the case of the corporation, since the legal entity of the corporation itself intervenes between the owners and the business. Ownership is divided into a number of shares owned by different people. The shares themselves can be divided up into different classes each carrying varying control and profit participation rights.

The state-owned corporation. Here, there is a simple vesting of control and the right to profit in the state under the provisions of the relevant statute. Because of the socio-political implications of state ownership and monopoly, and of differing objectives, this form is not further considered except where specifically stated.

Creation of further ownership funds

Additional ownership funds in a business can be created in three ways:

1. By the subscription of new funds to the business.
2. By allowing profits to be retained in the business rather than distributing them as a dividend.
3. By allowing the increased value of fixed assets, realized or potential, to remain in the business.

Because of the limitations on liability effected through the corporate structure there are, in the UK, limitations upon the ability of the owners to withdraw capital from a business. This is effected by the legal provision that repayments of capital to shareholders are prohibited, and that dividends can only be paid out of realized profits.

The owners' functions

Shareholders are in law members of the company. That is to say they occupy the same relationship to the corporate body as the owner to the sole proprietorship. Let us now examine the function of the owners and the role they play.

Control of the affairs of the business. The owner, whether partner or sole proprietor, exercises the power of control over the affairs of the enterprise. This includes the power of direction and the ownership of assets. While these rights are still ultimately exercised by shareholders, in the corporate structure they may be modified by:

1. Adjustment of ownership rights between different classes of owner.
2. Rights over assets and claims on income which the owners have specifically assigned to other people, e.g., in return for a loan.
3. The delegation of authority to individuals or groups of individuals. In the corporate structure, this is necessary since it would not be practicable for the general body of shareholders to exercise managerial functions.

The owner as the risk bearer. The owners' claims on a business are subordinated to the claims of all other people. They are, therefore, the principal risk bearers of the business. They are the first to suffer loss and the extent of the owners' funds at risk is a measure of the cushion against loss for creditors. The owners' funds at risk extend to the whole of their private fortunes in the case of proprietors and partners, and in the corporate structure the amount of the capital the shareholders have agreed to subscribe for, together with other owners' funds accumulated in the company.

Regulation of the receipt of income by the owners

The sole proprietor and the partner may withdraw funds from the business up to the extent of the original capital subscribed and accumulated profits. There is no need for special protection for creditors in either case since the private fortunes of the owners are at risk. Drawing more than the above amount from the business would leave it insolvent, and lead to trouble in the subsequent bankruptcy hearing.

In the limited liability company, funds paid to the owners are lost to the creditors. There is, therefore, a basic point in law which prohibits the repayment of capital to the owners without the sanction of the High Court. [Section 66 *et seq.* Companies Act 1948.]

Payment of dividends in excess of profits earned would effectively be a distribution of capital to shareholders. In such a case, the directors would be held personally liable to reimburse the company with the amounts so paid out. [Re. Exchange Banking Co: Flitcroft's Case (1882), 21 Ch D. 519.]

The basic preconditions for the payment of a dividend to shareholders are:

1. There should be available profits from which the dividend can be paid.
2. The directors recommend that a dividend be paid and specify the rate of payment.
3. There are no other prohibitions on the payment of dividends.

The last requirement usually stems from legislation introduced to combat inflation. In the UK and other countries dividend control has often been included in a package designed to control all forms of income and prices. The Companies Act 1980 defines distributable profits more closely, basically requiring losses to be recouped before dividends can be paid.

Availability of profit

Profits earned in previous years but not paid out to shareholders are available for the payment of dividends in any subsequent year. Such profits include not only balances carried forward in the profit and loss account, but also appropriations from that account to general reserves, dividend equalization reserves, plant replacement reserves, etc. As long as the origin of the funds was revenue profits, they are available, except where they have been used for the purpose of subscribing for new shares in a scrip issue, or to redeem redeemable preference shares.

Where the company is carrying forward a substantial loss from earlier years and has now reached the profit-earning stage, the board must decide its dividend policy. If the past losses are large, it may be years before they are recouped from profits. On the other hand, there may be substantial capital reserves already created, or which could be created by revaluing assets, against which the revenue loss could be offset.

If the board wishes to recommence payment of dividends it has two alternatives:

1. To set off the past losses against the capital reserves leaving current profits free for distribution.

2. To write off the past losses against the issued capital thus effectively writing down the nominal value of the share capital shown in the balance sheet. This would require the sanction of the court. [Section 66, Companies Act 1948.]

Realized capital profits held in capital reserves can be paid out as dividends provided the articles so allow.

Procedure for approving dividends

The authorization of the dividend rests with the shareholders. This authority is modified in two ways. Firstly, provision may be made for the directors to recommend and pay interim dividends without further authority. Secondly, the director's recommendation for the total dividend submitted to the shareholders at the Annual General Meeting usually cannot be increased. This is due to provisions to this effect being included in the articles. [Section 114, First Schedule, Table A, Companies Act 1948.]

CLASSES OF SHARE CAPITAL

A company may divide its authorized share capital in any way that it thinks fit and attach to each class those claims and rights which it thinks proper. There is no common definition of classes of shares. Each issue must be interpreted through that company's own articles of association. The following must, therefore, be read with this proviso in mind.

Non-cumulative preference shares

The shareholder has the right to be paid up to a fixed rate of dividend before any dividend is paid to subordinate classes of share. On liquidation, he gets back his capital (or a defined amount per share) before any repayment can be made to subordinated shareholders. Where there are a number of classes of preference share, the articles set out the rights and priorities between each.

Because of their preferential rights to dividend and capital, the holders of preference shares usually do not have the right to vote except in special circumstances, e.g., when the dividend is in arrear, or in respect of specific resolutions.

The normal ownership rights are, therefore, considerably modified as to control and interest in profits. They have become more akin to loans, which is what some people consider them to be. This is a mistake since they bear ownership risks and the same requirements for the payment of their dividend as other shareholders.

Cumulative preference shares

This class of share has, in general, the same characteristics as the non-cumulative preference share. The only difference is that, whereas a non-cumulative dividend is lost if not paid at the due time, with the cumulative preference dividend the amount accumulates until the company can pay the arrears.

Redeemable preference shares

These are shares redeemable by the company provided that the redemption is made out of profits otherwise available as dividends. An amount equal to the redemption cost must be set aside in a 'capital redemption reserve fund' which has the same effective status as paid-up capital. [Section 58, Companies Act 1948.]

Ordinary shares

Ordinary shares commonly carry the full characteristics of owners' funds. Within the class lies the voting control of the business; the residual profits after all other claims belong to them, and they are the first to suffer losses.

Voting and non-voting ordinary. The class as a whole can be divided into ordinary shares carrying votes and those without votes. This device concentrates the control of the business into the hands of a small group of people, the shares all having the same rights other than votes. Sometimes different slices of ordinary shares carry different voting rights. This is frequently the case where two or more companies jointly own a subsidiary company, their rights as between each other being adjusted in this way.

The non-voting share is looked upon with disfavour in most financial circles as it disenfranchises the majority of owners and new issues by listed companies are prohibited by the Stock Exchange. While making the company bid-proof, it also makes the board less accountable for their actions as remaining shareholders cannot remove them. There is frequently a price differential between the voting and non-voting ordinary shares arising from their respective capacity to exercise ownership rights, the right to vote commanding a premium. Examples of such differentials at 28 August 1979 are:

Great Universal Stores	Voting	410p
	'A'	406p
Decca	Voting	310p
	'A'	295p
Acrow	Voting	114p
	'A'	55p

Split-level capital. This is a form of regulating ownership rights developed by investment trusts. Recognizing that investors have different objectives, mainly because of taxation, the promoters of such companies have segregated aspects of income and capital growth and assigned the whole of each to a single class of share. Thus, all the income goes to the holders of 'income' ordinary shares, and all the capital gain goes to the holders of 'capital' shares.

This device tends to maximize the market value of the company as a whole. If one group of shareholders (possibly tax-exempt shareholders, e.g., pension funds) receives all the income, and another group which is subject to high tax rates receives all the capital growth with its relatively (to them) low tax rate, the value of the company is likely to be higher than when the gains are not separated.

Participating preference shares

This is a hybrid class incorporating aspects of both preference share and ordinary share. The normal form is that the share has a preferential dividend in the usual way but, upon a specified event, it participates in profits to the extent provided for. This might occur when a given level of profit is reached, or perhaps when the ordinary dividend has reached, say, 50p per share; then for every extra 2p per share dividend paid on the ordinary shares, an extra 1 per cent is paid to the participating preference shareholders.

Founders' or deferred shares

Use can be made of this class of share when the company's shares are being brought to the market for the first time. The value that the vendors put on the potential of the business may not be matched by the value the market would put on it, until it has proved itself.

The value on sale of a part of the owner's holding may be improved by splitting the share capital into ordinary shares and founder's shares. The latter receive no dividend until a certain level of profit or dividend payment on the ordinary shares is reached, when they can be converted into ordinary shares. This is also a useful device where the majority shareholder, for tax reasons, does not wish to receive income.

METHODS OF RAISING SHAREHOLDERS' FUNDS

In the private company structure, the shareholders regulate the provisions under which new funds are raised from their own number with very little formality other than the registration and stamp duty requirements. New issues offered to the public must be accompanied by a prospectus, the legal provisions governing the issue of which are set out in the Companies Act 1948, sections 37 to 46.

Obtaining a Stock Exchange quotation

To have its shares listed, the board must satisfy fairly stringent requirements laid down by Council of the Stock Exchange. These formalities are handled by an issuing house. Briefly, the company must be of a sufficient size, both in terms of profit and the number of shares on offer; there should be a record of profit over preferably 10 years; accounts over that period will be vetted by the reporting accountant for the issue. The issuing house itself must be satisfied that the company is satisfactory in every way since its own reputation suffers when one flops shortly after issue.

To escape the close company provisions of the Finance Act 1965, it is necessary for at least 35 per cent of the shares to be in the hands of the public and quoted and dealt in on a Stock Exchange in the UK. Currently the Stock Exchange requires 25 per cent of the shares to be offered to the public.

There are various ways in which the shares of a company can be brought to the market:

A placing.   Through its brokers, some shares are made available to the market, while a number are placed with firm investors. The number made available to the market must be sufficient to provide a basis for dealings.

An introduction.   The shares are already widely held and all that is required is the quotation. The brokers make shares available if required to support dealings to provide a market.

An offer of sale.   The prospectus published contains an invitation to the public to purchase the shares on offer at a named price. This method requires the issuing house to fix the price at which the shares will be sold. They try to arrange matters so that the price fixed is just below the level at which the market price will settle after early dealings. The problem is to fix the price low enough to attract enough applications from the public, and high enough to get the best price for their client.

This method has frequently resulted in massive oversubscription of issues, sometimes to the extent of 100 times or more. The paperwork generated and deciding on a basis of allotment to applicants are difficulties for the issuing houses.

The sale by tender.   This is similar to the offer of sale. Instead, however, of the issuing house fixing the selling price, it merely fixes the lowest price at which it will sell and invites the investor to nominate the price at which he will subscribe for the shares.

The issuing house then examines the tenders at the close of the offer and, working from the highest tender price downwards, determines the highest price above which there are sufficient applications to absorb the number of shares offered. This is called the 'striking' price and all the shares allotted are issued at this price. Sometimes the striking price is lower than that specified above. This is particularly so where an issue at that price would result in the shares being held by a very small number of people, seriously restricting dealings.

The method has not been altogether successful. Investors have become aware that by putting a very high bid in their tender they can ensure that they receive an allotment. When sufficient people do this the issuing house is again faced with a problem. If the striking price is fixed in the usual way, there is a danger that the price will not be sustained in early market dealings and the company have an unhappy start as a quoted company.

Rights issue. Where a quoted company wishes to raise additional funds from its shareholders, normal practice is to do so via a rights issue. This process avoids disturbing the relative voting rights of individual shareholders as the new shares are offered to the existing shareholders in proportion to the number of shares already held.

The new shares may be offered at any price between nominal value and market price. For obvious reasons they cannot be sold at a price higher than the current market price, and the issue of shares at a discount on the nominal value can only be carried out with the sanction of the court.

Practical reasons dictate that the price fixed should be a reasonable margin below the existing price. Unless this is the case, there is little inducement for the shareholders to take up the new shares. Moreover, the market price may move downwards during the period over which the issue is made making it even more unattractive. The precise sale price depends on an assessment of the effects of the issue on the earnings per share value. The higher the price at which the shares are sold, the fewer need to be issued, and consequently the earnings are not so diluted.

Share quotations during rights issue. During the period of the issue, shares are quoted as follows:

> 'Cum-rights' price: The purchaser buys the old shares plus the
> right to buy the new shares.
> 'Ex-rights' price: The purchaser buys only the old shares.

When the shares have gone 'ex-rights', there is a market for the rights until a date some weeks after the last date for subscribing for the new shares.

The market price for the shares ex-rights can be calculated by the following formula:

$$\left[\text{Subscription price of new shares} + \left(\text{Cum-rights price} - \text{Subscription price}\right) \times \frac{\text{Total number of shares before issue}}{\text{Total number of shares after issue}}\right] = \text{Market price 'ex-rights'}$$

Example: The market price of the ordinary shares of Terlawns Ltd is £2.50. The board make a rights issue of one for one at £1.50 per share. The ex-rights price will be:

$$£1.50 + [(£2.50 - £1.50) \times \tfrac{1}{2}] = £2.00 \text{ 'ex-rights' price}$$

If the shareholder does nothing about the rights issue, the value of the shares he holds declines from £2.50 per share to £2.00. If, however, he does not wish to subscribe for the new share he can sell the rights on the market for 50p to recoup this decline.

A new investor to the company can acquire shares in two ways during the period of the rights issue. He can purchase through the market old shares ex-rights for £2.00, or he can purchase rights for 50p each in the market and pay the subscription price of £1.50.

The value of the rights can be calculated in the following way:

$$\frac{\text{Market price} - \text{Subscription price}}{\text{Number of shares needed to give right to 1 new share}} = \frac{\text{Value of rights}}{\text{(per 1 old share)}}$$

Taking the values for Terlawns Ltd the rights value would be:

$$£2.00 - £1.50/1 = 50p \text{ per old share}$$

Scrip or bonus issue

The scrip issue is not concerned with raising additional shareholders' funds but with rearranging the way in which the shareholders' funds are shown on the balance sheet and the number of units into which they are divided. Where substantial revenue and capital profits have been retained and permanently employed, they can be incorporated into the issued capital by this means. When so capitalized, such profits are no longer available for distribution to the shareholders except under the same conditions as the original capital.

The process presents a solution to other problems. Although earnings accrue by virtue of all the shareholders' funds employed, they are often expressed as a percentage of the nominal capital only, with consequent misunderstandings of the company's real level of profitability. Also, the resulting high percentage of earnings and dividend results in a 'heavy' share price. Many investors avoid investing in shares that have a market price above £2–£3. A scrip issue brings prices down to more marketable levels. *Example:* The following is a summary of the balance sheet of Scrippo Ltd as at 31 December 19x2:

Authorized capital	
1 500 000 £1 Ordinary shares	£1 500 000
Issued capital	
500 000 £1 Ordinary shares	500 000
Capital reserve	950 000
Retained profits	440 000
Total shareholders' funds	£1 890 000
Represented by:	
Net assets	£1 890 000

To bring the issued capital more into line with the real value of the shareholders' funds employed, the board proposes a scrip issue of 2 for 1. The funds needed to subscribe for the new shares, to be distributed free of any further cost to the shareholders, will be taken from the capital reserve, the balance being capitalized from retained profits.

After the issue, the balance sheet would appear as follows:

Authorized and issued capital	£
1 500 000 £1 Ordinary shares	1 500 000
Retained profits	390 000
Total shareholders' funds	£1 890 000
Represented by:	
Net assets	£1 890 000

Note that the issue has not changed the value of shareholders' funds employed nor the value of net assets. It simply divides existing shareholders' funds into three times the number of units.

There is considerable confusion regarding the precise function of the scrip issue, fostered no doubt by flamboyant headlines of 'free handouts' to shareholders. What is given to the shareholder is already his by right; only the form is being changed.

The ex-scrip issue price of the share can be calculated in the following way:

$$\text{Pre-issue price} \times \frac{\text{Old number of shares}}{\text{New number of shares}} = \text{Post-issue price}$$

For example, if the price of Scrippo's share was 45p before the scrip issue, the new price is:

$$45p \times \frac{500\,000}{1\,500\,000} = 15p$$

There is one sense, however, in which the scrip issue can be used for another purpose. With the penal rates of taxation in many countries, particularly the UK, where the top slice of income has been taxed at 90 per cent or more, income is much less valuable than capital gains since the latter are generally taxed at lower rates. How then can income be converted to capital gain?

One way is for the company to pay no dividends and out of the enhanced value of retained profits make a small scrip issue. The shareholder receives no income. If he desires a monetary return from the investment, he sells the scrip issues and is only taxed on the capital gain element, which in the UK is at 30 per cent. In the UK, if a shareholder is given the *choice* of taking a cash dividend or a scrip dividend and he opts for the latter, he will be taxed as though he had received a cash dividend.

Share split

Where the share price is 'heavy', but the company is not sufficiently well endowed with capital and revenue reserves for a scrip issue, it can achieve an improved market rating by splitting its shares. For example, a company with 1 million £1 shares at issue could divide the capital into 4 million 25p shares.

As the shareholders' funds are now divided into four times the number of units, the share price is a quarter of the pre-split price, other things being equal.

BORROWED FUNDS

The annual value of funds raised by quoted companies over the period 1969–77 is shown in Table 12.1. In the late 'fifties only some 10 per cent of total funds was in the form of debt. The *percentage* of *total* capital employed financed by debt shown in Table 12.3 shows that this percentage peaked in 1971 and has since declined. The market value of long-term debt quoted on the London Stock Exchange is shown in Table 12.2.

Table 12.3

*Percentage of capital employed financed by debt
for over 1000 major UK companies*

Year	Capital employed	Long-term debt	Long-term debt to capital employed (%)
	£ millions	£ millions	
1969	21 349	4 443	20.8
1970	22 454	4 767	21.2
1971	22 428	5 250	23.4
1972	27 769	5 912	21.3
1973	32 081	6 672	20.8
1974	35 918	6 892	19.2
1975	40 707	7 339	18.0
1976	46 917	8 007	17.1
1977	52 131	8 551	16.4

Source: *Annual Abstract of Statistics,* HMSO

Characteristics

Unlike the shareholder, the person who merely lends money to a business is not a member of the company. At no time does the lender of money take on any of the characteristics of ownership. He remains purely and simply a *creditor.* In return for the use of the funds he provided, the company (or partner or proprietor) cedes three rights to him:

1. The right to receive a fixed rate of interest on the sum loaned at the specified dates.
2. A prior claim on certain defined assets of the business (this is sometimes dispensed with where the borrower has a first-class credit rating).
3. The right to be repaid the sum owing on the due date.

These rights are contained in the formal contract recording the loan, and are enforceable at law by the lender. The enforcement may take the form of appointing a receiver under the terms of the loan, the receiver taking over from the company those assets which are the subject of the charge, or proceedings may be taken through the courts in the normal way to enforce the debt.

The distinction between owners' funds and borrowed funds is thus quite clear. Owners can get no return from the business unless there are available realized profits. Lenders' returns, on the other hand, are not subject to the state of the profit and loss account. They look to the contractual terms only in their relationship with the business.

FORMS OF BORROWING

Mortgages

The owners of the business can raise funds by mortgaging the land and buildings it owns in the same way that a private individual mortgages his home. The mortgage deed records the rate and dates on which interest is payable, and how the principal will be repaid.

Mortgage debenture

In the large business the debenture form of mortgage is used in order to draw upon a number of lenders. The amount borrowed can be split up into any number of units, each ranking *pari passu* in the same way as share capital.

Where there are to be many debenture holders, a trustee is appointed to exercise the debenture holders' rights on their behalf against the company.

Debenture with a floating charge

Both the mortgage and the mortgage debenture suffer from a major disadvantage from the management point of view. The assets charged cannot be sold or otherwise disposed of without the consent of the debenture holders. While this may not be a burden where only land and buildings are concerned, it does present problems where management wishes to use other assets, such as plant and machinery or current assets, as security for the debenture. Such assets are constantly changing and it would be clearly impracticable to obtain the debenture holders' consent each time.

To overcome this, a form of *floating charge* can be used. Instead of charging specific assets, the debenture defines *classes* of assets to be charged. It then provides for the company to be able to deal with those assets in the normal course of business without any further formality. This position continues as long as the terms of the loan are adhered to by the borrower.

Should the borrower default, the charge on the assets 'crystallizes'. Then, the floating charge becomes a straightforward charge upon the assets in the classes covered which the borrower owns at that time. The rights of ownership are then effectively transferred to the lenders until such time as they have recouped the sums owing to them. Any surplus assets are then returned to the owners.

Loans secured and unsecured

Companies with first-class credit ratings may borrow money on a secured or even unsecured basis without the intermediary of debenture trustees, etc.

REPAYMENT PROVISIONS

Unlike share capital, loans are made for a specified period of time at the end of which the sum must be repaid. There are a number of repayment methods that can be incorporated in the loan terms.

'Balloon' payment.   By this method, the whole of the amount borrowed is repaid in a lump sum at the end of the loan period.

Annual repurchase.   A specified sum is set aside each year from earnings and is applied to the purchase of the debentures in the market. The debentures thus bought are usually cancelled.

Annual drawings.   Again out of earnings set aside for the purpose, some debentures are redeemed each year at par (or other specified value). The debentures to be repaid in this way are drawn by ballot.

Sinking fund.   A sum is set aside from earnings each year which together with the accrued interest will provide the sum needed at the end of the loan. The sinking fund is usually invested outside the business to ensure that *cash* is available for the purpose when required.

Insurance policy.   A policy is taken out with an insurance company which matures on the date of the repayment of the loan. This method is very useful where the business is dependent upon the services of its director(s) and would collapse or be seriously affected should they die. Provisions can be built into the policy for the sum secured to be paid on the happening of a specified event, e.g., the death of the managing director.

SOURCES OF BORROWED FUNDS

Insurance companies

Insurance companies form a major source of borrowed funds. The 20–25-year life cycle of the industrial debenture fits in well with the funds flow pattern of such institutions. They have fixed commitments themselves, due to the maturing of policies, which can be met from the funds provided by loan repayments.

Amounts that the insurance companies have lent in the form of debentures and loans are shown in Table 12.4.

Table 12.4

*Extract of insurance company and pension fund
investments 1974–78*

Year	Insurance companies: Debentures	Mortgages and loans	Pension funds: Debentures	Mortgages and loans
		£ millions		
1974	2720*	3162	517	33
1975	2783*	3198	578	32
1976	2695*	3157	592	42
1976	1957			
1977	2447	3212	658	28
1978	2287	3231	585	72

* Book values. In subsequent years market value.

Shareholders and other investors

Debentures and loans (particularly the latter) are often offered on a rights basis to the shareholders of the company. They may be offered directly to the public in the same way as shares.

Industrial and Commercial Finance Corporation (ICFC)

This body is sponsored by the clearing banks for the purpose of providing medium- and long-term funds for companies, etc. which are too small to go to the market in the usual way. Sums as low as £50 000 are loaned and may go up to several hundred thousand pounds. Most of the funds provided are in loans, but a small part of the equity is often taken as well.

Frequently, the corporation nurses the small company right through to the stage where it goes public, the corporation acting as the issuing house.

Before lending money the firm is vetted by investigating accountants who report, not only on the financial standing of the business, but on management ability, the information systems that exist, etc., and in appropriate cases help is given in correcting deficiencies in management techniques.

Finance Corporation for Industry Ltd

This organization, sponsored by the banks and other institutions, is designed to supplement, but not replace, normal sources of borrowed funds. The amount must not exceed £25 million and it must be shown that it cannot be borrowed from other sources.

Estate Duty Investment Trust (EDITH)

Shareholders in family-held companies face serious problems should a major shareholder die. His holding may have to be sold to meet capital transfer tax payments, with consequential effects upon the control and management of the business. To alleviate these problems, EDITH was set up with the purpose of providing funds by acquisition of shares while at the same time allowing the family management to remain.

Technical Development Capital (TDC)

The objective of this organization is to assist inventors and promoters of specialized developments who would have difficulty in finding finance from more conventional sources. Funds are loaned and shares taken up to bring the project to a commercial footing. It is a subsidiary of ICFC.

Others

Potential borrowers may also approach pension funds, clearing banks, merchant banks, and other specialist organizations.

Ship Mortgage Finance Co. Ltd
Agricultural Mortgage Corporation Ltd
Lands Improvement Company
Commonwealth Development Finance Co. Ltd

The above institutions specialize in the provision of loans for the purposes indicated in their title. Additionally, merchant bankers and other finance companies often have subsidiaries designed to meet specialized needs. [For further reading see *Money for Business*, Bank of England and City Communications Centre.]

Private loans

Loans may often be obtained from individuals, either directly or through solicitors or accountants who are placing clients' funds.

Building societies

Building societies may be prepared to lend on mortgage in the usual way.

METHODS OF RAISING LOANS

Offer of sale

The offer of sale operates in very much the same way as the offer of sale of shares. The issue is advertised with a prospectus and the public invited to subscribe. Unlike the share issue, it is quite normal for debentures and loans to be issued at less than par. For example, each £100 debenture might be sold for £98.50.

The offer at less than par achieves two purposes. Firstly, it provides a small guaranteed capital gain over the life of the loan. Secondly, the interest rate on the loan is not quoted at a smaller fraction than $1/4$ of 1 per cent. To provide for intermediate rates the price of the issue itself is adjusted, i.e., a 20-year 7 per cent loan issued at 99 provides a rate of $7 \times 100/99$ plus the capital gain. Assuming the investor looks to the before-tax yield only, this would be 7 per cent $\times 100/99 + 1/20 = 7.12$ per cent.

Placing

The debenture or loan is placed with a single institution or a small group of institutions without a formal offer of sale (although if they are to have a quotation on the Stock Exchange a prospectus is needed).

Private loan

The company and its advisers negotiate directly with the lender and mutually acceptable terms are agreed.

CONVERTIBLE LOANS

The convertible loan is a hybrid between owners' funds and borrowed funds. Although the funds are raised as straightforward borrowing, the loan provisions give the lender the right to convert his loan into ordinary shares at specified dates and at specified rates during its currency. Any part of the loan not converted after the latest conversion date continues as an ordinary loan.

Because of their partly 'owners'' characteristics, such issues are more frequently offered on a rights basis to existing shareholders, or used as the consideration on the acquisition of a company.

Example: Converto Ltd raises £1 million by means of a 20-year 7 per cent Convertible Loan 19x4/x8. The terms of the loan enable the lenders to convert on the following terms:

On 30 June 19y1, at the rate of 60 25p ordinary shares per £100 nominal of loan stock

On 30 June 19y3 at the rate of 56 ordinary per £100

On 30 June 19y5 at the rate of 52 ordinary per £100.

If conversion is not made by 30 June 19y5, the loan stock then continues as a straightforward loan with no conversion rights.

Uses of convertible loans

There are two principal reasons for the use of convertible loans. The first is where the issue of new shares would unduly dilute the earnings on the existing equity and this would create difficulties in raising funds by a rights issue. Since the convertible loan gives the lenders the right to interest in priority to dividends, the return is much more secure, and so it may be more practicable to raise new funds in this way. On top of the secured income, the lenders have the conversion rights which, if the company puts the funds to use profitably, will have some value.

The other factor is our old enemy taxation. Loan interest is deductible before tax and, therefore, attracts tax relief. Dividends cost the net amount out of after-tax profits. If new money is to be raised from shareholders, why raise it in the form of shares straight away? Why not a convertible loan so that a part of the return to the owners attracts tax relief, at least for some years? If the loan is a 'subordinated loan', i.e., it ranks *after* ordinary creditors, it is more likely to remain in the hands of the shareholders, thus not interfering with the credit rating of the business. Indeed, it is hardly distinguishable from equity, except that the fixed income it provides is relievable against corporation tax in the paying company.

The appropriate conversion price

In the previous example of Converto Ltd, the relative conversion prices at each of the conversion dates would be:

30 June 19y1 = £100/60 = £1.67 per share   Based upon a market
30 June 19y3 = £100/56 = £1.79 per share   price of £100 for the
30 June 19y5 = £100/52 = £1.92 per share   loan stock

Note that the effective cost of conversion rises with the passage of time. There is, therefore, an incentive to convert early. In view of the tax position previously mentioned, it is better if the holders convert at the latest date since more tax relief is obtained.

Market valuation of convertible loans

As long as the market value of the company's shares is less than the appropriate conversion price, the convertible loan tends to be valued on the basis of a straightforward loan, plus a small addition for conversion rights. This is largely determined by the current interest rates.

When the market price of the share exceeds the relevant conversion price, the loan is valued as though converted into shares at the next conversion date. It now follows that investors have two routes into the company: through the acquisition of shares in the normal way, and by acquiring convertible loan stock for conversion.

13

The capital structure

SOURCES OF FINANCE FOR BRITISH COMPANIES

The proportion of new capital raised from different sources by UK companies is shown in Fig. 13.1. This highlights the dramatic change in the proportion of new funds raised by borrowing over the period. The effect that this change in financing policy has had on the proportions of *total* capital employed originating from each source was shown in Table 12.3. The percentage of capital employed financed by debt remained fairly static at over 20 per cent until 1973, falling to 16.4 per cent by 1977.

Figure 13.1

Sources of new capital for UK companies 1967–77

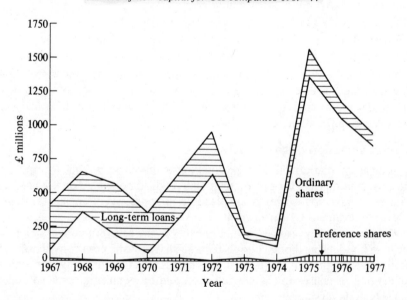

Source: *Midland Bank Review*

MAXIMIZING RETURN ON EQUITY

The policy of management as to the sources of funds used has an effect on the return on ordinary shareholders' funds. This was seen in Chapter 2 when the ratios for X Ltd were examined. There, the return on capital employed of 7.1 per cent after tax was lifted to a 9.47 per cent return on equity. For the years 1969–77, the average return on capital employed for UK companies was 9.8 per cent and the return on equity over the same period was 11.8 per cent (see Tables 2.1 and 2.2).

The gearing up in the capital structure is, therefore, important in the financial policy given the right conditions. Whether or not gearing is beneficial for the equity holders will depend upon:

1. *The effect on return on equity.*   This depends on the relationship between the cost of fixed interest/dividend funds and the ROCE.
2. *How it influences the risk of failure.*
3. *How it affects control of the enterprise.*
4. *What the market assessment of these factors is as expressed in the P/E ratio.*

Modigliani and Miller[1] consider the total value of a company independent of gearing, the increasing return on equity being cancelled out by the market's increasing risk rating for the shares. On this basis, when V is the market value of the business, D the market value of the debt, and S the market value of the share capital, then:

$$V = S + D$$

Then follows the proposition that, taking the company as a whole, the expected return on ordinary shares where there is gearing can be expressed by:

$$i = p^k + (p^k - r) \, D/S$$

where i = yield on ordinary shares, p^k = the capitalization rate for earnings, and r = the interest cost of debt.

Assume that a company has earnings of £5000 per year, the debt being £25 000 on which 6 per cent is paid, and the rate of earnings is 10 per cent. From this the valuation of the equity is £25 000, e.g.:

$$V = S + D \text{ and } V = £50\,000$$

(This follows from the capitalization rate $5000 \times 100/10$.)

$$\text{Therefore, } S = £50\,000 - £25\,000 = £25\,000$$

---

[1] 'The Cost of Capital, Corporation Finance and the Theory of Investment', *The American Economic Review*, June 1968, p. 261

The expected return would be:

$$i = p^k + (p^k - r) D/S$$
$$= 0.10 + (0.10 - 0.06) \, 25/25$$
$$= 0.10 + 0.04 \times 25/25$$
$$= 0.10 + 0.04$$
$$= 14 \text{ per cent}$$

The assumption that the increased return from gearing is exactly compensated by increased risk does not seem valid. Many companies would experience a negligible increase in risk within certain ranges of gearing; the effects of inflation in continually eroding the real cost of debt service and repayment is not adequately recognized. It is quite true that there is a point for each company at which an increase in gearing is exactly offset by increased risk, as the level of gearing is pushed up. This level varies with different companies. Within that level, the beneficial effects of gearing are likely to more than compensate for the slight increase in risk. This appears to be substantiated by the data for a random group of companies shown in Table 13.1.

Table 13.1

Effect of gearing upon P/E for a random selection of 121 companies

Percentage gearing[1]	Number of companies	Average P/E	Average times dividend covered
0	37	12.0	1.6
1– 5	23	14.9	2.1
6–10	20	14.4	1.8
11–15	13	14.3	1.6
16–20	9	12.3	1.6
21–25	7	15.0	1.3
26–30	6	11.7	1.4
31–35	5	14.4	1.3
36–40	0	—	—
over 40	1	50.3	0.4

[1] Percentage of fixed interest and fixed dividend cost to available earnings.

It is suggested that, in practice, setting an optimum financing structure by mathematical formulae is not yet practicable. Management's tasks are to establish broadly: the effect of gearing upon shareholders' return; the practical limitations to risk bearing by the company; and the personal attitudes to risk of management and shareholders; then, within this framework, to devise a policy likely to produce the best long-term gains to the owners.

ROLE OF MANAGEMENT IN RAISING FUNDS

The management which turns its back upon borrowing is doing a great disservice, not only to the equity holders by denying them the potential benefits of gearing, but also to the growth potential of the business. By limiting the market valuation of the equity, such a policy would make the cost of funds to the business higher than they need be and more difficult to obtain.

This limiting factor is very real. The rating of ordinary shares in the market is expressed largely (though not exclusively) by the price/earnings ratio. If gearing lifts the earnings per share (which it should do in the right conditions), it lifts the share price. A rising trend in share price, in normal conditions, makes the raising of new shareholders' funds easier and less costly.

GEARING

When a company makes use of fixed interest borrowing and fixed dividend shareholders' funds, it creates a situation where, of the total return earned on the capital employed, a fixed amount only is required to service the debt or provide the cost of the fixed dividend. After these commitments are met, the whole of the balance of the earnings accrues to the benefit of the ordinary shareholders. The theoretical basis for gearing is that, if the business earns more on the capital employed than it has to pay for the use of funds, the difference helps to increase the return on equity. If, for example, a company is earning 10 per cent on the capital employed, but is borrowing a part of that capital at 6 per cent interest then, ignoring tax, the 4 per cent difference between the rates accrues to the ordinary shareholders.

Let us see how this works out in practice. If we were concerned with setting up a business which required a total capital of £1 million, one could look at a number of different methods of raising the amount required. Taking two alternatives only: one, which we can designate the 'all equity' alternative, consists solely of ordinary shareholders' funds; the other, designated 'mixed capital', provides for 40 per cent of the required funds to be raised by a 6 per cent debenture and the balance by equity. If we now further assume that the profit expected from the enterprise is £150 000 p.a. then, ignoring tax, the relative return on capital employed and the return earned on equity funds for each alternative is shown in Fig. 13.2.

Figure 13.2

Effect of gearing on return on equity **40/60**

	All equity	Mixed capital
	£	£
Ordinary shares of £1 each	1 000 000	600 000
6% debenture	—	400 000
Capital employed	£1 000 000	£1 000 000
Expected annual profit	150 000	150 000
Debenture interest	—	24 000
Profit available to ordinary shareholders	£150 000	£126 000
Return on capital employed	15%	15%
Return on equity	15%	21%
Earnings per share	15p	21p

As can be seen from this comparison, the introduction of the 6 per cent debenture into the financing situation would increase the return on equity from 15 to 21 per cent and the EPS from 15p to 21p per share.

DIVISION OF EARNINGS BETWEEN DIFFERENT SOURCES OF CAPITAL

The way the earnings of the business are divided up when gearing is applied is shown in Fig. 13.3. This sets out in graphical form the same data used in Fig. 13.2. The horizontal axis represents the capital employed and shows how it is divided between the different sources in the mixed capital financing. On the vertical axis is shown the return in terms of return on capital employed and return on the various sources of funds. The rectangle *abcd* represents the earnings on the whole of the capital employed, i.e., 15 per cent on £1 million, or £150 000. In the mixed form of capital, the debentures have provided the first £400 000 of the capital and have the first claim against the profits for the 6 per cent interest. They, therefore, absorb the first £24 000 of the profit, or the area *efgd*.

Figure 13.3

Allocation of earnings in a geared company

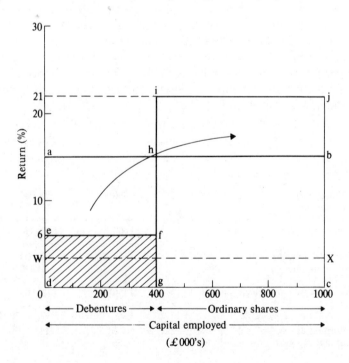

As there are no sources of funds other than equity, all the remaining profit belongs to the equity holders, i.e., the area *abcgfe*. The area of profit *ahfe*, representing the excess earned on the debenture funds over and above their cost, moves over to form *ijbh*, adding to the return earned on the equity funds.

The key to the success of gearing is the return on capital employed (*a*) being higher than the return on fixed cost funds (*e*). The wider the gap between the two, the greater is the effect of gearing on the return on equity. If the return on capital employed was only WX, the adverse effects can be left to the reader's imagination!

EFFECT OF GEARING ON THE VALUATION OF THE BUSINESS

Because of its effect upon the EPS, gearing also has a major influence upon market valuation. Again, examine the effects of the level of gearing used in Fig. 13.2. At the 'all equity' position, the earnings gave a return of 15 per cent. Assume that the market rating for a company of this type gives a P/E ratio of 6.67. The valuation of the business if the funds are all equity funds is, therefore, £1 000 000 (£150 000 × 6.67).

Taking the 'mixed capital' situation and assuming the market rating would continue on a P/E ratio of 6.67, the market valuation would be:

Ordinary share capital Available earnings £126 000 times		
P/E ratio of 6.67 =		£840 420
Debenture (assuming par value)		400 000
Total market value of the business		£1 240 420

The above figures were derived on the basis that under either of the forms of financing the market assessments of required earning yield and P/E ratio would be the same. This assumption might not remain true. These ratings for a company tend to be pulled in opposite directions by two contrary factors. The addition of gearing has made the earnings on the equity less certain than they would be under the all equity financing, since there would be a prior fixed charge upon total earnings. This increased risk may tend to be reflected in a lower P/E ratio. On the other hand, investors see a management formulating a dynamic financing policy which, if successful (i.e., earnings reach or exceed the forecast), will provide a rapidly increasing share value.

LIMITATIONS OF RISK

If gearing can have such beneficial effects upon the return to the equity holders and on the valuation of their shares, why not pursue it to its ultimate, where almost all of the capital required is borrowed? In other words, the type of financing pattern shown on Fig. 13.4.

Superficially, such a capital structure appears very attractive to ordinary shareholders. But consider the realities of the situation. Lenders of money will not normally allow themselves to be put into such a position where they are assuming the risks of the equity holders but getting none of the rewards. In the 'mixed capital' situation, the debenture holders would know that the first £600 000 of losses would be absorbed by the equity holders before they themselves would be affected. The value of the shareholders' funds in effect form a 'cushion' to shield the debenture from loss. Furthermore, the interest on the loan is covered 6.2 times whereas in Fig. 13.4 it is covered only 2.5 times. The capital loaned by the debenture holders is covered nearly 1.7 times in the former case, but only slightly over once in the latter. Lenders themselves, therefore, tend to prevent a company overcommitting itself to borrowing since they try to keep within certain standards of income and asset cover for the funds they lend.

Figure 13.4

Extreme gearing in a company

	£
100 ordinary £1 shares	100
6% debentures	999 900
Capital employed	£1 000 000
Annual rate of profit	150 000
Debenture interest	59 994
Available to ordinary shareholders	£90 006
Return on equity	900%

From the shareholders' point of view, the level of gearing set out in Fig. 13.4 is much less attractive than it first appears. Should the annual profits prove to be only £50 000 instead of the £150 000 forecast, the business will be unable to service the interest cost of the debt, and also, if such a level of profits persisted, to provide the funds to repay the amount borrowed. The stake of the shareholder in the company is so small that only a relatively small setback in earnings may eliminate it altogether and so put the business into the hands of its creditors.

The overborrowing outlined above is not untypical of the business which is started on a shoestring by one or two individuals with no capital and partly explains their high failure rate. The years until profit retentions have considerably broadened the equity base are critical.

EPS over a range of earnings

In assessing the relative merits of different forms of finance, it is useful to examine the effect that they have on the EPS over a range of earnings. This method of presentation enables management to see at a glance what the relative EPS values are at any level of profit.

Let us take the same figures as were used in Fig. 13.2. Assume two different levels of earnings for the company and calculate for each what the EPS would be. At a profit level of £24 000 the EPS would be as follows:

	All equity		Mixed
	£		£
Profit	24 000	Profit	24 000
		Less: Interest	24 000
	———		———
Available for equity	24 000		Nil
Number of shares	1 000 000		600 000
EPS	2.4p		Nil

At a profit level of £150 000, the relative EPS would be:

	All equity		Mixed
	£		£
Profit	150 000	Profit	150 000
		Less: Interest	24 000
	———		———
Available for equity	150 000		126 000
Number of shares	1 000 000		600 000
EPS	15p		21p

Having arrived at the two points on the EPS/earnings scale for each of the alternatives, we can now plot these on a graph, as in Fig. 13.5. This shows on the horizontal axis the range of earnings to be covered and on the vertical axis the related earnings per share. Taking the all equity position first, when earnings are £24 000 the EPS would be 2.4p. This is shown at A. When profits are £150 000, the EPS would be 15p and is shown at B. If these two points are joined by a straight line (which should intersect the two axes), one can read off the EPS for any level of earnings shown on the graph.

The same process is repeated for the EPS values for the mixed capital which were 'nil' and 21p respectively. The resultant curve cuts the horizontal axis at the value which represents the earnings required to cover the cost of interest. The resulting graph is essentially a 'break-even chart' for the financing decision. Up to an earnings level of £60 000, the all equity form of capital gives a better EPS but at higher levels of earnings the beneficial effects of gearing become more important and the debenture alternative gives a higher earnings per share.

TAXATION

So far in the discussion of gearing, the problem of taxation has been avoided. In real life, however, taxation has a number of vital effects upon the business.

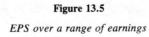

Figure 13.5

EPS over a range of earnings

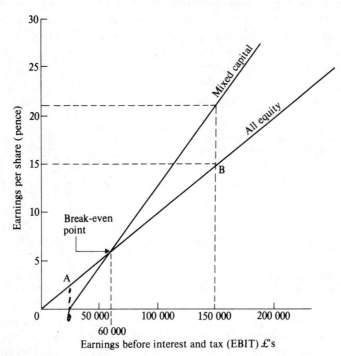

In particular, in the case of financing problems, one cannot avoid the fact that taxation considerably affects the relative cost of different sources of funds.

The way in which profits are taxed and the implications for the cost of funds are explored in Appendix A. In the UK at the present time (1980) the way in which the imputation system is applied to corporate earnings and dividends is shown in Fig. 13.6.

Figure 13.6

Tax burden on profit

	£
EBIT	1200
Interest on loans	100
Earnings before tax	1100
Corporation tax at 50%	550
Earnings after tax	550
Dividend (net)	300
Retained earnings	250

With a corporation tax rate of 50 per cent, the effective net cost of paying interest of 18 per cent is only 9 per cent. From the shareholders' point of view total net dividends of £300 are received and, if the basic income tax rate is 30 per cent, tax credits totalling £128.57. Thus, the dividend represents a gross dividend of £428.57 from which tax of £128.57 has been deducted.

The practical effect of the present tax system for the company is that, when paying interest, it saves an amount equal to the corporation tax rate on the amount paid, whereas the cost of paying a dividend means a cash outflow of an amount equal to the net cost of the dividend. How this difference in cost effects the EPS is shown in the following example.

Consider the case of a company which has an issued capital of £1 million all in ordinary shares of £1 and a current rate of earnings of £125 000 with a tax rate of 50 per cent. Assume that it needs to raise a further £1 million in order to develop its business and the proposals include an issue of 1 million £1,6 per cent preference shares and the issue of £1 million 6 per cent debentures.

The effect on the ordinary shareholders' interest is set out in Table 13.2, columns (c) and (d). It can be seen that, if the preference share alternative is adopted, the earnings remaining for the equity holders would amount to £2500, whereas if the debenture alternative is adopted the earnings available to the equity would be £32 500.

The effect of each of the above financing alternatives can also be shown on a graph similar to that in Fig. 13.5. With the EBIT level used in Table 13.2 of £125 000, the relative EPS values would be 0.25p where the preference alternative is used, i.e., £2500/1 000 000, and 3.25p for the debenture alternative. These two values provide A and B on the graph shown in Fig. 13.7. The EBIT required to cover the cost of the preference dividend and the debenture interest respectively is:

$$\begin{array}{cc}
\textit{Preference dividend} & \textit{Debenture interest} \\
£60\,000 \times 100/50 & £60\,000 \\
= £120\,000 & \underline{\hspace{2cm}} \\
\underline{\hspace{2cm}} &
\end{array}$$

These two values provide C and D on the graph which show where the respective curves must intersect the horizontal axis. Joining A and C, and B and D, we can now read off the EPS for any range of EBIT for each of the alternatives.

From the graph, it can be clearly seen that in terms of return to the ordinary shareholder the debenture alternative is preferable at all levels of earnings. The only problem involved is the possibility of the EBIT falling below the £60 000 cost of interest in the short term, and in the long term of its not being adequate to generate sufficient funds to provide for the repayment of the loan on its due date.

Now add a further choice to the problem, that is to raise the £1 million by a

Table 13.2

Calculation of EPS values for financing alternatives

(A) EPS values at an EBIT of £125 000

	(a) Present	(b) Rights issue	(c) 6% preference issue	(d) 6% debenture issue
EBIT	£125 000	£125 000	£125 000	£125 000
Interest	—	—	—	60 000
Profit before tax	125 000	125 000	125 000	65 000
Tax at 50%	62 500	62 500	62 500	32 500
	62 500	62 500	62 500	32 500
Preference dividend	—	—	60 000	—
Equity earnings	62 500	62 500	2 500	32 500
Number of shares issued	1 000 000	2 000 000	1 000 000	1 000 000
EPS	6.25p	3.125p	0.25p	3.25p

(B) EPS values at an EBIT of £250 000

	(a)	(b)	(c)	(d)
Equity earnings at A above	62 500	62 500	2 500	32 500
Plus additional after-tax earnings on a further £125 000 EBIT (125 000 less 50%)	62 500	62 500	62 500	62 500
Equity earnings	125 000	125 000	65 000	95 000
Number of shares	1 000 000	2 000 000	1 000 000	1 000 000
EPS	12.5p	6.25p	6.5p	9.5p
Required to cover loan repayment				50 000
Uncommitted earnings				45 000
Uncommitted EPS				4.5p

rights issue at par. The increase in the number of shares to 2 million will automatically halve the existing EPS at all levels of EBIT. The EPS values for all three alternatives are shown in Table 13.2 at two levels of EBIT to provide the basic figures for the graph in Fig. 13.7.

From the information presented so far on the financing problem, the following points can be made:

1. The break-even point as between the rights issue and the debenture issue is an EBIT of £120 000, and as between the rights issue and the preference issue almost £240 000.
2. To maintain the existing EPS of 7.5p (at £150 000 EBIT), profits would have to rise to £210 000 under the debenture alternative, to £270 000 under the preference alternative, and to £300 000 under the rights issue alternative.

Figure 13.7

Effect of alternative financing methods on EPS

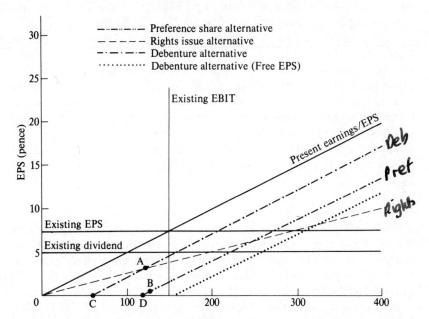

3. Earnings will not cover the cost of the preference dividend if they fall below
   £120 000, or the debenture interest if they fall below £60 000.

Let us now take into account two further facts in our analysis—the level of
dividend that the board wishes to maintain on the issued ordinary shares, and
the EBIT that is required to cover the retention of funds for the ultimate
repayment of the debenture.

The dividend level is of importance to both board and shareholders. A
reduction in the dividend paid has a significant effect upon the market price of
the shares. Moreover, once a reduction is made, the adverse effects on the
market price of the shares tends to persist for some years after the cuts have
been restored. The board should, therefore, select a method of financing
which does not seriously imperil the dividend rate.

The whole of the earnings after tax and prior charges is not free for the
payment of dividends under the debenture alternative, since funds must be
put aside for the eventual repayment of the debenture if an increasing level of
capital employed is to be maintained. The board should, therefore, be concerned also with the 'free' EPS after making the required provisions out of
after-tax profits for the amortization of the loan. Remember that the EBIT
required to cover this item must make provision for a *net of tax* figure equal to

the annual amount required. Taking the example in Table 13.2, if we assume the debenture would have a 20-year life, the amount to be put aside each year would be £1 000 000/20 = £50 000. The EBIT required to cover this amount (with tax at 50 per cent) is £50 000 × 100/50 = £100 000.

On the graph in Fig. 13.7 the required dividend line has been drawn (assuming a dividend rate of 5p per share). From this, it can be seen that earnings must rise to nearly £160 000 merely to cover the cost of the dividend under the debenture alternative, to £220 000 under the preference alternative, and to £200 000 to maintain the dividend rate under the rights issue alternative.

Adding in the line representing the 'free' earnings per share (the calculation of which is included in Table 13.2), it can be seen that to provide free earnings to cover the required dividend rate the EBIT would have to rise to £260 000, and to maintain a free EPS equal to the existing EPS would have to rise to £310 000.

Risk

The assessment of probabilities of ranges of EBIT introduces into the problem the concept of risk. The major element of risk, that the company will run out of cash, is dealt with in some detail in the next chapter, but already one can see some useful guidelines. If there is a serious possibility of earnings before interest and tax falling below £310 000 over a large proportion of the currency of the debenture, then the preference issue is preferable; if EBIT is likely to fall below £240 000 over a lengthy period of time, the rights issue alternative is preferable. Over the short term, where debt repayment considerations are not so important, the debenture alternative is preferable at all levels of EBIT over £120 000.

CONTROL

A final decision as to which source of capital to use for financing the business cannot be made without consideration being given to the effect that equity financing may have upon the controlling interests in the company. If all shareholders are to contribute to a rights issue in the normal way, control is not affected since the proportionate holdings remain the same. If, however, for any reason, the controlling shareholders are not putting new money into a proposed issue of voting shares or where the shares are to be issued as the consideration in a takeover bid, then the dilution of voting power of the existing shareholders may change the ability to control the business.

Close company

The urge to issue new equity shares in the case of a close company may come from its desire to escape the close company penalties. If more than 35 per cent of its voting shares are in the hands of the public and are dealt in and quoted on a UK Stock Exchange, the company cannot be a close company. Other considerations in the financing decisions may be overruled by the need to cease to be a close company.

Flexibility

The financing decision that is being examined at any one time is not unique, but is one of a series of financing decisions to be taken over the life of the company. The decision taken now has some impact on future decisions. One of the objectives of the current decision should be to leave the options as widely open as possible for the future. If, for example, in the present decision one opts for a high-risk, high-return solution in which a large part of the funds employed are in the form of debt, the options in the next financing decision are restricted, particularly if the present decision has gone sour in the meantime.

14

Using borrowing capacity

The decision on financing is not easy. The future pattern of earnings is not known with any certainty. Taxation patterns may change with considerable effects upon the cost of funds. In approaching this choice, management should try to be methodical, so that all factors are taken into account. A useful step-by-step assessment would require one:

1. To establish the amount of debt the business could support and the risks involved, over likely ranges of earnings.
2. To rank in order of desirability each of the financing choices available, e.g., through measuring the relative EPS values.
3. To assess the effect on the return on equity of dividing the owners' funds into different 'slices', each with different claims on earnings.
4. Having established the most desirable combination of funds, to bring the balance of the capital structure into line with that combination as soon as possible.

THE RISKS OF BORROWING

The use of borrowed funds in the capital structure involves the business in extra risks. As seen in Chapter 12, the major characteristics of borrowed funds are that the providers are *creditors* of the business. Should the business fail to meet its commitments, it is exposed to the risk of the lender, by legal process, taking over the business—a risk not present when the funds are all owners' funds.

The order of priority of claims on the assets of the business is laid down by statute. Each party's claims are governed by the following rules:

1. *Costs of liquidation.* These have priority over all other claims.
2. *Preferential creditors.* These are paid in priority to all debts other than 1. They cover rates and taxes up to one year, including value added tax, wages and salaries for up to four months, and similar items.
3. *Secured creditors.* This class comprises those creditors who have some specific charge against some of the assets of the business, e.g., a debenture holder.

Such creditors are entitled to realize the assets charged to them and reimburse themselves from the proceeds. To the extent that their claims exceed the amount so recoverable, they rank as unsecured creditors.

There may be degrees of ranking within classes who have charges against the same security, e.g., first and second mortgages. The second mortgage only gives rights subordinate to those of the first mortgage.

4. *Creditors.* This class comprises all creditors who have not been given priority in some way. To obtain satisfaction of the amount due, the creditor must apply through the courts for a judgement summons and finally, if that remains unsatisfied, take bankruptcy or liquidation proceedings. Their claims always take precedence over those of the owners.

5. *Subordinated creditors.* This is a little used class. It ranks after all other creditors, but before owners.

6. *Preferential shareholders.* These are shareholders with a preferential claim against the assets as against the ordinary shareholders. There may be a number of preference shares of different classes at issue at one time, and the articles will regulate the ranking of their respective claims.

7. *Ordinary shareholders.* These are the equity holders and as such they rank behind all other claims on a liquidation.

The risks of borrowing are founded upon the possibility that in the future the *cash* available in the business will not be sufficient to meet the obligations the business has assumed. To the stream of payments for wages and salaries, goods and services, etc., the business is adding through borrowing an additional outflow of funds for interest and debt redemption. Thereby, it increases the possibility of that event happening.

As there are two parties to a loan, the lender and the borrower, each has his own assessment of risk and it must be looked at from both points of view. These assessments of risk are unlikely to coincide in view of the difference of commitment of each party to a loan.

The risks of the lender. Typically, the lender spreads his funds over a number of loans rather than committing them in a single tranche. This is particularly true of the institutional lender who has a large volume of funds spread over a wide range of loans. Even with the individual lender, it is unlikely (or should be) that all his funds are tied up in a single loan.

The major risk from the lender's point of view is that he may lose that part of his funds loaned out to a single client. The part at risk with the individual loan may be only a very small part of his total funds. The fact that a loan goes sour does not endanger his whole business as a lender, but is something foreseeable and included as one of the costs of the business. The professional lender's view of bad debts is that it is a cost that can be estimated and allowed for. His problem is then to exercise control of the amount of bad debts arising to ensure that the amount allowed for in the budget is not exceeded.

While, therefore, the lender will not welcome bad debts, they are not critical to his existence and his assessment of the risk factor is made in the light of this situation.

The risks of the borrower.   The risk to which the borrower is exposed is that if he fails to meet his commitments to a lender *the whole* of the business is at risk. Moreover, if the business operates in the form of a sole proprietorship, partnership, or unlimited company, not only are the business assets at risk but also the private funds of the owners. Only in the case of the limited liability company and the public corporation are the risks limited to the business itself (though even this is modified where the directors or shareholders have given guarantees to creditors).

The risk cannot be minimized by spreading the borrowing over several loans. Loan terms usually contain provisions that, where liquidation proceedings are taken or a receiver appointed, the loan automatically falls due. Thus, when one loan goes sour, all are likely to become immediately due and the borrower is in the same position as with a single loan.

A further distinction between risks is that whereas the lender is in most cases a professional lender who is continually investigating and deciding upon loan situations, with the borrower the experience is a very infrequent one.

This has had the rather unfortunate result that in the past the assessment of the right level of borrowing for a business has been from the point of view of the lender rather than that of the borrower. Even the institutional advice sought by the borrower tends to be heavily oriented in that direction. Yet, it can be seen from the risks to which each party is exposed that they might become critical for the borrower at an earlier point than for the lender.

ASSESSMENT OF RISKS

Which risks are pertinent to the loan?

In negotiating a loan, the risk limitations should be those imposed by the party most at risk, i.e., in most cases the limiting factor should be the possible effects upon the borrower. It is pertinent in this context to consider to what extent borrowers do in fact try to assess the risk to their business, and to what extent the risk factors tend to be assessed in the light of the lender's business.

Borrowers are usually borrowers because they have a specific purpose in view—the establishment or extension of their business. They see the need to employ new funds and have a view as to the return that employment of funds will bring to the owners. If borrowing is an essential part of that extension of activity, management is more concerned with the *possibility* of obtaining the funds it requires than wondering whether the risks are too great.

Frequently, it is left to the business's outside advisors to dissuade management from assuming risks it should not bear.

The dangers inherent in relying on the lender's assessment of risk have not been readily apparent in the UK, since debt financing has been avoided by most businesses except to meet specific requirements. Indeed, the Victorian abhorrence of debt is still evident in many boardrooms.

But will this position now change? As was seen earlier, debt financing has assumed a much larger role in company financing since the early 'sixties and is likely to continue to be a predominant feature of corporate finance, for two reasons. The immediate change in the cost of different sources of funds caused by the Finance Act 1965 alerted management to the advantages from the point of view of tax saving, although this advantage has been reduced by the introduction of the imputation system (see Appendix A). It is even now becoming recognized that, where the call for funds is to be made to shareholders, there may be advantages in part of those funds being expressed in loan form.

A further powerful factor which has boosted the use of borrowed funds has been inflation. It is now appreciated that in inflationary conditions it is profitable to borrow money now and repay it in 20 years' time with the same number of pounds but with only half the purchasing power. Moreover, the effect of inflation over the intermediate years is to reduce gradually the real cost of servicing the debt. This was illustrated in Table 5.1.

Risk differentials between companies and industries

There is no one acceptable debt ratio for all businesses or even for all companies within a single industry. Each class of business has its own risk characteristics. These are largely dependent upon the degree to which the business is subject to the usual commercial risks. Companies operating in the financial sphere, where returns can be forecast with some certainty and the risk of forecasts not being met is relatively low, have very different risk characteristics than a firm operating in, say, the fashion industry where earnings can be very volatile.

Quite apart from differences between industries, firms within each industry may exhibit similar differences. Some firms may have a policy of renting land and buildings, of leasing plant and equipment. This not only reduces the assets backing for loans, it also adds considerable commitments to the cash flows of the business which can put the service of debt at risk. One business might be operating only as a subcontractor to other firms, whereas another might be involved in marketing its own proprietary products.

There can, therefore, be no single 'right' level of borrowing, either for businesses generally, or for different industries. Each business must be looked at separately and an assessment made of its capacity to service debt in the light of the risks peculiar to it.

MEASURING DEBT CAPACITY

Setting the level of debt capacity considered as sustainable is one of the most critical decisions management must make. Critical, because setting the level too high exposes the business to the risk of failure and setting it too low means the return on equity is not as high as it might otherwise be.

In the past, two basic criteria have been used in testing the debt capacity of the business, both of them oriented to the requirements of the lender rather than the borrower. One is a measurement of the number of times earnings cover the cost of interest, the other is concerned with the number of times the assets of the business cover the outstanding debt.

Interest cover

The higher the interest cover the greater the fall in earnings that can take place before the company must call upon reserves to pay the interest. Its basis as a measurement tool is that, as the number of times covered reduces, the risk of failure increases.

If it is to be useful as a measuring device it should, however, provide one with a scale against which the level of risk can be measured. But what is the appropriate number of times that the interest should be covered? Should it be 4 times, 10 times, or 40 times? Or, indeed, can it even be said at all that there is a 'right' number.

To try and provide answers, recourse has been had to standards that have proved to be satisfactory in the past. This historical outlook provides some lessons as to what is and is not practicable. It also raises some important questions. For example:

1. Are the conditions which proved successful in the past likely to continue in the future? Since 1938, inflationary factors have been at work in most countries, automatically reducing the cost and risk of borrowing. How vulnerable would businesses be if the trend was halted, or even reversed?
2. How different are the risk factors of the company under consideration from those of the companies setting the pattern in the past?
3. How relevant is the experience of the past? An ultra-cautious attitude may have provided such a wide interest cover that failure was bound to be extremely rare. If the earnings cover had been halved perhaps the risk of failure would still have been minimal.

Calculating earnings cover

Since interest attracts tax relief, the earnings that are available to meet the cost of interest are the before-tax earnings.

Example: Allborrow Ltd has the following loans at issue (in order of priority of claims):

4 per cent first mortgage	£400 000
6 per cent second mortgage	£250 000
7 per cent secured loan	£800 000
7½ per cent unsecured loan	£500 000

Earnings before interest and tax are £220 000. The earnings cover for each of the loans is as follows:

Loan	Interest cost	Available earnings	Times covered
4 per cent first mortgage	£16 000	£220 000	13.75
6 per cent second mortgage	£15 000	£204 000	13.6
7 per cent secured loan	£56 000	£189 000	3.4
7½ per cent unsecured loan	£37 500	£133 000	3.55

Although the times covered provides a means of measuring the cover for each 'slice' of loan capital, it remains true that *all* the interest charges must be covered at all times, otherwise there is a progressive movement to enforce claims. For example, in the case illustrated above, the total interest cost of £124 500 is only covered 1.77 times.

Asset cover

The asset cover measures the number of times the available assets cover the amount of loans outstanding. To this extent, it is a measure of the security which the lenders enjoy.

Example: Assume that the balance sheet for Allborrow Ltd used in the previous example is as follows:

	Balance sheet value		Break-up value	
	(£000's)		(£000's)	
Fixed assets:				
Land and buildings		750		750
Plant and machinery (net)		1238		619
		1988		1369
Current assets:				
Stocks and work in progress	1432		358	
Debtors	1331		1198	
Cash	34		34	
		2797		1590
		4785		2959
Creditors:				
Trade creditors		935		935
		3850		2024
Loans		1950		1950
Net worth		1900		74

The number of times the available assets at balance sheet values cover the various loans can now be calculated as follows:

4 per cent first mortgage (secured on land and buildings only)

750/400 = 1.875 times

(There would also be a supplementary claim against the remaining assets on an unsecured basis.)

6 per cent second mortgage

350/250 = 1.4 times

7 per cent secured loan (secured on all assets but subject to the above prior claims)

Assets available: £4 785 000 less £650 000 mortgages on land and buildings = £4 135 000

Cover is, therefore, 4135/800 = 5.17 times

7¹/₂ per cent unsecured loan

Assets available: £4 785 000 less prior claims £1 450 000 = £3 335 000

Unsecured creditors: Loan £500 000 plus trade creditors of £935 000 = £1 435 000

Cover is, therefore, 3335/1435 = 2.32 times

How valid is the asset-cover rating?

The balance sheet is based on the going-concern concept. However, assets, particularly those very specific to the firm and its products, may in fact have very little value to any other business. On a forced sale their realizable value may prove to be only a fraction of the book value. Processed and partly processed goods may be virtually unsaleable. What looks to be a very good cover on paper proves to be very illusory in practice. On the other hand some assets, e.g., buildings, may have values much higher than those shown in the balance sheet.

Using the previous example of Allborrow Ltd, let us assume that on a forced sale plant and machinery would realize 50 per cent of the book value; stocks a quarter of the book value; and 90 per cent of debts would be recovered. If the costs of liquidation were 10 per cent of the realized values, the creditors would not get their money back in full. The realized value of the assets would be the £2 959 000 shown on page 169. The costs of realizing those assets at 10 per cent would be £295 900. This sum is greater than the remaining equity value, therefore the balance of £221 900 would reduce the amount available for ordinary creditors and the unsecured loan stock.

In practice, the situation would probably be worse than that shown. The crunch often comes only after a series of years of unprofitable trading eroding the owners' funds. This inevitably leads to a diminution of the asset cover since the reduction in the value of the owners' funds reduces the cushion protecting the creditors against loss.

Recognizing this feature, many borrowing terms provide that the borrower shall at all times retain a stated level of cover for the loan. Should that cover not be maintained, the lender can enforce his rights in the same way as for any other breach of the loan conditions.

The greatest criticism of this measurement is that it does not try and measure the *debt capacity* of the business at all. It is concerned solely with the protection that the lender seeks against the possibility of loss should he need to enforce the conditions of the loan. It is dealing with the 'post default' position, whereas what the borrower needs is a measurement of the risk of default itself occurring.

When is the business most at risk?

The major risk for any business which borrows is that it will quite simply run out of cash and be unable to meet its commitments as they fall due. This situation is more likely to happen when the industry passes through a period of recession. It may have cash problems at other periods, but usually can overcome them in other ways since it has a record of increasing earnings. In the recession, this pattern of earnings is broken and the possibilities of satisfying cash needs from other sources drastically limited.

The interest-cover basis of measurement takes cash flow into account to a certain extent, in that profits form one of the major constituents. They are not its sole source, however, and where the level of activity in the business changes significantly, other cash flows may be set in motion which wield much more influence. The more important are those resulting from changes in the amount of funds locked up in assets and those provided by creditors.

The earnings cover for interest is, therefore, of use to management only in conditions where the level of activity is reasonably stationary. Profitable expansion is unlikely to present problems since it should prove possible to attract additional shareholders' funds to fill the cash needs. It is the unprofitable contraction which is the danger, a condition typically occurring in a recession.

Recessional analysis

The steps in the use of recessional analysis in the financing situation are as follows:

1. Assess the likely extent and maximum duration of a recession.
2. Define the ability of the business to adjust its cost structure to that change in volume.
3. Define what changes are likely to take place automatically in the working capital items.
4. Decide what response management will make in its policy towards investment in fixed assets, and how long it would take to recognize the situation and implement the decision.
5. How would management adjust dividend policy in the face of lower profits?
6. Ascertain commitments that the directors would want to continue in any circumstances.

7. Calculate the consequential effects of all the above on the cash flows during a period of recession.
8. What level of debt will the minimum cash flows support?
9. Assess the probabilities of such a recession being encountered.
10. Define the degree of risk management is prepared to accept.

In the US, there is then a further step available. When the level of debt the business can support within the acceptable risk levels is established, that amount can be borrowed irrespective of need. If, as a result of this policy, the company has substantial surplus funds they can be used to purchase the company's own shares. Thus, at one stroke the gearing level can be dramatically increased and the number of shares reduced, with considerable effect upon the earnings per share.

This option of purchasing the company's own shares is not open to UK companies and the consequential adjustments must take place over a period of time, but with the same objective in view—to maximize the earnings per share within the limitations of risk.

Example: Maxiborrow Ltd is currently thinking about a major expansion proposal requiring the investment of £200 000 in new buildings and £300 000 in new plant and machinery. The company is already overdrawn at the bank to the extent of £105 000. In view of the company's current cash flow of £175 000, the board has been thinking in terms of raising additional shareholders' funds to the extent of £750 000 by means of a rights issue of 3 for 8 at £2.50 per share.

At a recent board meeting, Mr A, recently appointed to the board, suggested raising the funds instead by means of borrowing, pointing out that with the going rate of interest of 6 per cent and tax relief at 40 per cent the cost to the company would only be 3.6 per cent.

The deputy chairman opposed this policy arguing that the company has always avoided debt, and anyway he 'likes to sleep at night and not worry where the next £100 is coming from'. Mr B supported this argument by pointing to the major recessions that affected the company's business in 1935–38, and again in 1948–53 and 1974–78.

Following the discussion, the financial director was requested to produce a report on the following matters:

1. What would be the comparative effects of the different financing alternatives, i.e.,
   (a) a rights issue of 3 for 8 at £2.50,
   (b) the issue of a 20-year debenture at 6 per cent to raise the required £750 000?
2. Assuming that the loan alternative was chosen, what would be the likelihood of the company's not being able to meet its interest commitments?

As a preliminary to his report, the financial director has obtained information and guidance on a number of points including:

1. The maximum risk position occurs if the recession starts as soon as the new capital has been committed, i.e., 19x2.
2. The duration of the recession, if it came, would probably be three years. In the first year, the level of sales is likely to fall by 20 per cent, in the second year 40 per cent, and in the third year 30 per cent below normal.
3. To help the company maintain its competitive position, gross margins would probably fall to 35 per cent in the first and third years and 30 per cent in the second year.
4. Fixed costs would remain unchanged, other than depreciation which would be affected by changes in the capital investment programme.
5. Variable costs would remain constant at 10 per cent of sales value.
6. It is unlikely that the extent of the recession would be apparent in the first year and the dividend would be unchanged. In any subsequential change, management would not want to reduce the dividend rate below 12.5p per share.
7. A minimum cash balance of £30 000 should be maintained.
8. Management estimates that the normal plant replacement programme could be halved for up to three years without endangering efficiency. Because of delays in effecting the adjustment, it is unlikely that it could be made effective before the second year.
9. Stock levels are likely to remain at 50 per cent of cost of goods sold; debtors at two months' sales and creditors at one quarter of cost of goods sold.
10. The effective rate of tax is expected to be 40 per cent over the period.

The financial director decided that the time scale involved if the recession occurred at the earliest time would be the following:

19x1 Acquire new plant, etc.
19x2 First year of recession
19x3 Second year of recession
19x4 Third year of recession
19x5 Normal sales level
19x6 Bring in benefits of new investment

The balance sheet and profit and loss account at the end of 19x0 were as follows:

Balance sheet as at 31 December 19x0

	£000's	£000's
Uses of funds		
Fixed assets:		
Land and buildings		160
Plant and machinery (net)		700
		860

Balance sheet as at 31 December 19x0 (contd.)

Current assets:		
Stock and work in progress	792	
Debtors	440	
	—	1232
		2092
Current liabilities:		
Bank overdraft	105	
Creditors	396	
Tax provisions	157	
Dividend	160	
	—	818
Net assets		£1274
Sources of funds		
Share capital £1 shares		800
Capital reserve		130
Retained profit		344
		£1274

Profit and loss account for the year to 31 December 19x0

	(£000's)	£000's
Sales		2640
Cost of goods sold 60 per cent		1584
Gross profit		1056
Fixed costs (excluding depreciation)	300	
Variable costs 10 per cent of sales	264	
Depreciation	70	
	—	634
		422
Tax at 40 per cent		157
		265
Dividend		160
Retained profit		£105

The first step is to look at the effect on the EPS values of the two financing alternatives shown in Fig. 14.1. The debentures alternative has clear advantages at any level of EBIT above approximately £160 000. In view of the current level of earnings and the new earnings accruing from the additional funds, the choice should fall upon this alternative *provided it does not put the company at too much risk.* This has provided management with a scale of return preferences as between the alternatives.

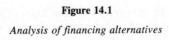

Figure 14.1

Analysis of financing alternatives

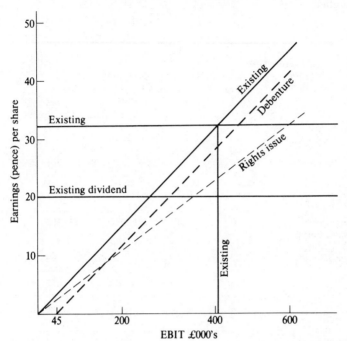

Turning now to the risk, Fig. 14.2, A, B, and C shows the effect if a recession is encountered. Part A of this figure shows the forecast profit and loss account, part B the consequential changes that would appear in the balance sheet, and part C the movement of cash.

On the basis of the cash forecast, it is apparent that there would be inadequate cash resources in the years 19x3, 19x4, and 19x5. This does not necessarily mean that there should be no long-term borrowing and that the rights alternative should be chosen. Management must now make some judgements about:

1. What sources of funds could be used if the situation as forecast arose. Could the gap be bridged by short-term funds?
2. What is the *probability* of a recession arising as early as 19x2? Bearing in mind that the business is generating funds of over £75 000 p.a., if the onset of the recession does not occur until one or two years later the firm might have sufficient cash to get through. The probability of a recession in the near future might be so remote that management would be prepared to accept the risk of it happening.

3. What is the probability of any recession that occurs being the maximum recession shown above? 'Mini-recessions' may be more probable, but less damaging.

Figure 14.2A

Recessional forecasting

Forecast profit and loss accounts (£000's)

	19x1	19x2	19x3	19x4	19x5
Percentage of normal	100%	80%	60%	70%	100%
Sales	2640	2112	1584	1848	2640
Cost of goods sold	1584 (60%)	1373 (65%)	1109 (70%)	1201 (65%)	1584
Gross profit	1056	739	475	647	1056
Fixed overheads (excl. depreciation)	300	300	300	300	300
Variable costs 10% sales	264	211	158	185	264
Depreciation	100	100	95	90	91
	664	611	553	575	655
Net profit	392	128	(78)	72	401
Tax 40%	157	51	—	—	158
Profit after tax	235	77	(78)	72	243
Dividends (all payable the following year)	160	160	100	100	100
Retained profit	£ 75	(83)	(178)	(28)	143

When management has formed some judgements on these matters, it is in a position to assess the risks disclosed and compare them with the gains to be won for the equity holders through gearing. There is no automatic decision. It must be a matter of management judgement as to what course it takes in the light of their own capacity to accept risk and possible adjustments of investors' valuation of the shares.

The process of recessional forecasting may seem to involve a great deal of work. Undoubtedly, it does. But it is suggested that in the process management is called upon to look at the business in a slightly different way, gaining an insight into likely trends together with the decisions with which they would be faced if hard times came for the company. This is no bad thing. It highlights the danger points and perhaps leads to some useful contingency planning.

Figure 14.2B

Forecast balance sheets in recession period (£000's)

	19x1	19x2	19x3	19x4	19x5
Uses of funds					
Fixed assets:					
Land and buildings	360	360	360	360	360
Plant and machinery (net)	1000	1000	955	915	924
	1360	1360	1315	1275	1284
Current assets:					
Stocks, etc.	792	686	554	601	792
Debtors	440	352	264	308	440
Cash	30	30	30	30	30
	1262	1068	848	939	1262
	2622	2428	2163	2214	2546
Current liabilities:					
Creditors	396	343	277	300	396
Tax	157	51	—	—	158
Dividends	160	160	100	100	100
	713	554	377	400	654
Net assets	£1909	1874	1786	1814	1892
Sources of funds:					
Share capital	800	800	800	800	800
Capital reserves	130	130	130	130	130
Retained profits	419	336	158	130	273
	1349	1266	1088	1060	1203
Funds required	560	608	698	754	689
	£1909	1874	1786	1814	1892

Forecasting the future is always difficult, particularly in times of inflation. The figures used in the example are what management thinks are the 'most likely' values. The usefulness of the analysis can be improved by also looking at alternative possible values.

Figure 14.2C

Recessional cash forecasts (£000's)

	19x1	19x2	19x3	19x4	19x5
Profit before tax	392	128	(78)	72	401
Tax payments	(157)	(157)	(51)	—	—
Dividends paid	(160)	(160)	(160)	(100)	(100)
Depreciation	100	100	95	90	91
New plant:					
Expansion	(300)	—	—	—	—
Replacements	(100)	(100)	(50)	(50)	(100)
Building extension	(200)	—	—	—	—
Stock changes	—	106	132	(47)	(191)
Debtor changes	—	88	88	(44)	(132)
Creditor changes	—	(53)	(66)	23	96
Annual cash movements	(425)	(48)	(90)	(56)	65
Requirement for minimum					
cash balance	(30)				
Bank overdraft	(105)				
Cumulative cash requirement	(560)	(608)	(698)	(754)	(689)
Amount to be borrowed	750				
Cumulative surplus/					
(deficiency)	190	142	52	(4)	61
Net cash requirements for debt					
service	(13)	(27)	(27)	(27)	(27)
	($^1/_2$ year only)				
Cumulative cash requirements					
for debt service	(13)	(40)	(67)	(94)	(121)
Overall surplus/(deficit)	177	102	(15)	(98)	(60)

15

Managing shareholders' funds

The business is a vehicle for the creation of value for its owners. Management, therefore, has a much wider brief than the creation of value within the business and should be concerned with the problem of transferring that value to the owners. One can readily think of cases where, for various reasons, intrinsic values fail to emerge in the share price. This chapter examines some of the problems associated with that transfer and, in particular, how dividend policy can be an instrument of management.

INVESTMENT OBJECTIVES OF SHAREHOLDERS

One cannot consider the long-term objectives of shareholders without distinguishing between them from the points of view of investment objectives and tax status.

The tax status

The basic influence of tax status lies in the choice between income and capital gain. The tax structure may well make the relative values different for different classes of shareholder.

The high tax bracket investor. A shareholder in the top income brackets may well pay up to 75 per cent in the UK of dividend income in taxation. Capital gains on the other hand are more lightly taxed in most countries. In the UK, the highest rate for personal capital gains tax is 30 per cent. This indicates that such an investor will prefer capital gain rather than income.

Example: A business earns £100 p.a. and can earn 10 per cent on funds reinvested in the business. An investor can also earn 10 per cent on funds that he manages. It is assumed that any profit ploughed back will work through into the share price, i.e., every £1 ploughed back will appear as an increase of £1 in the market value of total shareholders' funds.

Using this example to illustrate the case of a tax rate on income of 75 per cent and a capital gains tax rate of 30 per cent, the net values accruing to him over a five-year investment period would be:

| All earnings paid as dividends | | | | No dividends paid |

Year	Gross £	Tax £	Net £		
1	100	75	25		£100 per year earnings com-
2	100	75	25	Net present value	pounded to the end of the fifth
3	100	75	25	£25 × 3.791 =	year amount to £610. Sale of
4	100	75	25	£94.77	shares with a capital gain of
5	100	75	25		£610 less capital gains tax of

£610 less capital gains tax of 30% = £427 with a net present value of £427 × 0.621 = £265.20

On the assumption used in the example, one would expect a clear preference on the part of such taxpayers to receive their return in the form of capital gain rather than the underlying earnings as dividends.

The basic rate taxpayer

The differences between the net present value of the different forms of income for this class of shareholder are not so great since the gap between the two tax rates is less. Assuming the basic rate is 30 per cent and the taxpayer pays the 15 per cent investment income surcharge, and that the capital gains tax rate is 30 per cent, the relative values for the situation outlined in the previous example would be:

All earnings paid as dividends	No dividends paid
Net dividend £100 less 45% tax for 5 years = £55 × 3.791 = £205.50	Data as previous example. Present value £265.20

Once more, on the same assumptions, one would expect the shareholder to prefer the profits to be retained and emerge as capital gain rather than be distributed as dividends. The gap between the two has closed considerably from that shown for the high-tax-rate investor. On the tax rates used, it can be shown that the investor would need to earn 29.1 per cent more on funds he controls than could be earned by the company [(265.2−205.5)100/205.5]. This factor remains constant at different time intervals of investment.

With the relationship so far explored between the levels of tax on dividends received by shareholders and the rate of tax on capital gains, at all levels where earnings are positive the return to the shareholder is higher, *provided that the earnings work through into the share price* and that the return the shareholder can earn by managing his own funds does not exceed by a calculable percentage that earned by the business on internal investment.

The tax-exempt investor

The investor who pays no tax will have a different scale of values for income and capital gain to that of taxpayers. This class is very important, embracing pensions funds and similar tax-exempt institutions and charities.

All earnings paid as dividends	No dividends paid
Net present value of £100 each year for 5 years £100 × 3.791 = £379.1	Capital gain £610 × 0.621 = £378.8

In fact, as one would expect, ignoring the rounding off differences, the net present value is the same whatever dividend policy is followed.

Because under the above assumptions no investor has a preference for dividends, the maximum return for investors is achieved if all companies retain profits and pay no dividends. Other work (for example, see Fig. 15.1) indicates that this scale of preferences does not apply in real life. One can consider some of the factors which explain this apparent disregard of their interests by shareholders, e.g.:

1. Can the company always earn as much as the investor?
2. Do retained profits always work through into the market price of the share?
3. Is there a risk preference on the part of shareholders, e.g., a bird in the hand is worth two in the bush?
4. Many investors want to receive an income.
5. What proportions of funds come from each class of investor?
6. Market movements affecting the share price.

Attainable returns

Many investors no doubt think that they can outperform the market and, therefore, gain an edge over the company's earning capacity. As has been shown, when the tax rate is 45 per cent, this differential must exceed 29 per cent and the higher the tax rate the higher the differential.

Risk

Earnings left in the business may be lost if they are used unprofitably or the company runs into a period of difficult trading. Moreover, the market for one reason or another may change its rating for the company, more than outweighing the benefit of the retained earnings.

Investment requirements

One might, therefore, divide shareholders into two classes according to investment needs. On the one hand are the top-rate taxpayers and the more sophisticated basic rate taxpayers who are not concerned with income as such, but who are concerned to maximize the long-term values of their investments. On the other hand are the tax-exempt funds and those private investors who need income.

This polarization towards the extremes of high and nil dividend payments is reinforced by a study made in the context of the American market by C. Austin Barker on the price behaviour of stocks (shares in UK terminology), where differing patterns of stock and cash dividends are paid. Where stock dividends were accompanied by increased cash dividends, the stocks maintained an overall increase of 8–9 per cent. Where there was no increase in cash dividends, value fell by approximately 12 per cent. Where there were no dividends at all, prices rose by 21 per cent within six months after the stock went 'ex cap'. [*Harvard Business Review*, 'Evaluation of Stock Dividends', C. Austin Barker, July/Aug. 1958.]

THE INFLUENCE OF EARNINGS AND DIVIDENDS ON SHARE PRICE

While recognizing the rationality of the previous arguments for maximizing the returns to shareholders, one must also recognize the realities of the market price. In the UK, since 1965 the basis for assessing the share price has moved to the P/E ratio. It is interesting to examine the actual relationships between the percentage of earnings paid out as dividends and the P/E ratio. This is shown in Fig. 15.1 based on the payout ratios and P/E ratios for companies in the 'Building' section of the *Financial Times* for 29 August 1979. Some

Figure 15.1

Effect of payout ratio on P/E — building and construction companies

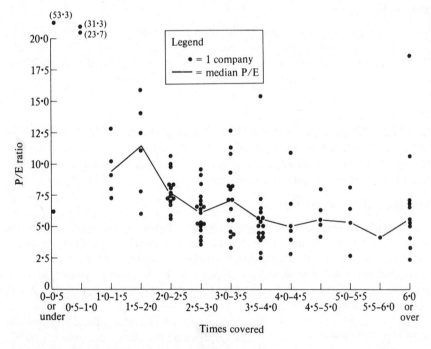

Source: *Financial Times,* 29 August 1979

companies have been omitted because, for various reasons, either the P/E ratio or payout ratio or both were omitted from the table for the day. The payout ratio is indicated in the *Financial Times* tables by the 'times covered' for the dividend, e.g., a dividend twice covered by earnings has a payout ratio of 50 per cent of earnings.

Each dot on the graph represents one company being placed upon the coordinates for payout ratio and P/E. The solid line has been plotted by reference to the median P/E for each step in the payout ratio scale, e.g., for the group in the 2.5 to 3.0 times covered range there are 18 companies for which the median P/E is 6.1.

The downward trend in the P/E as the percentage of earnings paid out falls is clearly evident on this chart. A P/E of approximately 11.2 when the dividend is covered between 1.5 to 2.0 times declines to 5.5 when it is covered between 3.5 and 4.0 times. If a few 'high flyers' were omitted from the averages, the curve would be almost smooth until the sample got too small at either end of the scale.

It is clear from this chart that *on balance* shareholders prefer income to retentions. This should not disguise the fact that the benefits of retentions for those paying high rates of tax are so overwhelming that some consideration should be given to providing special facilities for them. In the UK, attempts were made in 1967 to make such provision by some companies who arranged that shareholders could have the option of a cash dividend or a stock dividend. This was firmly rejected in the 1968 Finance Act. It is still open to a company, however, to treat all shareholders the same and pay no cash dividends. One would expect to see some companies emerging which specialize in catering for the needs of this class of shareholder.

THE LEGAL BASIS OF DIVIDENDS

Internal constraints

The decisions on the basic dividend policy rest squarely with the board and not the shareholders. The directors usually have the power to declare and pay interim dividends, to place such funds as they think desirable to reserves, and recommend the payment of the balance as a final dividend. While the approval of the dividend rests with the shareholders in general meeting, their powers are so circumscribed that in fact the directors determine the dividend policy and shareholders can only influence it by changing their board.

As was seen in Chapter 12, there is a statutory prohibition on the payment of dividends, other than from realized earnings, without the sanction of the court.

External constraints

Apart from constraints arising from internal requirements and basic law, there may be specific constraints upon amounts that can be paid.

Statutory. The legislature may pass laws limiting dividends payable. An example was the prices and incomes legislation in the UK, providing for dividend limitation. In some countries, there are requirements that a proportion of earnings must be retained and placed to reserves.

Non-statutory. Lenders and others to whom the business has obligations may incorporate into the terms of the loan, etc., instrument specific limitations upon the payment of dividends, in order to protect their own interests.

Tax. Where the tax statutes provide for a differential tax structure for earnings retained and those paid out, this may seriously influence the dividend decisions of the board.

FORMULATING THE DIVIDEND POLICY

One of the first questions that management should consider in defining its dividend policy should be 'To what type of investor is our company to be oriented?' Unless this is clearly defined the final policy is likely to be indeterminate.

The need for a consistent pattern

A dividend policy is aimed at maximizing the long-term return for shareholders in the class decided upon. The process should commence with an assessment of the needs of those shareholders along the lines already outlined.

The market price of the share is influenced by a number of factors. Stability and certainty of income can be major aspects in formulating market sentiment. A reduction or omission of a dividend can have profound repercussions on the share price for a number of years afterwards. A pattern of dividends fluctuating between wide extremes is considered less favourably than the same *total* payments divided on an even trend.

In its desire to maximize shareholders' values, management draws a balance between a specific payout ratio and the need to show a consistency in the pattern of dividends. Having set the framework within which it operates, the actual dividend payments are designed to move progressively along the trend line rather than conform to short-term fluctuations. Obviously, management is much better equipped to carry out such a policy if it has a clear view of its own long-term objectives and profitability targets.

The adoption of this approach to a dividend policy lays the primary stress upon the claim of dividends upon earnings. The retention of earnings then becomes subsidiary to that need.

The need for retained earnings

The need for retained earnings arises from two factors. The effect of inflation is to increase the cost of assets when renewed. Just to remain in business, therefore, the company must usually retain some earnings over and above the depreciation provided on an historic cost basis.

Secondly, companies want to grow and this requires some of the additional funds to be provided by equity holders. As a claim on earnings this is not a must, since all earnings could still be paid out and the required equity funds provided by a rights issue. However, most boards think that the extraction of funds from shareholders is much less painful if carried out by retention of current earnings. The possible danger of this argument is that management may think that such funds are cost-free, whereas if they resort to a rights issue they must be subjected to the market tests of profitability.

There is, of course, an extremely important interface at this juncture between the inward-looking aspect of financial management, dealing with the profitability of investment within the firm, and the outward-looking aspects of the firm's relations with its owners and the environment. The normal marginal concepts would argue that internal investment should proceed to the point where the (decreasing) return on further investment matches the (rising) cost of capital. This argument has the appearance of orthodoxy, but must be viewed cautiously.

Much hinges on the definition of the cost of capital used. If it is the weighted average cost of capital and the equity funds have been assigned a cost based upon the P/E ratio, the wrong conclusions may be drawn. For example, assume that one is considering a company with a dynamic growth record and, therefore, with a high P/E ratio of, say, 33; further, that all the capital employed is in the form of equity. This would impute a cost of capital of 3 per cent. If the company works on this basis and accepts investment projects with returns down as low as 3 per cent, its dynamic growth prospects are seriously impaired and the market value of the shares would move sharply downwards. The proposition can only be true where the cost of equity funds is taken as the long-term return required on them to maintain the existing P/E ratio.

The return required by investors is a constant factor. Therefore, the further a firm pushes the investment of funds and assuming that the marginal return on investment is declining, the lower the growth prospects for the return on shareholders' funds. As this prospect of income declines, the current P/E ratio adjusts downwards accordingly.

The competition for funds

Retentions and dividends are normally looked upon as being in competition for the funds available; funds spent on dividends reduce the amount available for investment. Superficially, this is true, but are there other aspects of the decision which may influence the volume of funds management can call upon?

The chart in Fig. 15.1 showed that the higher the payout ratio, the higher the P/E. Let us consider the implications of this for the volume of funds available for investment. Let us say that XOL Ltd has £1 million of shareholders' funds with earnings of £100 000 p.a. On the current payout ratio/P/E relationships for the industry, a payout of 50 per cent would give a P/E of 10 and a payout of 80 per cent would give a P/E of 14. The relevant market values of the equity would then be:

50 per cent payout ratio   £100 000 × 10 = £1.0 million
80 per cent payout ratio   £100 000 × 14 = £1.4 million

The only other difference between the two valuations would be the fact that there is £30 000 less for reinvestment where the payout ratio is 80 per cent. The increase in the market value of the equity, however, will facilitate raising additional funds externally which may more than make up for this small loss.

Consider the case if XOL Ltd proposed to take over another company at an agreed price of £400 000, the consideration to be satisfied by an issue of its own shares. If the P/E is 10, it must offer new shares equivalent to 40 per cent of its existing equity; if it is 14, it must only offer 400 000 × 100/1 400 000 = 28.5 per cent. This provides a clear gain to the existing shareholders of XOL Ltd.

The constraints of liquidity

The need to conserve liquid funds may at times impose restraints upon the company's ability to pay dividends. This problem is most acute where the

Figure 15.2

Industry payout ratios – building and construction industry

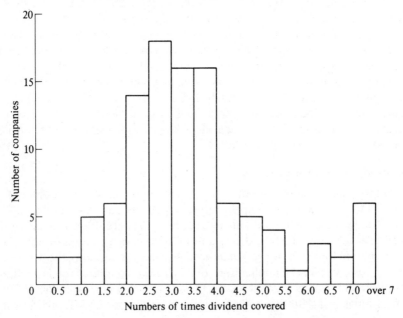

company has not only a critical liquid position but also a declining level of profitability, with a level of long-term debt making it impossible to raise new long-term funds. Management is forced to fall back upon the conservation of all liquid funds generated in the business until the crisis is past.

Dividend policy trends in the UK

Figure 15.2 represents the distribution of payout ratios for the group of companies included in Fig. 15.1. This indicates that there is a fairly wide range of dividend policies in this particular industry, the top of the distribution curve being fairly flat over the range 2 to 4 times covered.

Table 15.1 illustrates the trends in overall dividend policies by over 1000 major British companies over the period 1969 to 1977. It must be remembered, however, that the latter years cover a period of dividend restraint and a period of high inflation which would lead companies to retain a higher proportion of earnings measured on the historic cost basis.

Table 15.1

Trends in the payout ratio for major British companies
1969–77

Year	Percentage of available earnings paid out
1969	56
1970	54
1971	53
1972	41
1973	31
1974	35
1975	40
1976	40
1977	30

Note: Dividends prior to 1973
are gross. From 1973 on, they are net.

Part 3
Corporate strategy

16

Corporate strategy

In a sense, this chapter should have been the first of this book. All decision making, at whatever level in the business, stems from decisions on the corporate strategy. It has only been left until this stage to enable a framework of financial measuring techniques to be built up.

It can be argued that a decision which is properly the province of the board is not appropriate to a book on financial management. The author makes no apology for this for two reasons:

1. Although the process of setting the strategy is carried out at general management level, the evaluation of the alternative proposals is expressed in mainly financial terms.
2. The major financial decisions, such as volume and types of capital and the application of evaluation techniques such as DCF, cannot be carried out except within the framework of an overall strategy.

Why a corporate strategy?

There are many similarities between military operations and running a business, but nowhere are they so striking as in the sphere of strategy. The *objective* of a war is quite clear: it is to defeat the enemy so that a negotiated or imposed settlement can be achieved which satisfies certain defined criteria. The overall objective of the participants is clear, although the criteria for a settlement may not be so well defined.

Within that main objective of hostilities, the chiefs of staff make an appraisal of the resources available and the resources deployed by the enemy; known strengths and weaknesses on both sides, e.g., the skills of particular commanders, industrial capacity, and so on. The role of the chiefs of staff is then to prepare a strategy which, taking all known factors into account, is most likely to bring the conflict to a successful and speedy end.

Politicians may put certain limitations upon the means that may be employed, e.g., exclude the use of poison gas, respect the neutrality of other countries, etc. This may limit the courses of action open.

Let us examine the steps discussed so far:

1. Define the objective of the war—in this case usually self-evident.
2. Define the criteria of acceptability in meeting that objective.
3. Delineate the constraints within which the planners must work.
4. Appraise the strengths and weaknesses of:
   (a) self and allies
   (b) enemy and his allies.
5. Devise a strategy which maximizes the possibility of achieving (a) above.

Note that the local commanders are required to conform to the general agreed strategy. They are not now left to wage war in their own theatre as they think fit but are (or should be) given specific tasks derived from the overall strategy and designed to facilitate its achievement. Left to themselves, each theatre commander would fight 'his war' in what he deems the right way and the result could well be uncoordinated efforts. The designing and imposition of an overall strategy brings the individual efforts together, aimed towards a common objective.

The reader has already discerned many similarities with the business world. Instead of the roles of politicians and chiefs of staff, we are talking about the role of the board of directors and senior management. Just as in war, a strategy is designed to integrate and coordinate the efforts of a number of people towards a common objective, so in business it is concerned with ensuring that all aspects of the business are working towards the same goal—making a profit.

The five steps outlined above for the military scene may now be slightly redefined for use in the business:

1. Define the objective of the business.
2. Define the criteria of acceptability for meeting that objective.
3. Define the constraints within which the business must operate.
4. Appraise the strengths and weaknesses of:
   (a) the firm
   (b) the environment.
5. Devise a strategy by which the objective can be reached.

WHAT IS THE OBJECTIVE?

Failure to meet the objective should mean failure for the business. It should be something which is vital for the continued existence of the business. In the private sector, this leads one to the inescapable conclusion that *all* businesses have the same single objective—to make a profit. If that objective fails, the business fails.

Other definitions of an objective which are sometimes used, e.g., 'To improve the market share to 60 per cent', or 'To become the leaders in technology in the industry', are not critical for the continued existence of the firm. Indeed, they may often be abandoned as targets when found to reduce profitability. Their efficacy as targets is totally conditioned by the long-term effects they have upon profitability.

The conceptual difficulty in accepting profit as the single objective probably stems from the attacks that have been made upon the profit motive and a feeling that it is somehow 'immoral'. This should be faced fairly and squarely. Nationalized industries in the UK are not devoid of the profit motive. Indeed, as noted later, Parliament specifically sets profit targets for them. The tragedy in the UK over the period since the Second World War has been that profitability has not been high enough. The plain truth is that, only if industry is efficient and profitable will it contribute to build up a prosperous nation. Whether we like it or not, our prosperity is linked with the prosperity of industry, nationalized or private.

Objectives in the nationalized industries

The nationalized industries are independent bodies controlling considerable resources in terms of assets and manpower, financed by the state, and responsible to a minister. The chairman and board members will not, therefore, be entirely responsible for defining the objectives of their industry, since these may be laid down by the minister or by Parliament. Because they are not responsible to shareholders, the objectives may include not only financial but also social criteria.

An overall view of the objectives of these industries is given in *The Nationalised Industries* (HMSO Cmnd 7131, 1978). After setting out the overall duty to provide specified services, as laid down in the Nationalisation Act, it proceeds to discuss the problems of control of the nationalized industries, their financial and economic objectives, and their relations with government. In the author's own words: 'It sets out proposals designed to reconcile the purpose of public ownership with the independence needed for vigorous and enterprising management; and to ensure that the nationalised industries employ resources efficiently to the benefit of the whole community.'

Profitability standards.   Over the past years attempts have been made to set rate-of-return criteria for the industries. However, government intervention for short-term political needs has tended to override these criteria. Such criteria have usually been for periods of from three to five years. Paragraph 56 of the White Paper then goes on to say:

The Government recognises, however, that it has the responsibility of giving each industry guidance on the financial framework within which it is expected to operate. It intends, therefore, to complete as soon as possible the process of setting and publishing new financial targets. . . .

Clear financial objectives will continue to be necessary so that the industries know what is expected of them by the government. Thus, they should serve both as an incentive to management and as one of the standards by which the success or failure of management can be judged—but only if the industries are left free from political interference.

Need for rate-of-return criteria.   Investment by the nationalized industries accounted for 14 per cent of total fixed investment in 1966. It is, therefore, vital for the national well-being that their investment decisions are judged on similar criteria to those in private industry, and that the quality of the appraisal/approval process be of the highest order. Again, from paragraph 57 of the White Paper:

> The main theme is that, in general, if the industries do not cover the full costs of supplying goods or services efficiently, resources may be diverted from more to less worthwhile uses. By using resources in the nationalised industries, the nation foregoes their use in other parts of the economy—that is it incurs an 'opportunity cost'.

And later in the same paragraph:

> The capital and other resources invested in the nationalised industries should produce a return to the nation comparable to that which they would have achieved elsewhere in the economy. Otherwise there will be a misallocation of resources and they will not make their full contribution to the growth of national output.

The government recommends that all nationalised industries use discounted cash-flow techniques, and have gone further than this in laying down a criterion or cut-off rate of return (described in the White Paper as a 'test rate of discount') of 10 per cent. This is calculated as being broadly equivalent to the average rate of return in real terms looked for on low-risk projects in the private sector, after allowing for different treatment in relation to taxation, grants, etc.

If, then, one accepts that profit is the objective of a business, the natural question is 'What level of profit on what volume of funds?'

MEASURING PROFITABILITY STANDARDS

Techniques for defining the rate of profitability to be set as the target for the business have been attacked from a number of different directions. Each technique has attracted its own adherents who have then proceeded to denigrate other techniques. This battle has been particularly acrimonious over the 'return on capital employed' and the 'return to shareholders' methods. Sitting on the sidelines is the newer technique of setting as a standard a 'net present value per share'.

A little thought discloses that ROCE and the return to shareholders are not incompatible or distinct measurements. They deal with the same underlying profitability, but express it from two different viewpoints, the manager's and the shareholder's.

It is quite true that in the long run the business must offer investors a return in terms of income and capital growth at least equal to the average for the market. If it cannot do so, it is unlikely to attract new funds into the business for growth. This is certainly a standard of profitability which must be used in setting the corporate strategy.

On the other hand, the business works through people and a manager's profit performance is normally assessed in terms of ROCE. The criterion of profitability should also, therefore, be expressed in terms of the ROCE that must be achieved by the whole business which can then be related to individual manager performance.

As was seen in Chapter 13, given the ROCE, the return on equity is determined by the gearing built into the capital structure. Since the return on equity is the major factor determining the long-term return to shareholders (the other is the proportion of earnings paid out as dividends), both methods measure the same basic profitability. The decisions that are needed are:

1. Return on capital employed target
2. Policy on gearing
3. Policy on the payout ratio for dividends.

Once these have been settled, the return to investors that would result from these decisions can be forecast, together with likely changes in the market's rating of the shares in terms of the P/E ratio.

Return on capital employed

One of the criticisms that is levelled against this measure is that it is based upon a valuation of capital employed which does not accord with real values because of the ravages of inflation and differing accounting treatment. This criticism is quite valid and is a further pointer to management that objectives cannot be set realistically unless the underlying measurements are based upon the real cost of assets used up.

It is also alleged that accounting practice differs so much as between different companies that the measure is meaningless. For example, depreciation policy is often quoted in this context. A little thought makes one realize that this is only partly true. Only when the company is first set up, or where there are major changes in the level of fixed assets is this the case. Where a balance of assets of differing ages is maintained there is no difference in reported profits.

It does not greatly matter if there are differences in reported profit because of differing accounting practices. While this may upset ROCE comparisons between companies, the individual company's ROCE modified for gearing and the payout ratio is tested against the income offered to investors. This is the critical test as to whether or not it is adequate, not what other companies earn.

Return to shareholders

Investors' assessments of what the share price should be are determined by their estimate of what the future pattern of EPS is likely to be, and what proportion of that EPS will be paid out as a dividend. When management has reached a policy decision on these matters, it is possible to estimate what the likely return to shareholders will be.

This can be only an estimate at best. The share market, generally, can move by substantial margins in either direction. It may reappraise the relative P/E ratios for individual companies and different industries. All one can say is that, given a pattern of EPS and the dividend policy of the business with all other factors remaining the same, the relative price movement over the planning period can be determined.

Example: Targo Ltd currently has a capital employed of £1 million with a financing policy and profits as shown in the first column of Fig. 16.1. The board has decided not to call upon shareholders for additional funds except through retentions. Earnings of 40 per cent are retained and, as the value of shareholders' funds increases, borrowing will be raised in minimum £100 000 issues to maintain the 50:50 ratio between shareholders and borrowed funds. The forecast cost of borrowed funds (after tax) is 4 per cent.

Figure 16.1

Measuring profitability target

Capital employed: At start £1 million
Target ROCE: 8% (after tax)
Gearing: 50% of capital employed to be borrowed at 4% after tax in minimum amounts of £100 000
Dividend policy: 60% of earnings to be paid out
Shareholders' funds: No additional amounts to be raised

(A) CALCULATION OF OVERALL RETURN TO SHAREHOLDERS

Years	1	2	3	4	5	6	7	8	9	10
	← - - - - - - - - - - - - £000's - - - - - - - - - - - - - - - →									
Capital employed	1000	1024	1049	1075	1201	1230	1260	1291	1423	1457
Profit (after tax)	80	82	84	86	96	98	102	104	114	117
Loans	500	500	500	500	600	600	600	600	700	700
Cost of interest	20	20	20	20	24	24	24	24	28	28
Profit for shareholders	60	62	64	66	72	74	78	80	86	89
Dividends	36	37	38	40	43	44	47	48	52	53
Retained	24	25	26	26	29	30	31	32	34	36
New borrowing	—	—	—	—	100	—	—	—	100	—
Valuation of equity if P/E is 20	1200	1240	1280	1320	1440	1480	1560	1600	1720	1780

(B) VALUATION OF SHAREHOLDERS' RETURN

(a) Purchase of 10% interest in the business at end of year 1 would cost £120 000.

(b) If held for nine years to the end of year 10 the return would be:

Year	Dividends	Capital gain	
	£000's	£000's	
2	3.7	—	
3	3.8	—	
4	4.0	—	
5	4.3	—	
6	4.4	—	
7	4.7	—	
8	4.8	—	
9	5.2	Realized	178
10	5.3	Cost	120
Total	40.2	Gain	58

(c) If shareholders' basix tax rate is 30 per cent, then the equivalent gross dividend

total $= \dfrac{40\,200 \times 100}{70} = 57\,171$. Total return $57\,171 + 58\,000$ capital gain provides

an overall return of 115 171 which gives an annual return of $(115\,171 \times 100)/9 \times 12\,000 = 10.7\%$.

(C) AFTER-TAX DISCOUNTED RATE OF RETURN (assuming shareholder pays income tax at 30 per cent and capital gains tax at 30 per cent)

Year[2]	Net dividends	Residual value (sale value of shares)	Capital gains tax	Cash flow	PV Factor for 6%	Present value
	£000's	£000's	£000's	£000's		£000's
1	3.7	—	—	3.7	0.943	3.49
2	3.8	—	—	3.8	0.890	3.38
3	4.0	—	—	4.0	0.840	3.36
4	4.3	—	—	4.3	0.792	3.41
5	4.4	—	—	4.4	0.747	3.29
6	4.7	—	—	4.7	0.705	3.31
7	4.8	—	—	4.8	0.665	3.19
8	5.2	—	—	5.2	0.627	3.26
9	5.3	178	17.4[1]	165.9	0.592	98.21
						124.90

[1] Based upon realized 178 less cost 120 giving a gain of 58 taxed at 30%.
[2] Discount years equivalent to years 2 to 10 in the previous table.

If the company maintains the ROCE at 8 per cent after tax on the new funds it will provide the pattern of earnings for equity and dividends shown in Fig. 16.1. Management must then consider whether the gross redemption yield of 10.7 per cent and the discounted after-tax rate of return of just over 6 per cent are acceptable returns as far as investors are concerned.

The key assumptions and decisions reviewed, should management not think the rate of return an acceptable one in view of returns offered by similar types of company, would be:

1. The ROCE
2. The gearing ratio and the cost of fixed interest (and if appropriate, fixed dividend) funds
3. The dividend policy for the payout ratio and its implications for the P/E ratio.

Net present value method

The first step in using this method is to survey the return offered by other companies in the market which are capitalized on the same basis. This, then, becomes the discounting rate. When the broad patterns of the corporate strategy have been determined, it is possible to estimate the likely pattern of earnings after tax but before financing charges. These are discounted to arrive at the present value of that stream of earnings. (In some circumstances, it may be better to express this as a value per share.)

The cost of debt service including debt repayment is discounted in the same way, so that one now has two values: the net present value of the earnings net of tax but before interest payments, etc. and the net present value of the forecast future pattern of financing through borrowing. The objective of the strategy is to maximize the former value and minimize the latter. If the net of these two values is greater than the present value of the business, the proposed strategy, if successful, will exceed the going market rate of return; if it falls short, the strategy will need further examination since the return is unacceptable.

CONSTRAINTS

Quite apart from the constraints that may be placed upon the activities of individuals and companies by law, management itself may decree that certain practices may not be employed and that staff must comply with certain standards of behaviour. Constraints that are frequently imposed impinge upon:

1. *Relations with staff.*   Specific practices in relation to employees may be laid down, or general guidelines set out.
2. *Trading practices.*   Guidelines on the use of undercutting, switch selling, price fixing, etc., in the home market. Overseas, the extent to which representatives are allowed to make use of local customs for obtaining business.
3. *Moral issues.*   Situations such as that outlined on page 48 where, with devaluation a possibility, the problem is to protect the firm's interests to

the maximum—or does one try to support the national interest at whatever the cost?

DEVISING THE STRATEGY

Measuring the profit 'gap'

The first step in devising the strategy is to measure the task. For private industry the measure of the task is the gap that exists between the level of profit achieved by the business without any major changes being introduced and the level of profit the target profitability measurement indicates should be earned.

Figure 16.2 shows the likely relationship that will exist between these two values. AA^1 shows the level of profit that must be earned if the profitability target is to be reached. BB^1 shows the likely level of profit for the business, assuming that no major changes are made in its structure.

Figure 16.2

The profit gap

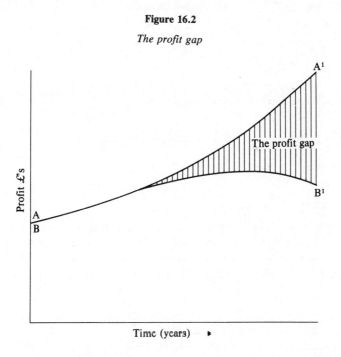

It is an old adage that when a business ceases to grow it starts to decline. Like many old sayings it contains a grain of truth. Each product or service a business provides passes through a life cycle. In the early stages, when it is being marketed for the first time, it takes time to gain acceptance and profitability is low. If it is a successful launch, profits increase until they reach the maximum, where they remain for some time. Depending upon the nature of the product, it sooner or later becomes less attractive to purchasers. New competing products emerge, customers' tastes change, the need for the product may cease altogether. Thus, profitability declines until the product is no longer viable.

The profile of a product life has, therefore, the appearance shown in Fig. 16.3(a). Some products may have a life cycle of decades, others of only a few years. Management should try to avoid having a mix of products, such as that shown in Fig. 16.3(b). While profitability is high at time X, by time Y all projects are in their final stages with nothing to follow on. Ideally, a range of

Figure 16.3

Product life

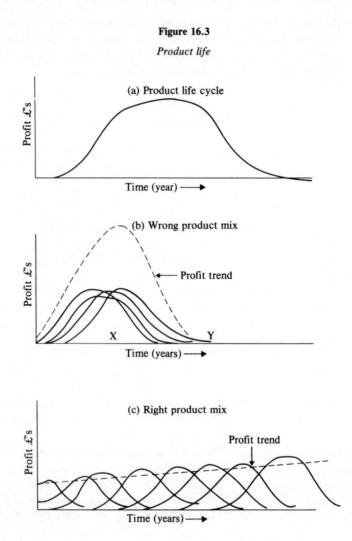

products all at differing stages in their life cycle, such as that shown in Fig. 16.3(c), should be maintained, so that profit does not fluctuate widely.

The decay rate of their products is a factor many managements will not face. Old products are clung to with an obstinate belief in their revival, instead of plans being made to bring forward a range of products to replace them. Too often, this has resulted in hasty last-minute attempts to put the profitability position right by 'buying in' expertise in the form of licensing agreements or by bidding for companies in an attempt to diversify. Such death-bed repentance has often lost a large part of the shareholders' funds.

Having defined the gap which exists between the trend of profits for the business as presently constituted and the desired level of profits, management faces the crucial problem of how that gap is to be filled.

Assessing the business

A preliminary to the devising of the strategy is an assessment of the business itself. On what has its success in the past been founded? What are the particular strengths and weaknesses that it possesses, both those of the past and those which could be developed in the future?

The strengths and weaknesses are related to the skills of the staff, to 'know-how', and to managerial abilities. It may have developed particular skills in organizing finance, in managing resources, facilities for specialized manufacturing operations through the equipment it possesses, skills in marketing products, etc.

The firm's past results may have been adversely affected by deficiencies in any of these factors. These deficiencies should be known so that steps can be taken to remedy them in suitable cases.

Assessing the environment

The environment offers either currently or prospectively opportunities to be exploited by a business which is alive to them. The identification of market needs, the development of advanced skills in manufacture, the development of new products, etc., are skills of the highest order. The business which can generate relevant ideas, which can select the profitable ones from among them, and put them into practice efficiently is likely to be successful in the future.

One of the features of modern society is the rapidity of change. It is estimated that the sum of human knowledge is doubling every 10 years, with consequential effects upon the requirements of society and the ability of firms to satisfy these new requirements. The firm which remains blissfully unaware of what the future holds may not be in business very long. The firm which can identify those future needs at the earliest stage and organize itself to satisfy them is the future leader in its industry or the creator of a new industry.

This need to look into the future is expressed in the technique of *technolog-*

ical forecasting. Currently practised in many parts of the world, it is designed to provide management with some idea of the likely direction and extent of changes in technology. This is obtained by close attention to developments in the realms of pure and applied science, allied with estimates of the time scale required to bring ideas to the stage of producing marketable products. This latter time scale is one which is continually decreasing. One has only to consider the time scale for developing the horse-drawn carriage, the steam engine, the motor car, the aeroplane, the space vehicle, to know this.

Management should consider not only what the technological age may have to offer for their business. As society changes so will its needs, or there may be existing needs not developed at all. The idea, and the exploitation of that idea through developing a market for it, may provide the basis for a prosperous business.

Figure 16.4

Formulating corporate strategy

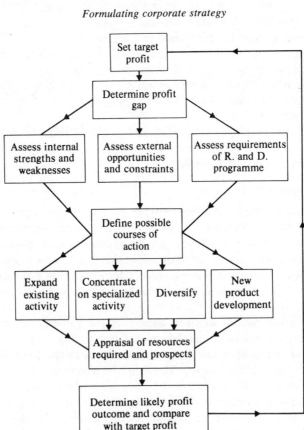

Determining the strategy

From the strategies open to it, management is faced with the choice of the one which can provide the target profit already established. As shown in Fig. 16.4, after the assessment of external and internal strengths the different courses of action are appraised in terms of the resource and other requirements needed to support that strategy. The final stage is an assessment of the proposed strategy to determine whether or not it meets the profit target set in the initial stages.

In this process of assessment, a number of factors should be considered. One of the most important is the flexibility underlying the proposed strategy. The more specific the strategy, the more difficult it may be to devise a viable alternative. Specialized machinery may be difficult to use profitably on other products; the single customer may be difficult to replace. The choice here is quite clear. Specific, highly specialized resources and markets may be the most profitable. On the other hand, the business is much more vulnerable. Taking into account the risks and uncertainties, it *may* be better to accept a lower return than could otherwise be achieved through employing less specific resources which, should the need arise, can be deployed more readily into other uses.

Continuing scrutiny of strategy

The devising of the corporate strategy is not a once-and-for-all task. Neither the business nor its environment is static but is continually changing, with the rate of change itself accelerating. Effective management requires a continuing review of goals and of the strategies set up, to test them against the actual or prospective changes to see whether they continue to be valid, and to sense the possibilities of new strategies emerging to meet new conditions.

The decision to wind up the business

It may be that after a full examination of all the possibilities open to the business, management cannot see any viable way of reaching the profit target they have set. This means that the business is only able to offer its owners a return lower than that which they could obtain elsewhere. Management has a clear duty, here, to consider the possibility of winding up the business before the owners' funds are lost. Obviously, there may be other factors to be considered, such as the re-employment prospects of employees. The difficulty is that management rarely recognizes the need to wind up and perse veres until overwhelmed by circumstances, to the cost of shareholders and employees alike.

17

Capital budgeting

In defining the corporate strategy, management has decided the extent and direction of the utilization of resources. Just as the chiefs of staff must be prepared to back up their strategy by an allocation of resources to the various theatres of war, so the board must be prepared to make broad decisions as to how the available funds are to be used. If the goals set in the strategy are to be achieved, some activities may have to be curtailed, others may have to be supported through an early unprofitable stage.

The link between corporate strategy and operations

The corporate strategy has set the framework within which the business will operate during the planning period. The day-to-day decisions on new capital investment are filling in that framework with the 'flesh' of production resources which may be more or less specialized. It is essential, therefore, that the projects approved should conform to the requirements of the strategy.

Since the majority of investment projects is initiated by line management, the corporate strategy is not something which should be confined to the board of directors. Each manager involved in putting it into effect should be aware of its broad terms, and, in more detail, the part that he has to play in the achievement of the target profit. Unless there is this awareness, the manager continues to regard his department, etc., in a manner which may not conform to this requirement. In this way, investment projects absorb man-hours in their preparation, only to be discarded when submitted for approval.

Allocation of funds to achieve maximum profitability

Within the context of the funds allocation determined by management, the aim of the capital budgeting process is to maximize the return along the lines outlined in Chapter 6. This is achieved by the two requirements of the capital budgeting system dealt with, e.g.:

1. By ranking projects in order of profitability.
2. By ensuring that investment is not made in projects which earn less than the cost of capital or other criterion rate.

Within the overall capital budget, the latter requirement must be further expanded. Not only must the individual project earn at least the cost of capital, but the budget for the year or other period must as a whole provide an overall return greater than that cost or other minimum criterion rate set.

This postulates that some view must be taken of the pattern of capital investment for the whole period rather than looking at each investment project in isolation. While this overall view might be of necessity imprecise, it should set an order of magnitudes for different classes of investment projects, e.g., 'normal' plant replacements may be set out in a global figure for the year. A typical capital budget for a year might look like that shown in Fig. 17.1.

Figure 17.1

The capital budget
Forecast requirements and approximate yields 19x3

Projects	Cost (£000's) (a)	Return (after tax)% (b)	Weight (a×b)
Launch new product XL	150	16	2400
Office block	50	—	—
Replacement machines	60	12	720
Replace power plant	90	14	1260
Acquire land for sports field	10	—	—
Replace lathes with automatics	75	10	750
Delivery vehicles to replace contractors	30	12	360
	465		5490

Average return on projects   5490/465 = 11.8%

If the criterion rate of return is less than 11.8 per cent then the mix of projects shown would be broadly acceptable. If it is higher then the programme for the year should be reviewed with a view to changing the mix of products to provide an acceptable return. This reviewing of projects should not of course be confined to the mix contained in the budget for the year. There are a number of ways in which the objective of an individual investment project can be achieved, and a part of the capital budgeting process should be devoted to an examination of all the viable alternatives that are open to the business.

Assume, for example, a project could be carried out at a relatively unsophisticated level with an investment of £10 000 and a rate of return of 20 per cent, or in a more sophisticated form for £20 000 and a rate of return of 15 per cent. While the latter return in itself might be acceptable, the return on the incremental investment of £10 000 should be examined. The investment of this extra £10 000 has a rate of return of approximately 10 per cent only. When this is compared with the return that can be earned on other projects, it might well prove to be more desirable to invest this £10 000 in another project which can earn 13 per cent than to invest it in the more sophisticated form of the original project. [See *Discounted Cash Flow,* 2nd edn, M. G. Wright, McGraw-Hill, 1973, pp. 82–90.]

LEASING v. BUYING

When the decision has been made to go ahead with a particular project, another decision may be appropriate in certain cases. This is whether or not to lease the plant, etc., rather than to buy it outright. Many businesses may not have a choice of action. The lease-or-buy decision has far-reaching effects on the general financial structure which may limit the decisions available, for two basic reasons:

1. It may be 'last resort' financing to acquire the use of assets in this way.
2. The use of leasing reduces the owned assets of the business and raises an obligation to pay rentals. This influences the ability of the business to raise capital by borrowing.

Where the business does have a choice as to whether or not it will use leasing, the objective of the appraisal system is to establish whether the use of funds to acquire ownership offers sufficient advantages over leasing to provide a rate of return that is comparable to or better than other uses.

Cash flows which are relevant in the leasing decision

The incremental principle applies just as much to this situation as to other investment problems. One is concerned to isolate the differences in cash flows as between the two alternatives.

In other investment problems, net cash investment is measured by the net cost of the assets to be acquired, i.e., net of investment or other grants and the realization value of existing assets. In the leasing decision, receipts from the disposal of assets are not relevant, being common to both alternatives. Only if there will be a difference in the amount received, e.g., through a trade-in as against a cash sale, will it be relevant.

In calculating the operating and residual cash flows, the first step is to identify the differences between the two alternatives. If the asset is purchased, there is no rent to pay; as the asset is owned, capital allowances and grants can be claimed; at the end of the project, owned assets have a residual value. In each of the cases, there would be tax consequences.

Example: Tracto Ltd is replacing one of its machines and a DCF appraisal has shown that the savings would provide a return in excess of the criterion rate of 10 per cent. Because of the large demands upon the company's funds, management is considering leasing the machine rather than buying it. The cost of purchase would be £10 000 and the company expects that it would qualify for first-year allowances of 100 per cent. The life of the machine is expected to be five years, having a residual value at the end of £1000.

A leasing organization has offered to lease the equipment for five years at an annual rental of £1500 per year.

Assuming a tax rate of 50 per cent, should the company lease or buy?

The net present value of the future cash flows is less than the net cash investment, therefore the investment of funds through purchase of the machine would not provide a large enough rate of return through savings on lease costs to warrant their use in this way. The decision should be to lease the machine.

Assuming here that the sum of the net present values had been £10 928 rather than £7928, i.e., it indicated purchase would satisfy the criterion rate, this would not provide the final decision. As with other investment projects, the return would be compared with the profitability indices for other projects under consideration, so that the higher yielders can be selected.

(A) Capital allowances

	£
Cost of machine	10 000
First-year allowances 100%	10 000
Written-down value for tax purposes	nil
Residual value	1 000
Claw-back of capital allowances	(1 000)

(B) Net cash investment

Cost of machine	£10 000

(C) Annual and residual cash flows

Year	Leasing payments saved	Tax on increased profit	Capital allowances	Tax saved	Cash flow	PV factor 10%	Present value
	£	£	£	£	£		£
1	1 500	—	10 000	5 000	6 500	0.909	5 908
2	1 500	(750)	—	—	750	0.826	620
3	1 500	(750)	—	—	750	0.751	563
4	1 500	(750)	—	—	750	0.683	512
5	1 500	(750)	—	—	750	0.621	466
6	—	(750)	—	—	(750)	0.564	(423)
	7 500	(3 750)	10 000	5 000	8 750		7 646
Residual values:							
Sale of machine					1 000	0.564	564
Claw-back of capital allowances		(1 000)	(500)	(500)	0.564	(282)
		9 000	4 500	9 250			7 928

There are a number of points to be noted about the example:

1. Cost savings, etc., related to the original decision to acquire the asset are not relevant to this decision.

2. The 'saving' or profit increase in this case is the net cost of leasing saved. As between the two alternatives, this would have the effect of increasing the tax bill if the asset is acquired.
3. The benefit of the capital allowances accrues to the owner of the asset, as does the residual value.

USE OF FUNDS IN THE FINANCING DECISION

Capital investment appraisal may be called into play where it is proposed to use a part of the firm's funds to provide the costs of changing one form of finance for another, e.g., to replace preference share capital with borrowing. The DCF technique may also be used where it is required to compare alternative forms of debt finance.

Example: Finco Ltd is considering replacing its 7 per cent preference shares with a 9 per cent debenture. The net costs of the change are estimated at £15 000. The 100 000 £1 preference shares will be replaced by £100 000 debenture stock redeemable at the end of 20 years. The criterion rate of return is 10 per cent after tax.

Investment of funds requires	£15 000
Time horizon	20 years
Annual cost of preference dividend	£7 000
Annual cost of debenture interest	£9000 less tax relief at 52% = £4320

Present values:

Preference dividend years 1–20	£7000 × 8.514[1] = £59 598
Interest payments (gross) year 1–20	£9000 × 8.514 = £76 626
Tax relief on interest years 2–21	£4680 × 7.740 = £36 223
Net present value	£59 598 − 76 626 + 36 223 = £19 195

The net present value of the saving is greater than the cost of effecting the replacement of the preference capital, so it should go ahead.

It can also be argued that by reducing the cost of servicing fixed return funds, the improved cash flow increases the debt capacity, thus compensating for the investment of funds.

Quite apart from the appraisal of the investment of funds in the way just outlined, the discounting technique can be employed to appraise the relative

---

[1] The present value factors are those shown in Appendix C for £1 receivable each year. The tax relief is postponed 1 year, the PV factor being that for 21 years less that for 1 year.

costs of different loan alternatives. The objective is to select the loan proposal with the lowest discounted total repayment pattern (including repayment of capital). The smaller this present value, the lower the deduction from the present values of future earnings on which the capitalized value of the business is based.

Example: Fundon Ltd is considering borrowing the sum of £1 million over a period of 20 years. Two alternatives are being canvassed. One provides for the borrowing of the whole sum over the entire 20 years at $8^1/2$ per cent, the loan being repaid in a lump sum at the end. The other provides for the repayment of the sum of £50 000 per year from the end of the fifth year, the balance of the loan remaining being paid at the end of the twentieth year. In this case, the interest rate would be 8 per cent. The company can currently earn 12 per cent after tax on investments.

(A) Net present value of repayment, etc., under the first alternative

Annual cost of interest	£85 000 p.a. less tax at 50% = £42 500 p.a.
Present value	£42 500 × 7.469 = £317 433
Present value of capital repayment	£1 million × 0.104 = £104 000
Total net present value	£421 433

(B) Net present value of second alternative

Year	After-tax cost of interest	Capital repayment	Total debt service cost	PV factor 12%	Present value
	£	£	£		£
1	40 000	—	40 000	0.893	35 720
2	40 000	—	40 000	0.797	31 880
3	40 000	—	40 000	0.712	28 480
4	40 000	—	40 000	0.636	25 440
5	40 000	50 000	90 000	0.567	51 030
6	38 000	50 000	88 000	0.507	44 616
7	36 000	50 000	86 000	0.452	38 872
8	34 000	50 000	84 000	0.404	33 936
9	32 000	50 000	82 000	0.361	29 602
10	30 000	50 000	80 000	0.322	25 760
11	28 000	50 000	78 000	0.287	22 386
12	26 000	50 000	76 000	0.257	19 532
13	24 000	50 000	74 000	0.229	16 946
14	22 000	50 000	72 000	0.205	14 760
15	20 000	50 000	70 000	0.183	12 810
16	18 000	50 000	68 000	0.163	11 080
17	16 000	50 000	66 000	0.146	9 636
18	14 000	50 000	64 000	0.130	8 320
19	12 000	50 000	62 000	0.116	7 192
20	10 000	250 000	260 000	0.104	27 040
		1 000 000			495 038

The net present value of alternative A is lower than that of B and, therefore, is more attractive. This arises because the business can earn a high return on investments and, therefore, it is advantageous to retain the funds in the business as long as possible. The earnings on the funds of A more than compensate for the small difference in cost.

RISK AND UNCERTAINTY

The future is never certain and this fact must be recognized in the capital budgeting process if it is to be really meaningful. The final choice of projects should take into account both the indicated rate of return and the assessment of the risks involved. One of the most difficult decisions is the choice between the low risk, low return investment and the high risk, high return investment. The objective of the capital budgeting system should be to provide management with an adequate risk profile of each investment proposal.

Appraisal: probabilities

Faced with the choice between two projects each with an indicated DCF rate of return of 10 per cent, management would want to know the probabilities in each case of the rates being higher or lower than that indicated. If this can be depicted as shown in Fig. 17.2 the choice would obviously lie with project A. This project has a much higher probability of exceeding the forecast rate and a lower probability of being less than does project B.

Figure 17.2

Probability in project selection

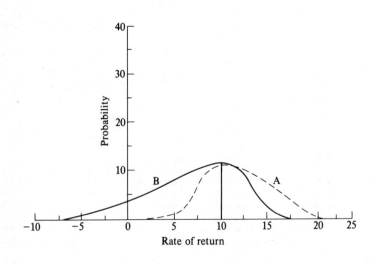

Measurement by manual methods

The scope for measuring probabilities by manual methods is restricted by the ability to manipulate the volume of data required. In a limited way, it can be done by delineating the extremes of possible rates of return as well as the probable rate. Instead of only one value being provided for each factor in the appraisal, three values are provided called the 'possible best', the 'most probable', and the 'possible worst'. (So far we have been using only the 'most probable' values.) The information for a project can then be set out in the following way:

	Annual cash flows	Investment	Years' life
Best	£1800	£8 000	8
Probable	£1500	£10 000	7
Worst	£1200	£13 000	5

The worst, probable, and best values are now combined into a solution rate of return for each to provide an indication for management as to the extent to which the rates of return may vary from the forecast rate. It has not provided, however, an indication of the probability of any particular rate being earned.

Measurement by simulation techniques

The advent of the computer has provided the resources needed to manipulate large volumes of data and use can be made of this in the capital investment decision.

So far, in dealing with investment projects, the appraisal has been preceded by a forecast of the effect that the course of action being considered will have upon the cash flows, both initially and annually. This forecasting of cash flows can be combined with the appraisal process when a computer is used. Instead of starting with the forecast increase in profit, for example, one can start with the sales and cost volumes in whatever detail is required, and the computer will work through to the profit and cash flows and calculate the rate of return.

The simulation process starts with an estimation of the range and probabilities of values for each factor considered. Sales value, for example, may be one factor. The upper and lower limits to sales are established and probabilities placed upon intermediate values being achieved. This process is repeated for all of the factors and, where necessary, interrelationships between two or more factors established, e.g., sales volume and direct costs.

The technique then proceeds by a *random selection* of values from each of the factors and the combination of the selected values into a rate of return. The process is repeated a hundred or so times with the random selection of values for each factor taking into account the probabilities estimated for each. As each computer run produces a rate of return, it is accumulated to provide a probability distribution curve for the range of rates of return. [For further reading see *Discounted Cash Flow,* 2nd edn, M. G. Wright, McGraw-Hill, 1973.]

SENSITIVITY ANALYSIS

The probability distribution of rates of return just outlined provides management with a broad outline of the possible outcomes of the project in total and has, therefore, extended the basic information required for the decision. What may prove of more use to management is an analysis of the effects of changes in the values of any of the underlying factors. For example, the rate of return has been calculated taking into account a given volume of sales. What would be the effect upon the rate of return if a competitor enters the market and volume suffers a 20 per cent overall decline?

Where the computer holds all of the basic data relating to a project, it is quite easy to change the value for one of the factors, holding all other factors constant, and recalculate the rate of return. Moreover, because of the speed of the computer, this can be repeated a number of times with different ranges of change for that factor, so that a trend in the rate of return can be established. The results of this type of analysis are shown in Fig. 17.3. This illustrates a project in which the forecast rate of return is 10 per cent and the effect of varying the values of three of the factors is shown.

Figure 17.3

Sensitivity analysis

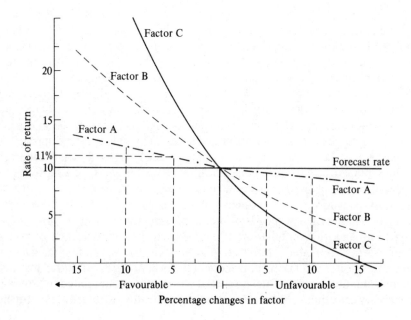

Percentage changes in factor

Looking first at factor A, the values are changed for each of a series of runs on the computer, say by 5 per cent stages both upwards and downwards. As the rate of return for each run is calculated, it is plotted on the chart; for example, a 5 per cent favourable change lifts the rate of return to 11 per cent. When the rate for each value has been calculated, the forecast rates of return can be connected by a curve which shows the effect of intermediate changes in the value for the factor over the whole range.

This process is repeated with factors B and C and the appropriate curves drawn. The slope of each of the curves indicates the relative *sensitivity* of the rate of return to changes in the value of that factor. In the illustration, factor A has little effect upon the rate of return, factor B affects it to a considerable extent, and with factor C the rate of return is highly sensitive.

This process has achieved two purposes:

1. Management can now isolate each factor and, where the rate of return is shown to be highly sensitive, it can vet the forecasts more closely or call for further investigations before committing the business to a course of action.
2. It has identified the areas of the project which need the closest management control if it is authorized. The management information and control system in this case would provide a much greater degree of control of factor C than of factor A. Parameters may also be set for the factors which trigger off management action. For example, a $7^1/_2$ per cent unfavourable movement in factor C might call for a full report to the board for reappraisal of the whole project. The bad aspects should not be singled out for treatment. A similar favourable movement might indicate that the company has a real money spinner in the project and that further resources should be committed to exploit the potential more fully.

Flexibility and other factors

The analyses of a project such as those outlined may indicate areas of uncertainty or risk which the business should try to avoid. Management should in the normal course of events examine alternative ways of carrying out the project to improve profitability. This examination should include ways of achieving the purpose of the project with less risk. This is not to say that risk should be avoided at all costs. The management that is not prepared to take risks is not worth its salt. The risks, however, should be calculated ones and unnecessary risks avoided where possible.

THE COST OF CAPITAL

One of the requirements of the investment appraisal system is that it prevents the investment of funds in projects where the forecast rate of return is less than the cost of capital. Although in most cases the criterion or cut-off rate of return is well in excess of the cost of capital, this cost always forms the lowest acceptable rate.

Capital in this context is the value of the shareholders' funds in the business, plus borrowing. In other words, it is the usual definition of capital employed. In setting the objectives of the business, management specifies the proportions in which sources of funds are to be used. This proportion is used in determining the cost of capital in future.

Note that it is not proposed that the cost of capital raised specifically for a particular project should be used as the cost of funds for that project. All funds contribute to a pool of funds available for investment and from that point they cannot be distinguished from each other. The pool of funds is then appropriated to specific uses. If borrowing is used now for a particular project, future fund raising may have to rely on equity funds to maintain the debt/equity ratio.

If one considered solely the source of the funds used on each project, one using borrowed funds at a cost of, say, 5 per cent would be acceptable if it yields 5½ per cent, whereas another earning 9 per cent might be rejected because it used equity funds at a cost of 10 per cent. This would make nonsense of an appraisal system.

Calculating the average weighted cost of capital

The calculation of the weighted average cost is shown in Fig. 17.4. The balance sheet values of funds are set out and provide the basis for the weighting. The net cost column takes into account the differing rates and tax treatment of the different sources of capital used. The interest on the unsecured loans and debentures attracts tax relief and this reduces the cost to the net after-tax value. Preference dividends on the other hand do not attract tax relief and the cost is the net dividend per share.

Figure 17.4

The weighted average cost of capital

Source	Book value	Weight	Net cost with tax at 50%	Weight × cost
	£			
8% Unsecured loan	200 000	2	4%	8.0
7% Debenture	100 000	1	3½%	3.5
*7% Preference shares	100 000	1	7%	7.0
Ordinary share capital	300 000 ⎱	6	10%	60.0
Reserves	300 000 ⎰			
				——
				78.5
				——

Weighted average cost of capital 78.5/10 = 7.85%

*Net dividend rate

The real problem in the process is to calculate the cost of ordinary shareholders' funds. This cannot be just the dividends payable to shareholders, since a shareholder holds his investment to obtain income and capital gain. The measure of the cost of equity funds to the business is the return it must hold out to an investor to induce him to put his capital into the business. To an extent, this is measured by the P/E ratio, but this does have some defects. The 'price' part of the ratio is an indication of the market's expectations as to the *future* trend in earnings. The 'earnings' aspect on the other hand is a measure of *past* earnings. As was shown in Chapter 15, the company with a high growth rate has a high P/E ratio, but this is not indicative of the cost of new shareholders' funds. The real cost is the anticipated total return investors expect from such an investment.

It would seem logical to use as the cost of equity funds the average return achieved by investors over a period. As indicated in Table 2.2, the average return on the book value of equity funds from the company's point of view has been around 11 per cent. Other studies have indicated that the achieved gain by investors has been around 9 per cent after tax in recent decades. This latter figure includes gains from the effects of inflation, so the figure of 9 per cent may be of the right order.

The really crucial point is that, if a company has a high P/E because of past and expected future performance, management must set the cut-off rate at such a level that that performance is achieved. If it fails in this, the retribution is soon evident in the new level of the P/E.

The criterion or cut-off rate of return

Too much attention has been focused upon the cost of capital in the past, to the detriment of the real problem of deciding what is to be the minimum acceptable rate of return. Certainly, this must not be less than the cost of capital and in most cases must be substantially in excess of it, an excess large enough to render rather meaningless the academic arguments as to what precisely is the cost of capital.

Firstly, management may set quite clear-cut goals as to its return on capital employed, and, in relation to those goals, set the criterion rate or rates of return. Thus, the return is determined not by what costs are but by what management wants the return to be. The only regard that management then has to costs is to ensure that the target performance standards set are adequate in terms of those costs

If it is desired to construct the criterion rate of return from the ground upwards, there are additional factors to be considered, i.e., inflation and uncertainty.

INFLATION

The effects of inflation are insidious and must be taken into account in most estimates of future events. Project selection is based on bringing future values back to present values; therefore, if all those future values are affected in the same way by inflation, it can be ignored. To bring them back to present values, one must first convert the estimates of future values to real values at today's prices and then discount in the usual way. The problem arises where some of the values are not affected in the same way by inflation.

Ability to adjust prices to inflation

Where the business is carried out on the basis of long-term fixed-price contracts, or there are statutory prohibitions on price changes, etc., clearly the effect of inflation is to reduce future profits. Costs will be rising and prices stable. In this case, it is suggested that the expected increase in costs should be built into the forecasts and the final profit figures converted to pounds at today's value before the discounting takes place. There will also be problems if some costs are inflating at a different rate to the general rate of inflation.

Capital allowances

The one factor that remains constant in every case is the allowance against taxable profits in respect of the depreciation of fixed assets. Revenue authorities generally do not accept that inflation exists and tax both income and capital gains on that basis. This means that, in general, in inflationary conditions firms are taxed on book profits which exceed their profits in real terms. The greater the acceleration of tax relief for depreciation, the less will be this effect. In the UK the 100 per cent first-year allowances given in place of depreciation is the ultimate in acceleration and minimizes the inflation effect. In other countries, it points to the use of depreciation methods giving the greatest acceleration.

Care must be exercised in the appraisal of projects where a substantial part of the cost consists of land and buildings. This class of asset is likely to rise substantially in value during the period of the project due to inflationary and other factors. It will form the major part of a very large residual value at the end of the life of the project. While the project as a whole may meet the rate of return criterion, the gain in value of the land and buildings may obscure the fact that the business part of the project does not.

Consider the case of a company appraising a project which requires the investment of £100 000 in buildings and a similar amount in plant and machinery over 10 years. The year-by-year cash flow is expected to be £15 000 p.a. Because of its site, management expects that the buildings will be worth £400 000 at the end of 10 years, following recent trends. The plant will have no residual value and the criterion rate is 10 per cent.

On a conventional basis the net cash investment would be:

Land and buildings	£100 000
Plant (net)	100 000
	£200 000

The evaluation of the cash flows can be abbreviated as follows:

Present value of cash flow years 1−10 = £15 000 × 6.145

= £92 175

Residual value £400 000 × 0.350 = £140 000

Total present value = £232 175

On this basis, the project meets the criterion rate of 10 per cent and would be acceptable. A little thought shows, however, that the trading activity is not profitable enough on its own. Taking out of the calculations the values in respect of the land, the project can be analysed as follows:

	Trading activities		Land investment
	£		£
Net cash investment	100 000		100 000
Cash flow from trading discounted at 10%	92 175	Residual value	140 000
Total present value	92 175		140 000
Profitability index 92 175/100 000	= 0.922	140 000/100 000	= 1.4

Businessmen who have large investments in properties, e.g., farmers, hoteliers, etc., should consider the above implications when looking at such projects and segregate the two activities combined in the project, as shown, to make sure that the underlying trading profitability is adequate.

18

Problems of valuation

There is no question but that the valuation of a business is one of the most difficult decisions to make. The value is conditioned to a large extent by the purpose for which it is made. If one is effectively buying a future stream of earnings, different factors are relevant, compared with a valuation related to security for a loan. The first requisite of the valuation process is a clear definition of the purpose for which it is required.

The business is the sum of a group of people with different abilities and characteristics, of productive and marketing capacities, of opportunities and skills. Although its appraisal results in a financial figure, that appraisal should be determined by all the factors, internal or external, which might affect the value in any way. In many cases, the business is quite clearly valued on an assessment of the ability of the management.

Value must also be judged in the context of a continuously changing range of external factors. For example, if one is trying to decide on the multiple of earnings which is applicable to the business under consideration, reference is made to the multiples being applied to similar businesses by the market. But those multiples are themselves changing. As the market moves up or down, the P/E ratio changes with it.

In the last resort, value is what people think it is. Any analysis is in the final test subject to the values that the world at large is prepared to place upon it. This has been most clearly evidenced in the past by the attempts of issuing houses to fix the price of shares for a new issue. However carefully they may assess what is the right value for that share, the final word is said by the people who are prepared to buy it. The margins of error have not been small ones. Frequently, in past years, one has seen dealing in a new issue quickly run up to a premium of anything up to 100 per cent of the issue price. If the professionals find it so hard to calculate the value for the business, how much harder it must be for the non-professional.

PURPOSES OF VALUATION

One can distinguish a number of situations in which one is required to make a judgement on the value of the business. They are:

1. *Purchasing a complete business.*   What is relevant to the valuation in this case is the return that the investment of funds in the purchase will provide, as compared with what could be earned in similar investments elsewhere.

2. *Purchasing the controlling interest in a business.*   Basically, this has the same purpose as the purchase of an entire business. As the control of the business is gained without the expenditure of the same amount of funds as would be needed to purchase 100 per cent ownership, the part purchased may have a higher value than its strict proportion of the whole.

3. *Marketing a company's shares.*   The value that must be put on the business is one which interests sufficient people in buying the shares, but not so many that it is several times over-subscribed. The latter situation indicates that the shareholders who are selling a part of their holding have not received as much for the sale as they might have done.

4. *Buying a share in a business.*   Here one is putting money into a business which individually one is not able to control in any way. The basic factor to be determined is, given the management ability that exists, together with other factors, what is the likely pattern of income receivable in terms of income and capital gain.

5. *To acquire assets.*   The purpose here is to acquire a business or a part of one in order to obtain the assets that it holds.

6. *For capital transfer tax (CTT) purposes.*   An unlisted business requires a value to be placed upon its shares for CTT purposes, since in this case there is no market price available.

7. *For the purpose of obtaining insurance cover.*   This will be largely concerned with the costs of replacing the relevant assets.

8. *As security for a loan.*   The lender is not concerned with the earning capacity of the business in this case, but with the realizable value of the assets should he be forced to foreclose on the loan.

One can distinguish three approaches in the valuation of the business, one or more of which may be relevant in each situation.
These are:

1. By placing a value on the assets with no reference to earnings.
2. By a combination of projected earnings and capitalization rate.
3. By reference to market value.

VALUATION OF ASSETS

The *book value* of the assets is of little value in this context. It is based upon historic costs and influenced by the depreciation and valuation policies of the business. It is no guide as to the value of such assets to a purchaser to use in his own business or as to what they are likely to realize if sold on the open market.

Forced sale

The *purpose* for which the asset valuation is required should be borne in mind. The creditor is concerned with the amount that the assets would realize if he is forced to foreclose. This will bring the most disadvantageous value to the owner, unless the firm is very lucky and the sale coincides with a demand for that asset. In addition to these disadvantages, there are the costs of realization to consider.

Break-up value

More favourable values may be realized where the decision to break up the company is quite deliberate. This decision may be taken because the directors estimate that a higher value can be obtained for the business in this way than if sold on an earnings or market-value basis. This decision was taken by some property investment companies in the UK. On the introduction of corporation tax, the earnings accruing to shareholders under the company structure were less than could be earned by other forms of investor, notably the tax-exempt fund. The portfolio had a higher value to these other investors than to the holders of the company's shares. A board of directors concerned with max-imizing the value of the business for its owners would come to the conclusion in such a case that the higher value should be realized.

CAPITALIZED VALUE OF EARNINGS

In arriving at the value of a business by this method, there are two principal difficulties: what level of earnings to use, and what multiple of those earnings to apply to arrive at the value.

The level of earnings

The level of earnings that is relevant to the decision is the level of earnings generated in the future. The only level of earnings currently known is that earned in the past. What one requires to know is how and to what extent past earnings are likely to be affected in the future. Some of the principal factors which may influence that future level are:

1. *The class of industry or commerce within which the business oper-ates.* Attention will be devoted to the general economic trends in the indus-try, whether it is contracting or expanding and if so at what speed. The volatility of the industry is also considered at this stage, although it is much more relevant when deciding the multiple to be applied to earnings.

2. *The activities of competitors.* If competitors are gaining in market share, is their strength such that it is likely to continue or can it be reversed?

3. *The research and development programme.* The future business that can be obtained may be crucially affected by the success or failure of the R. and D. effort. An appraisal of the projects at present being worked upon

together with a judgement of the likely success/failure rate should be made.

4. *Management.* Is the existing management to remain or will it be replaced by a new team from the purchasing company? What are their likely relative skills? Is the management solely dependent upon one man with little or no management succession?

5. *Spread of products.* A business based upon a single product is at the mercy of changes to a greater extent than a more broadly based business.

6. *The organization structure.* Does this seem logical for the business and is it likely to be an effective one in practice? Will it fit in with that of the acquiring company?

7. *Key management personnel.* This group largely influences the continuing profitability of the business. Are they with you or against you? In at least one case in recent years—that of the bid for Edwards High Vacuum—the attitude of the senior staff of the business was decisive in resisting a bid, even when agreed by the board.

Are the skills and judgement of the managers those required for that class of business? Is there adequate management succession?

8. *Management information systems.* Are the control and information systems adequate for their purposes or will they need to be revamped considerably to be made effective?

9. *Capital demands.* Is the business to be acquired adequately capitalized or will it need a further injection of funds to realize the level of profits forecast?

Readers will begin to recognize that the question of future earnings can only be adequately ascertained by a process similar to that employed in devising the strategy for a business.

The multiple of earnings

In general, the multiple to be applied to the ascertained earnings is determined by the going rate for similar enterprises. This may be difficult enough in the case of a quoted company where there are similar quoted companies against which it can be compared. As was seen in Fig. 15.1, if one was trying to establish the proper P/E ratio for a building and contracting company, there is a range from around 7 times earnings up to 30 times earnings from which to choose.

In the case of the unquoted business, it is even more difficult to determine the right earnings multiple since other factors such as the saleability of the business must be considered.

Having determined the future level of profits and the multiple of earnings to be applied, the calculation of the value is simple. Assume the business we wish to purchase is expected to average earnings of £100 000 p.a. in the immediate future, rising to some £120 000 in five years' time with prospects of a continuing upwards trend. Also assume that the average P/E ratio for that class of business is 10 and that the forecast level of profits indicated follows the likely trend for the industry as a whole. The value of the business would then be:

$$(100\,000 + 120\,000)/2 \times 10 = \text{\pounds}1\,100\,000$$

The more the business being appraised diverges from the trends for the whole industry, the less relevant is the industry P/E ratio as an indication of the multiple to be used. Value is also affected by whether one is a seller or a buyer. When fixing the sale value for a new issue, one must bear in mind that one has to persuade sufficient investors to buy the share at a single point in time. This can only be achieved by pitching the price a little below the level at which one expects the market to settle. On the other hand, if one is making a bid for a business, one has to persuade shareholders content with their investment to sell them. Since the bidder's interest draws attention to possible latent values in the business, this offer has to be pitched somewhat above the price ruling before the bid becomes public.

Assessing the price for a share issue

When making an issue of shares, one must relate a number of variables in setting a price for the issue. Firstly, the trend and level of future earnings is not known for certain but will fall between upper and lower limits. Secondly, it is rarely possible to obtain a strictly comparable quoted company which one an use as a yardstick for setting the P/E ratio. Thirdly, when the known factor is the amount of cash the issue must raise, the related unknown is the number of shares to be issued to raise that sum. This can only be decided when the earnings and P/E are known. This latter point is not so important in a rights issue, since all the existing shareholders would be treated equally. It is important in cases where the new shares are to be issued to third parties.

A useful technique for the display of information in this decision situation is shown in Fig. 18.1. The objective of the presentation is to enable the EPS, P/E ratio, and share price to be read off for any number of new shares to be issued, related to a specific funds need. In this example, the EPS and P/E ratio are shown for two levels of earnings so that an appreciation of the effect of variable earnings can be assessed.

Example: Assume that Shariss Ltd, an unquoted company, has at issue 100 000 ordinary shares and a current level of earnings of £50 000 after tax. The company needs to raise an additional £250 000 which, because existing borrowing is high, must be in the form of equity. The present shareholders do not have the funds available to subscribe to a rights issue and the new shares are, therefore, offered to the public. It is estimated that earnings should expand to £80 000 after tax when the new capital is fully employed.

Ignoring the expenses of the issue, the key variable is the number of shares

Figure 18.1

Assessing issue price of shares

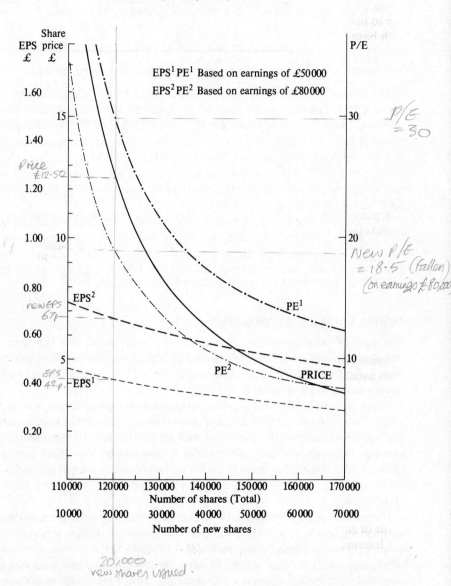

to be issued to raise the £250 000. This variable is plotted on the horizontal axis of the graph in Fig. 18.1 The related EPS, price, and P/E values for some of the range of possible numbers of shares to be issued can now be calculated, i.e.:

Number of shares to be issued	Total number of shares	Price at which shares must be issued to raise £250 000	EPS when earnings are £50 000 p.a.	Price/earnings ratio
		£		
10 000	110 000	25 per share	45.5p	55
40 000	140 000	6.25 per share	35.7p	17.5
70 000	170 000	3.57 per share	29.4p	12.14

The values for the price are shown on the 'price' curve, those for EPS on the curve EPS[1], and for the price-earnings ratio on PE[1]. These three curves, therefore, represent the values for the price, EPS, and P/E over the whole range of likely issue size. For example, if one was considering issuing 20 000 shares, the price would be £12.50 and the EPS would be approximately 42p, giving a P/E of 30. If the forecast range of earnings is achieved, the EPS would rise to nearly 67p and the P/E fall to about 18.5, as shown by PE[2] and EPS[2], both based on earnings of £80 000.

Management and its advisers can now concentrate attention on comparative P/Es for similar companies. Assuming that similar companies appear to have a P/E of around 19 on the basis of current earnings and with similar growth prospects, the number of shares to be issued is 35 000, which would provide an EPS of 37p and a price of £7.14.

MARKET VALUE APPROACH

The market value approach is based on the assumption that the price that reflects the balance between sellers and buyers of the company's shares is the best indicator of value. This immediately rules out its application to businesses which are not quoted.

There are other difficulties in accepting market price as an indicator of value. Even though some shares are quoted on a stock exchange, the number of deals is so small that the market cannot really be said to be representative of value as between a willing seller and a willing buyer. The small number of deals usually means that there is a wide spread between the buying and selling prices and one is faced with a decision as to where in that range the value should fall.

The market price is influenced by a number of factors outside the domain of intrinsic value. As was seen in Chapter 15, the market price is significantly influenced by the dividend pay-out ratio. In Fig. 15.1, the average for building companies suggests that when 50 per cent of earnings are paid out as a dividend, the market assesses the company on a P/E of 12, but when the whole of earnings are paid out the P/E would be 16. Which of these values, or any intermediate value, is to be used as the measure?

Short-term market influences also affect the current market price. An investor unloading a long line of stock, a technically oversold or undersold market, etc. produces reactions in the share price. Even weekend press comment can have a considerable short-term impact one way or the other.

While it is possible to sell or buy small quantities of stock at the ruling price this is not so for large holdings. The holder of 5 or 10 per cent of the shares of a business may find difficulty in disposing of that holding at the market price. If it is attempted to complete the disposal in a short period of time, it can easily force the price down.

THE BUSINESS AS THE SUM OF NET PRESENT VALUES

This follows the same approach as that used in measuring profitability targets by the present value method. It looks upon the business as a series of streams of cash flows over future years from investment projects and for financing costs. These streams are discounted back to present value, the net sum of the present values forming the present value of the business as a whole.

Conceptually, this method has some attractions. The capital employed can be considered as a series of investment projects started in the past and still in being. Each of those investments has a forecast stream of future cash flows based upon the amounts included in the assessment when they were approved as adjusted for any subsequent changes.

Set off against this series of inwards cash flows is the present value of the cost of servicing debt. The net of the two is the present value. It is attractive because it brings together two 'optimizing' aspects. Firstly, by maximizing the return on capital employed, one increases the present value of the cash flows. Secondly, by looking at the cost of debt service in terms of its net present cost, one tries to minimize the deduction from the inward cash flows.

One problem immediately arises when discounting is considered. At what rate is one to discount the future cash flows? This must be assessed externally from the company, since it must be a return acceptable to a possible purchaser. One is, therefore, forced back to examine market returns to see what is the present 'going rate' for return on investments.

19

Mergers and takeovers

Mergers and takeovers are the conditions in which two businesses come under the same effective control and are managed as members of the same group or are actually combined into a single company. Mergers tend to denote parity of status in the negotiations preceding the merger. The takeover tends to denote the situation in which one business offers to buy out the owners of another, often against the wishes of the board of directors or groups of shareholders. The dividing line between the two is indistinct. A number of situations which are presented as mergers are effectively takeover bids. The directors of the taken over company, being unable to control effectively the course of events in their business, are glad of the opportunity to come to an arrangement with another business which preserves their self-esteem by presenting the operation as a merger.

The process presents difficulties because it highlights the difference in interests of the directors, controlling shareholders, and the general body of shareholders. Nowhere else in the business management area is this fact more apparent than in the contested takeover bid. The directors of the company subject to a bid may have little or no financial stake in the business that they manage, and may be more concerned to preserve their office than to serve the interests of the owners of the business. The controlling shareholders are in a position to deny the advantages of a bid to the remaining shareholders or to sell effective control via their holding at a price the remaining shareholders cannot match.

In Britain since the late 'sixties, the trend has been to bigness. Unlike the activities of Sir Charles Clore in the 'fifties, which were designed to unlock the real value of the assets being used, the recent trend of mergers seems to have been for the sake of bigness itself. This trend has often been instigated by government or organizations sponsored by government. It is now being appreciated that big is not necessarily beautiful.

REASONS FOR MERGERS AND ACQUISITIONS

The process of acquiring another company should only take place after the identification of the need in the course of devising the corporate strategy. It should not happen merely as a convenient way of making use of surplus liquid funds or in a desperate attempt to disguise the unprofitability of the underlying business. If unexpected opportunities arise to buy business on what appear to be very favourable conditions, the corporate strategy should be re-examined to make sure that the proposal conforms to the long-term requirements of the business.

Among the reasons why a firm may decide to merge with another, one can identify those detailed below.

Diversification

This follows the need of a narrowly based business to reduce the risks by broadening its activities. To reduce such risks effectively, the acquired business must not be subject to the same risk-promoting factors as the parent, even though it may operate in a different field.

Diversification has received a tarnished image in recent years because, on a number of occasions, managements, who have seen their traditional products becoming obsolete, have used this process to invest heavily in acquisitions to bolster up future profits. While this may often be useful in practice, it is a process which must be approached with care. Too frequently, there is a facile assumption that management expertise can be carried over from one type of activity to another. Failures have occurred through overestimating managerial ability and through entering into unfamiliar fields with no preconceived plan.

To secure scarce sources of supply

Where any of the resources the business needs are in short supply or subject to other difficulties, one solution is for it to acquire its own sources.

To secure economies of scale

An increase in volume can often lead to a reduction in operating costs by enabling a larger capacity plant to be used. For example, a 200 000 ton tanker costing, say, £6 million, with a crew of 35, is less costly than ten 20 000 ton tankers, each costing £1.2 million, carrying a crew of 20. Modern chemical plants are another example of the same principle.

To modify the firm's competitive position

The marketing strategy of the business is one of its most important elements. The merger technique can be used to further this strategy in the following ways:

1. *By filling gaps in the product range.*
2. *By filling gaps in the outlets that are available to the business.* For example, a firm that is weak in a particular geographical area may bid for another company which operates in that area.

3. *By acquiring marketing expertise.*   One company may buy another for the purpose of bringing in a strong marketing team which may prove effective for the combined business.
4. *By improving market penetration.*   In some conditions, e.g., where the marketing effort must support a substantial after-sales service and spares organization, the market penetration required to support such services may be achieved through a takeover.

Buy in management

Where the business suffers from inadequate management and it does not appear possible to rectify this in the near future, the problem may be resolved by merging with or bidding for a company with a good management team.

Improve the financial standing of the business

When two companies are joined together, two plus two do not always make four. When the strengths of the two companies are added together, the market may put a higher valuation on the combination than on the constituent parts.

To benefit from the undervaluation of another business

If the management of a business is unable or unwilling to maximize the value of that business in terms of the assets employed, other businesses may want to take advantage of that undervaluation.

The increased value may result from the elimination of loss-making activities which the previous management has been unable to do, to improve the return on assets, or where this cannot be done to sell the assets and if necessary to lease them back.

Achieve a monopoly position

The elimination of competition by absorption gives the firm a greater control over the market and market price. There are conflicting requirements in this situation. Firstly, the public interest must be considered since this may now conflict with the objectives of the firm. The strange thing is that governments, who should protect the public interest, are often the promoters of monopoly organizations. The public interest is best preserved by drawing a balance between the benefits of competition and the need for an orderly market.

Taxation

As far as the UK is concerned, the major objective here is to escape the close company requirements of the 1965 Finance Act. Although the effect of these has been ameliorated in recent years, there are still advantages in escaping through marketing the shares of a business. Where the business is small, this marketing can often only be achieved by merging with another business to provide a vehicle of sufficient size to obtain a quotation.

DANGERS OF MERGERS AND ACQUISITIONS

The Monopolies Commission

One of the hazards to be surmounted is a referral to the Monopolies Commission in the UK; or a prosecution under the antitrust laws in the USA, and similar bodies elsewhere. The merger may be prohibited, or allowed to continue unconditionally or subject to certain constraints. Codes of conduct such as those set out by the Takeover Panel must be observed.

Management control

The carrying over of management skill from one business to one enlarged by acquisition may prove to be more difficult than is at first thought. The more divergent the two businesses are in product, in manufacturing operations, in marketing, etc., the more likely it is that problems will arise. When the management of the business taken over is to remain, there may be personality problems in combining management teams. When it is resigning, there is the problem of replacing it with a new management style which may upset staff.

Conflict of objectives

This problem is only likely to arise where the acquisition has been made without a full previous examination of the acquisition against the criteria of the existing business objectives, e.g., a 'quality' company acquiring a 'mass production' company. This may prove to be a rational structure, but the blurring between quality and quantity aspects may lead to failure in both objects.

Effect upon capital structure and financial rating

Because of the long-term implications, consequential changes in this area should be carefully considered. Major points of concern include:

Dilution of earnings.   Will the enlarged equity so dilute earnings that the growth potential of the EPS is damaged?

Control.   The bringing together of two companies by merger or takeover through the medium of an exchange of shares may dilute the controlling interest to the point that it is no longer effective.

Financial rating.   This may be affected by the market's assessment of the dilution effects. If growth potential is affected, the P/E ratio may be downgraded for the enlarged group. Additionally, there is the problem of what the final P/E ratio is for the merged group, particularly where the companies to be merged have very different P/E ratios. If, for example, company A which has a P/E of 10 is merged with company B which has a P/E of 20, what will be the P/E for the new group? Will it tend to follow that of company A or that of B? If the former, it would lower the valuation of the group to less than that of the constituent parts.

Increased cost of management.   There are a number of managerial 'hurdles' at various stages in the growth of a business which require a substantial revision of management organization and methods if they are to be overcome. If the merger brings the group up to one of these barriers, management costs may escalate as a new structure of control is brought into being.

PRE-ACQUISITION STRATEGY

Overall company plan and objectives

It is stressed once again that a clear understanding of the role to be played by the acquisition is an essential prerequisite if it is to bring long-term benefits to the business. Each proposal for acquisition must be tested against these requirements and a selection made of the project(s) which maximize the success potential.

Maximize the value of the bidding company

The bidding company should be concerned not only with the valuation of the business to be acquired, but also with maximizing the value of its own business. The higher the market value of one's own shares the fewer of them need be issued in exchange for those of an acquired business, thereby reducing the effective cost. — *Issues cost money.*

Action which can be taken to achieve this includes the promotion of the company name and image and steps to improve profit performance during the run-up period to the acquisition. For many businesses, this is the single most important transaction that it ever engages in and has important long-term consequences.

Finding likely acquisition prospects

In surveying the field of potential acquisitions, the team searches for those which:

1. Fit in with the existing activities.
2. Conform with the corporate strategy.
3. Will improve the growth prospects of the shares.
4. Have an amount and form of consideration which is within the capacity of the business to satisfy.
5. Will not adversely affect control.

ACQUISITION TACTICS

The bid price

This is probably the most difficult part of the acquisition process. Where the business is being bid for on a going-concern basis, the same problems of valuation are present as were discussed in the previous chapter. They broadly divide into two decisions:

1. To decide what is the likely pattern of earnings that the addition will provide, and
2. the multiple that should be applied to those earnings to arrive at the capitalization value of the business.   (what P/E ratio ?)

Forecast of earnings.   In the particular circumstances of the takeover bid and merger, the following points require consideration:

1. The reliability of past reported earnings. Many firms have found that the earnings prior to acquisition have been inflated by high stock values which have been found in the event to be overvalued or worthless. A danger signal is a decreasing stock turnover in the years prior to acquisition.
2. How good a guide to the future is the past? Changes consequent to the acquisition may have important effects upon the earnings potential and any such possibilities should be taken into account.
3. Are there any special features of the business which affect its value? Is the plant obsolete and does it require renewal? Is there a good information system for management.
4. Specific management problems. Are the earnings of the company highly dependent upon the skills or personality of the existing management? If so, what steps could be taken to retain or supplant those aptitudes?
5. What savings will result from the merger of the two businesses?

Multiple of earnings.   The multiple of earnings is largely determined by the normal considerations for the valuation of a business modified only by any special considerations specific to the firms concerned.

Acquisition for break-up value.   Where the sum of the values of individual parts of the business is in excess of the whole, it may be acquired with the intention of breaking it up and disposing of all or some of the parts separately. In this case, the individual parts should be valued separately, either on a going-concern basis or asset-value basis, to arrive at an estimate for the business as a whole.

The objective is to sell the parts not required for retention on an asset basis or on a going-concern basis, as appropriate.

Cash and loan stock versus equity

The choice of the form in which the cost of the acquisition is settled should be based upon an analysis of the effects upon the capital structure and EPS, along the lines discussed in Chapter 13. Satisfaction of the purchase price by cash or loan stock ensures that the benefit of gains in future earnings will accrue to the benefit of the shareholders of the bidding company only. For the same reason, it may prove to be less attractive to the vendors.

Acceptance of a cash bid is a disposal for capital gains tax purposes, and the bid is worth the cash offer less gains tax liability for each holder. The acceptance of a bid in the form of loan stock or equity is not a disposal and, therefore, attracts no liability until the new stock is sold.

Where the earnings of the acquisition are very dependent upon the personalities of the existing management, an equity or part equity offering may be more desirable. This makes the ultimate value of the consideration that they receive to some extent dependent upon their continued efforts.

In some cases, the company has no choice in the matter. It may not have the cash resources and is already fully geared up. A bid must, therefore, be made on the basis of equity only. The test of acceptability as far as the bidder is concerned is the familiar one of its effect upon the EPS.

A general assessment of acceptability is obtained by comparing the proportion of the combined earnings provided by the acquisition and the proportion of the combined equity that its former shareholders will own. For example, in the situation illustrated below, equality is obtained if company A offers two of its shares for each share of company B. In this way, the percentage additions to both earnings and equity are the same:

	Company A	Company B	Combined	Company B as a percentage of the total
Earnings	£500 000	£200 000	£700 000	28.6
Number of shares	1 000 000	200 000	1 400 000	28.6
EPS	50p	£1	50p	
Share price	£5	£10	£5	

If company A can gain acceptance from the shareholders of company B with an offer of less than two for one, the shareholders of that company gain an advantage from the merger.

FINANCING ACQUISITION FROM SALE OF PART OF ACQUIRED COMPANY

In some cases, it may be possible to fund the acquisition in whole or in part from the disposal of the assets acquired. This situation can only arise when the management of a company which is the subject of a bid has been unaware of the real value of the business they have managed, or are unable to obtain from it the level of earnings that another management could obtain.

There are two circumstances in which the acquisition can finance itself. Firstly, while all the assets may be usefully employed in the business the use of some assets could be obtained without ownership through leasing in one form or another. Land and buildings may be sold and leased back, where necessary, releasing substantial sums to repay monies borrowed for the purchase or to extend the trading activities. If land and buildings are disposed of in this way it should not be forgotten that the value of such assets as a hedge against inflation has been foregone.

The second circumstance occurs when only a part of a business is required. Those parts not wanted can be sold, or the business closed down and only assets or goodwill sold. Assume that the company is divided into three divisions with assets and profits as follows:

	Division A	Division B	Division C	Total
Assets (net)	£2 million	£1.5 million	£2 million	£5.5 million
Profit	£250 000	£100 000	Loss £100 000	£250 000

On the assumption that total profits could be increased by 20 per cent to £300 000 and a 12-year purchase is appropriate, the purchase price would be £3.6 million. If the purpose of the bid is to acquire division A and it would be possible to sell division B on a P/E of 15 and to sell the assets of division C for 60 per cent of their book value, the amount realized would be:

$$
\begin{aligned}
&\text{Division B } £100\,000 \times 15 &&= £1.5 \text{ million} \\
&\text{Division C } 60 \text{ per cent of } £2 \text{ million} &&= £1.2 \text{ million} \\
& && \overline{} \\
& && £2.7 \text{ million} \\
& && \overline{\overline{}}
\end{aligned}
$$

If there were properties in division A with a sale value of £900 000, they could be sold and leased back, so recouping the whole of the cost of purchase.

Takeover code

As outlined earlier, a takeover battle puts management and controlling share-holders in a position in which their personal interest may well conflict with that of the general body of shareholders. It is not surprising, therefore, that there have been occasions when the parties in a contested bid have taken advantage of a privileged position in a way detrimental to other interested parties.

In the USA, this aspect is controlled by the Securities and Exchange Commission which has wide-ranging powers of supervision. In the UK, supervision is still on a voluntary basis with no formal sanctions available. The objective of the regulatory codes is to:

1. Ensure that all shareholders have equality of opportunity and treatment and that they are not denied the advantage of an approach by the tactics of the minority.
2. To ensure that information relating to bids and counterbids is made available within a reasonable time so that shareholders have the necessary information on which to make their decision.

Appendix A

The taxation of companies

There are two basic approaches to the taxation of companies. One approach is to separate entirely the taxation of the company from the taxation of income in the hand of the shareholders, there being no relationship between the two taxes. The other is to consider some of the tax paid by the company as meeting some of the shareholders' liability to tax. The former is often called the 'classical' system of tax and the latter the 'imputation' system. There are also variants of the imputation system which share the burden of tax in very much the same way.

The classical system

The company is taxed at the relevant rate of tax on companies. In addition, when the company makes a distribution of earnings to its shareholders out of after-tax earnings, that distribution is treated as income in the hands of the shareholders and is further taxed at their personal rates of tax. Distributed profits are therefore taxed twice—once as company earnings and again as personal income.

Example:

	£
Operating profit	110
Interest on long-term loan	10
Pre-tax profits	100
Corporation tax at (say) 50%	50
After-tax profit	50
Gross cost of dividend[1]	30
Retained profit	20

---

[1] Usually the company is obliged to deduct tax at source from the dividend and pay only the net amount to the shareholders. The tax so deducted is then paid to the tax authorities.

The imputation system

This system provides for part of the taxation paid by the company to be used to cover the basic tax liabilities of the shareholders. It can perhaps be best illustrated by the UK system of corporation tax, using a corporation tax rate of 52 per cent and a basic personal rate of income tax of 30 per cent.

Example:

	£
Operating profit	110
Interest on long-term loan	10
Pre-tax profit	100
Tax at 52%	52
After-tax profit	48
Dividend net	21
Retained profit	27

In the UK, dividends are paid as a net amount per share and, in addition to the net dividend, the shareholder receives a tax credit to cover the basic tax liability on the gross dividend. In the example above, the cost of the net dividend while the equivalent gross dividend is £30 is calculated as follows:

Gross dividend	£30
Less income tax at 30%	9
	21

From the shareholder's point of view, he has received a gross dividend on which the basic tax of £9 has been paid for him. He will have to settle any liability to higher tax rates himself. If he is a zero-rate taxpayer, he can reclaim the tax credits from the Inland Revenue, thus he gets in cash the gross value of the dividend.

From the company's point of view, the corporation tax that it has paid is imputed to cover the value of the tax credits that it has given to the shareholders. When a dividend is paid the company pays advance corporation tax (ACT) to the Inland Revenue—an amount to cover the value of the tax credits. However, provided that the company has sufficient UK taxable profits, ACT is not an extra tax but merely a prepayment of its total corporation tax. Thus, in the example shown above, the company would pay the corporation tax liability in two instalments: £9 would be paid when the dividend was paid and the balance of £43 some time after the end of the accounting year. (In practice, it is the ACT on *dividends actually paid* in the year which is used.) Only when a company does not have sufficient UK income does ACT become an extra tax.

The same balance of taxation can be achieved by taxing undistributed profits at the normal rate of tax on companies and those profits that are distributed at a lower rate. The dividends are then taxed as income in the hands of the shareholders, in the normal way.

From the financial management point of view, the principal difference between the two tax systems is the way that they affect the comparative cost of paying interest and paying dividends. Both systems provide for tax relief for interest paid, since interest reduces the pre-tax profit. However, the cost of paying dividends under the classical system is the *gross* cost of the dividend which is paid out of after-tax profits, whereas under the imputation system the cost of dividends is only the *net* amount paid out of after-tax profits. Therefore, when considering the relative cost of borrowed money and equity funds, there is a much greater cost advantage in borrowing money under the classical system than there is under the imputation system.

Appendix B

Present value of £1 receivable at the end of each period

Year   Percentage

Year	2	4	5	6	8	10	12	14	15
1	0.980	0.962	0.952	0.943	0.926	0.909	0.893	0.877	0.870
2	0.961	0.925	0.907	0.890	0.857	0.826	0.797	0.769	0.756
3	0.942	0.889	0.864	0.840	0.794	0.751	0.712	0.675	0.658
4	0.924	0.855	0.823	0.792	0.735	0.683	0.636	0.592	0.572
5	0.906	0.822	0.784	0.747	0.681	0.621	0.567	0.519	0.497
6	0.888	0.790	0.746	0.705	0.630	0.564	0.507	0.456	0.432
7	0.871	0.760	0.711	0.665	0.583	0.513	0.452	0.400	0.376
8	0.583	0.731	0.677	0.627	0.540	0.467	0.404	0.351	0.327
9	0.837	0.703	0.645	0.592	0.500	0.424	0.361	0.308	0.284
10	0.820	0.676	0.614	0.558	0.463	0.386	0.322	0.270	0.247
11	0.804	0.650	0.585	0.537	0.429	0.350	0.287	0.237	0.215
12	0.788	0.625	0.557	0.497	0.397	0.319	0.257	0.208	0.187
13	0.773	0.601	0.530	0.469	0.368	0.290	0.229	0.182	0.163
14	0.758	0.577	0.505	0.442	0.340	0.263	0.205	0.160	0.141
15	0.743	0.555	0.481	0.417	0.315	0.239	0.183	0.140	0.123
16	0.728	0.534	0.458	0.394	0.292	0.218	0.163	0.123	0.107
17	0.714	0.513	0.436	0.371	0.270	0.198	0.146	0.108	0.093
18	0.700	0.494	0.416	0.350	0.250	0.180	0.130	0.095	0.081
19	0.686	0.475	0.396	0.331	0.232	0.164	0.116	0.083	0.070
20	0.673	0.456	0.377	0.312	0.215	0.149	0.104	0.073	0.061
25	0.610	0.375	0.295	0.233	0.146	0.092	0.059	—	—
30	0.552	0.308	0.231	0.174	0.099	0.057	—	—	—

Year	Percentage								
	16	18	20	22	24	25	26	28	30
1	0.862	0.847	0.833	0.820	0.806	0.800	0.794	0.781	0.769
2	0.743	0.718	0.694	0.672	0.650	0.640	0.630	0.610	0.592
3	0.641	0.609	0.579	0.551	0.524	0.512	0.500	0.477	0.455
4	0.552	0.516	0.482	0.451	0.423	0.410	0.397	0.373	0.350
5	0.476	0.437	0.402	0.370	0.341	0.328	0.315	0.291	0.269
6	0.410	0.370	0.335	0.303	0.275	0.262	0.250	0.227	0.207
7	0.354	0.314	0.279	0.249	0.222	0.210	0.198	0.178	0.159
8	0.305	0.266	0.233	0.204	0.179	0.168	0.157	0.139	0.123
9	0.263	0.225	0.194	0.167	0.144	0.134	0.125	0.108	0.094
10	0.227	0.191	0.162	0.137	0.116	0.107	0.099	0.085	0.073
11	0.195	0.162	0.135	0.112	0.094	0.086	0.079	0.066	0.056
12	0.168	0.137	0.112	0.092	0.076	0.069	0.062	0.052	—
13	0.145	0.116	0.093	0.075	0.061	0.055	—	—	—
14	0.125	0.099	0.078	0.062	—	—	—	—	—
15	0.108	0.084	0.065	0.051	—	—	—	—	—
16	0.093	0.071	0.054	—	—	—	—	—	—
17	0.080	0.060	—	—	—	—	—	—	—
18	0.069	0.051	—	—	—	—	—	—	—
19	0.060	—	—	—	—	—	—	—	—
20	0.051	—	—	—	—	—	—	—	—
25	—	—	—	—	—	—	—	—	—
30	—	—	—	—	—	—	—	—	—

Appendix C

Present value of £1 receivable annually at the end of each year

Year

Percentage

	2	4	5	6	8	10	12	14	15
1	0.980	0.962	0.952	0.943	0.926	0.909	0.893	0.877	0.870
2	1.942	1.886	1.859	1.833	1.783	1.736	1.690	1.647	1.626
3	2.884	2.775	2.723	2.673	2.577	2.487	2.402	2.322	2.283
4	3.808	3.630	3.546	3.465	3.312	3.170	3.037	2.914	2.855
5	4.713	4.452	4.329	4.212	3.993	3.791	3.605	3.433	3.352
6	5.601	5.242	5.076	4.917	4.623	4.355	4.111	3.889	3.784
7	6.472	6.002	5.786	5.582	5.206	4.868	4.564	4.288	4.160
8	7.325	6.733	6.463	6.210	5.747	5.335	4.968	4.639	4.487
9	8.162	7.435	7.108	6.802	6.247	5.759	5.328	4.946	4.772
10	8.983	8.111	7.722	7.360	6.710	6.145	5.650	5.216	5.019
11	9.787	8.760	8.306	7.887	7.139	6.495	5.938	5.453	5.234
12	10.575	9.385	8.863	8.384	7.536	6.814	6.194	5.660	5.421
13	11.348	9.986	9.394	8.853	7.904	7.103	6.424	5.842	5.583
14	12.106	10.563	9.899	9.295	8.244	7.367	6.628	6.002	5.724
15	12.849	11.118	10.380	9.712	8.559	7.606	6.811	6.142	5.847
16	13.578	11.652	10.838	10.106	8.851	7.824	6.974	6.265	5.954
17	14.292	12.166	11.274	10.477	9.122	8.022	7.120	6.373	6.047
18	14.992	12.659	11.690	10.828	9.372	8.201	7.250	6.467	6.128
19	15.678	13.134	12.085	11.158	9.604	8.365	7.366	6.550	6.198
20	16.351	13.590	12.462	11.470	9.818	8.514	7.469	6.623	6.259
25	19.523	15.622	14.094	12.783	10.675	9.077	7.843	6.873	6.464
30	22.396	17.292	15.372	13.765	11.258	9.427	8.055	7.003	6.566

Year				Percentage					
	16	18	20	22	24	25	26	28	30
1	0.862	0.847	0.833	0.820	0.806	0.800	0.794	0.781	0.769
2	1.605	1.566	1.528	1.492	1.457	1.440	1.424	1.392	1.361
3	2.246	2.174	2.106	2.042	1.981	1.952	1.923	1.868	1.816
4	2.798	2.690	2.589	2.494	2.404	2.362	2.320	2.241	2.166
5	3.274	3.127	2.991	2.864	2.745	2.689	2.635	2.532	2.436
6	3.685	3.498	3.326	3.167	3.020	2.951	2.885	2.759	2.643
7	4.039	3.812	3.605	3.416	3.242	3.161	3.083	2.937	2.802
8	4.344	4.078	3.837	3.619	3.421	3.329	3.241	3.076	2.925
9	4.607	4.303	4.031	3.786	3.566	3.463	3.366	3.184	3.019
10	4.833	4.494	4.192	3.923	3.682	3.571	3.465	3.269	3.092
11	5.029	4.656	4.327	4.035	3.776	3.656	3.544	3.335	3.147
12	5.197	4.793	4.439	4.127	3.851	3.725	3.606	3.387	3.190
13	5.342	4.910	4.533	4.203	3.912	3.780	3.656	3.427	3.223
14	5.468	5.008	4.611	4.265	3.962	3.824	3.695	3.459	3.249
15	5.575	5.092	4.675	4.315	4.001	3.859	3.726	3.483	3.268
16	5.669	5.162	4.730	4.357	4.033	3.887	3.751	3.503	3.283
17	5.749	5.222	4.775	4.391	4.059	3.910	3.771	3.518	3.295
18	5.818	5.273	4.812	4.419	4.080	3.928	3.786	3.529	3.304
19	5.877	5.316	4.844	4.442	4.097	3.942	3.799	3.539	3.311
20	5.929	5.353	4.870	4.460	4.110	3.954	3.808	3.546	3.316
25	6.097	5.497	4.948	4.514	4.147	3.985	3.834	3.564	3.329
30	6.177	5.517	4.979	4.534	4.160	3.995	3.842	3.569	3.332

Index

Printed in Great Britain by
J. W. Arrowsmith Ltd, Bristol